PERSONALITY AND
ITS DISORDERS:
A BIOSOCIAL
LEARNING APPROACH

PERSONALITY AND ITS DISORDERS: A BIOSOCIAL LEARNING APPROACH

Theodore Millon, Ph.D.
George S. Everly, Jr., Ph.D.

JOHN WILEY & SONS
New York   Chichester   Brisbane   Toronto   Singapore

Library of Congress Cataloging in Publication Data:

Millon, Theodore.
  Personality and its disorders.

  "This book is an abbreviated version of the senior
author's Disorders of personality"—Pref.
  Bibliography: p.
  Includes index.
  1. Personality, Disorders of.   2. Personality, Disorders of—Classification.   I. Everly, George S.,
1950–   II. Millon, Theodore. Disorders of personality.   III. Title.

RC554.M543   1985   616.89   84-21995
ISBN 0-471-87816-2

Printed in the United States of America

10 9 8 7 6 5 4 3 2 1

PREFACE

We wrote this book because we feel that no other introductory text of abnormal psychology provides more than a single chapter on the most rapidly growing subject in psychopathology today—personality disorders. This book has been designed explicitly to fill that vacuum by providing a supplement to the basic abnormal or personality text. It details each of the major personality syndromes, less exhaustively than Millon's more scholarly book, *Disorders of Personality: DSM-III, Axis II*, but in sufficient depth to give beginning students a full sense of the character of the disorders.

Personality disorders have risen rapidly in importance in recent years, becoming *the* primary topic of interest for contemporary psychological researchers, theorists, and practitioners. Why has this growth occurred?

First, mental health clinicians in practice today employ their skills primarily in outpatient rather than inpatient settings. This means that the vast majority of clients with whom psychologists and psychiatrists work are no longer the severely disturbed "state hospital" psychotics on which most abnormal texts still focus, but they are the individuals seen in outpatient private office and community clinic settings. These patients experience rather "ordinary" family, work, and social problems that stem not from dramatic or unusual sources of pathology but simply from interpersonal difficulties and everyday maladaptive personality functioning.

Second, the official classification system, the DSM-III, published in 1980, has given the personality disorders a status equal to that of all other syndromes combined. Personality is now grouped into its own separate "axis," only one of two required for formal diagnoses. This placement also established the personality disorders as a context from which the more dramatic and severe forms of psychopathology could be more fully understood.

Personality disorders have a special significance at the introductory level: not the exotic and bizarre varieties of mental disorder that preoccupy graduate students or psychology interns, but rather, the forms of maladaptive behavior that undergraduate students are likely to encounter in the course of their everyday lives—in their families and among their friends. In addition to making abnormal and personality courses more meaningful and relevant to individual undergraduates, the "milder" pathologies of personality enable them to see the continuity that exists between the lesser and the more severe disorders as well as to trace the insidious manner in which the more severe pathologies unfold. We hope to demonstrate not only the developmental continuity between levels of pathological functioning, but also the interconnections that exist among overtly dissimilar syndromes, which are still approached as discrete clinical entities in many abnormal and psychiatric texts.

As noted, this book is an abbreviated version of Millon's *Disorders of Personality.* That volume not only remains in print but has become one of the all-time best selling texts on the Wiley-Interscience psychology list. Used primarily for graduate-level courses, the original, longer, and more detailed volume is clearly too focused to serve as a major text and too comprehensive to serve as a supplementary text for undergraduate abnormal or personality courses. Consequently, we abridged it so that it could usefully serve as a supplementary text. Significantly shortened, enlivened with numerous case histories, and enhanced by various pedagogic aids and chapter summaries, we believe this abridged version will prove both interesting and informative to the beginning student.

Despite its relative brevity, we sought to balance the scholarly thinking of a scientific discipline with the curiosity that attracts the undergraduate to the subject. There is no reason why the book cannot serve equally well as auxiliary reading for both majors and nonmajors alike by furnishing solid clinical underpinnings for those who wish to make psychology a career and by exposing a rich vein of "life" information for those seeking personal enrichment in their liberal arts education.

Coral Gables, Florida   *Theodore Millon, Ph.D.*
Baltimore, Maryland   *George S. Everly, Jr., Ph.D.*

Contents

PART One

THE NATURE AND CLASSIFICATION OF PERSONALITY

CHAPTER 1

The Nature of Personality

The quest for understanding has fueled the conduct of inquiry since before the time of Hippocrates in the 5th century B.C. One of the most fundamental questions ever to face those in search of understanding pertains to why people behave the way they do. Although the answer to this question surely lies in a multitude of interacting factors, the notion of *personality* offers some "order and congruence to all the different kinds of behavior in which the individual engages" (Hall & Lindzey, 1957, p. 9). Perhaps for this reason, the construct of personality has been formulated, reformulated, and endlessly debated for centuries. For students of human psychology, whether their specialization be clinical psychology, counseling, health, social psychology, psychophysiology, or other related specialties, an understanding of human personality and its disorders offers a wealth of relevant insight into human behavior. With this notion in mind, we have written this text to provide what we feel is a useful perspective on the nature of personality. Furthermore, we present a schema for classifying personality patterns. Finally, we examine the nature and classification of personality disorders.

WHAT IS PERSONALITY?

It seems appropriate to begin with in-depth discussion of human personality with a definition of just what the term personality is intended to encompass. Not only will such a definition prove useful in describing the construct itself, but it may prove useful in gaining insight into personality classification systems and personality disorders as well.

In the first years of life, children engage in a wide variety of behavior responses. Although children will display what appear to be constitutional characteristics at birth, their way of reacting to themselves and their environment tends, at first, to be changeable and unpredictable to observers. It seems that these behavior responses serve an exploratory function. In other words, each child is trying out and testing various behavior responses. Through a process of what Edward Thorndike (1935) called "trial and error" learning, the child learns which behavior responses are effective and which are not. From a learning perspective, the child discovers which behavior responses lead to reinforcement (pleasure) and which responses are ineffective or punishing (unpleasurable).

As the child develops and matures, a shaping process takes place. The child develops a repertoire of what are now empirically tested behaviors designed to achieve reinforcement that also avoid punishment. In time, those observing the child may note that the child fairly consistently practices specific behavior responses in a variety of different situations. At this point, the child may be said to be demonstrating a habit.

As the child continues to mature, he/she begins to exhibit a repetitive clustering, or grouping, of habits. This collective group of habits may be referred to as a trait.

Finally, the child's behavior becomes crystallized into preferred patterns of behaving. Not only do these patterns become resistant to extinction, but the very fact that they have been successful in the past makes them a high-priority response pattern. Thus, given a continuity in basic biological development and a range of experiences for selecting and adopting behavior responses, the child can be seen to develop a distinctive pattern of environmental and intrapersonal interaction that is deeply embedded and not easily eradicated. In short, these characteristics *are* the essence and sum of the child's personality.

A Definition of Personality

What then is personality? As we use the term, personality represents a *pattern* of deeply embedded and broadly exhibited cognitive, affective, and overt behavioral traits that persist over extended periods of time.

These traits emerge from a complicated matrix of biological disposi-tions and experiential learning. Lying at the core of personality are two processes: (1) how the individual interacts with the demands of the environment and (2) how the individual relates to self. We use the term *pattern* when referring to personality for two reasons: first, to focus on the fact that these behaviors and attitudes arise from a complex in-teraction of both biological dispositions and learned experience; sec-ond, to denote the fact that these personality characteristics are not just a scattered aggregation of random tendencies, but a learned and predictable structure of overt and covert behaviors.

This conception of personality, now central to the DSM-III,[1] breaks the long-entrenched tradition of viewing syndromes of psycho-pathology as pathological, alien entities or lesions that insidiously or abruptly overwhelm the individual so as to prohibit normal function-ing. We will expand on this theme when we discuss the concept of syndromal continuity.

Personality, Temperament, and Character

The term personality has historically meant many things to many peo-ple. To aid in our definition of personality, it may be of some value to contrast our notion of personality to the related concepts of tempera-ment and character, terms that are often used interchangeably with personality.

As noted above, *personality* as used in this text, refers to the pattern of deeply embedded and broadly exhibited cognitive, affective, and overt behavioral traits that emerge from a complex biological-en-vironmental formative matrix. This pattern persists over extended pe-riods of time and is relatively resistent to extinction.

Temperament, on the other hand, may be viewed as a biologically determined subset of personality. Each child enters the world with a distinctive pattern of response dispositions and sensitivities. Nurses have long observed that infants differ from the moment they are born. Parents, particularly mothers, are capable of noticing distinct dif-ferences in successive offspring. For example, some infants have pre-dictable cycles of hunger, elimination, and sleep, whereas other in-fants are far less rhythmic in those processes. Some infants suck vigorously at birth, whereas others must be assisted. Some infants are tense, whereas others seem relaxed and happy. Finally, some infants are energetic, whereas others are lethargic.

---

[1]*Diagnostic and Statistical Manual of Mental Disorders,* 3rd ed. Throughout we refer to this work as DSM-III.

The conclusion that infants differ dramatically at birth from a number of perspectives may be supported by more than just the observations of nurses and perceptive parents. Researchers have identified different patterns of activity among newborn infants that are manifested in electroencephalographic patterns, autonomic nervous system activity, and even sensory thresholds (Escalona, 1968; Murphy & Moriarty, 1976; Thomas & Chess, 1977; Thomas, Chess, & Birch, 1963).

It would appear as if such differences in patterns of behavior are more a function of biological factors than environmental factors. In other words, such patterns of behavior appear to be biogenic because they are manifested before postnatal learning experience can account for them. These biogenic foundations of personality development will be referred to as *temperament.* Temperament is most commonly defined as the raw biological materials from which personality will ultimately emerge. It may be said to include the neurological, endocrinological, and even biochemical substrates from which personality will begin to be shaped.

The other term that is often used interchangeably with personality is *character.* Character may be thought of as the person's adherence to the values and customs of the society in which he/she lives. The term character was derived from the Greek word meaning engraving and was used to identify the distinctive features of the individual's persona. The term later appeared in the psychoanalytic literature to reflect the integrating functions of the personality structure, that is, the ego (Fenichel, 1945).

Today, however, the term character appears to reflect a moral judgment of a person's behavior (Millon, 1981), that is, to what extent a person conforms to and manifests the social mores, ethics, and customs of his/her society. Character, then, can be seen to reflect numerous and diverse environmental influences. It is broader in scope than temperament but far narrower than personality.

In summary, within the context of this volume, we will view personality as a broader concept that can easily include temperament and character. Temperament will be viewed as the raw biological materials from which personality will be shaped, and character will be viewed as a subset of personality, broader than temperament, but narrower than personality and defined along societal guidelines.

NORMAL VERSUS ABNORMAL PERSONALITY PATTERNS

One of the most common encountered dilemmas facing students in the mental health professions involves the determination and differentiation of normal and abnormal behavior.

The most commonly used criterion for determining abnormality is the statistical criterion. From this perspective, abnormal behavior is any behavior that is deviant from the expected or accepted norm. The statistical criterion represents a *quantitative* analysis only. It fails to consider qualitative aspects. For example, if the normal, that is, statistically average, IQ (intelligence quotient) is 100, then a person with an IQ of 140 is just as "abnormal" as the person with an IQ of 60. Yet, the IQ of 140 is far more desirable, from a qualitative perspective, than the IQ of 60.

Perhaps a better way of viewing normal and abnormal behavior is to consider the *qualitative* domain. When considering mental health, normality may be conceived of as "the capacity to function autonomously and competently, a tendency to adjust to one's social environment effectively and efficiently, a subjective sense of contentment and satisfaction, and the ability to self-actualize or to fulfill one's potentials" (Millon, 1981, p. 8). Abnormality could then be noted by deficits in these qualities.

To continue, normality and abnormality are best conceived of as relative concepts. They may be thought of as representing points on a continuum or gradient rather than as discrete, nominal categories. Abnormal behavior is developed and shaped according to the same principles and mechanisms as those involved in the development of normal behavior. However, because of differences in biological dispositions and environmental influences, some individuals learn maladaptive cognitive, affective, and overt behavioral habits, whereas other individuals do not.

More specifically, an individual may be said to possess a normal and healthy personality when:

1. he/she displays an ability to cope with the environment in a flexible and adaptive manner.
2. the individual's characteristic perceptions of self and environment are fundamentally constructive.
3. the individual's consistent overt behavior patterns can be considered health promoting.

Conversely, an individual may be said to possess an abnormal and unhealthful personality pattern when:

1. the person attempts to cope with average responsibilities and everyday relationships with inflexibility and maladaptive behavior.
2. his/her characteristic perceptions of self and environment are fundamentally self-defeating.

3. the individual's overt behavior patterns can be shown to be health eroding.

Despite the variable nature of the normality-abnormality distinction, it may be useful to elaborate some criteria by which it may be made. In the following discussion, we will not concern ourselves with gross aberrations whose pathological character is easily identified. Rather, it is in that nebulous category of *apparently normal* personality that we wish to alert ourselves to subtly concealed signs of an insidious and pervasive abnormal process. Three criteria that point to the abnormal personality pattern include:

1. *Adaptive inflexibility.* The term adaptive inflexibility refers to the consistent tendency of the individual to relate to self and cope with the environment through inappropriately rigid and uniformly applied strategies. Such rigidity furthermore inhibits the development of a broad repertoire of coping skills. Not only is the individual unable to adapt to events, but this person also seeks to change the conditions of the environment so that they do not call for behaviors beyond his/her limited behavior repertoire.

2. *A tendency to foster vicious cycles.* Of course, all individuals tend to attempt to manipulate their environment to receive reinforcement and to avoid punishment. What distinguishes abnormal from normal personality patterns is not only inappropriate rigidity and uniformity in coping strategies, but also the tendency of those strategies to provoke or set into motion further self-defeating coping behaviors. Thus, abnormal personality patterns are, in and of themselves, pathogenic by intensifying preexisting difficulties.

3. *Tenuous stability.* Abnormal personality patterns are characteristically fragile and lack resilience under conditions of environmental pressure. (This notion is sometimes referred to as weak ego strength.) Faced with a recurrent series of ineffective attempts at coping, unresolved conflicts tend to reemerge. When this occurs, the individual is likely to revert to pathological ways of coping, to less adequate control over his/her emotions, and ultimately to subjective and distorted perceptions of reality.

In summary, we see that abnormal personality patterns may be differentiated from normal personality patterns by their adaptive inflexibility, their tendency to foster vicious cycles, and their tenuous stability, all of which inhibit effective coping, are essentially self-defeating, and may be viewed from a broader perspective as health eroding.

ORIGINS OF PERSONALITY AND PERSONALITY DISORDERS

It is a basic premise of this text that personality development is a function of a complex interaction of biological and environmental factors. The relative impact that each set of factors will have on a given individual's personality development will depend on the potency and chronicity of each factor's influence. This will certainly vary from individual to individual. It seems safe to suggest, however, that biological factors set the foundation that undergirds personality development, whereas environmental factors act to shape the form of their expression. Therefore, biological factors may set the parameters for personality development, but environmental factors serve to refine and ultimately dictate what we believe constitutes the essence of human personality (see Figure 1.1). We will now examine both sets of factors in greater detail.

Basic Biological Factors

It seems inconceivable that characteristics of anatomic morphology, neuroendocrine and endocrine physiology, as well as neurochemical function would not play a role in shaping the development of response behavior and, in a broader context, personality itself (Williams, 1983). It seems even more reasonable that significant deviations in such factors may indeed lead to personality dysfunction, that is, psychopathology.

Basic biological influences on personality development probably take two major forms: heredity and prenatal maternal factors.

Heredity. "Hereditary ailments are more common than anyone has expected. Medical investigators have now identified nearly 2000 genetic ailments caused wholly or partially by defective genes or chromosomes. It is estimated that 25 percent of the nation's medical problems are genetic" (Sorochan, 1981, p. 404). It is little wonder, then, that many psychopathologists agree that heredity must play a role in the development of human personality and its disorders. Psychopathological conditions such as bipolar depression, schizophrenia, Pick's disease, ruminating obsessive cognitive behavior, pathological risk-taking behavior, and some stress-related disorders appear to have genetic foun-

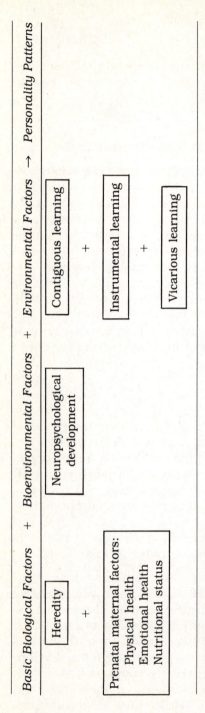

Basic Biological Factors + *Bioenvironmental Factors* + *Environmental Factors* → *Personality Patterns*

Heredity

+

Prenatal maternal factors:
Physical health
Emotional health
Nutritional status

Neuropsychological
development

Contiguous learning

+

Instrumental learning

+

Vicarious learning

Figure 1.1 The origins of personality.

dations (Everly & Rosenfeld, 1981; Faber, 1982; Gottesman & Shields, 1972; Kallman, 1953; Slater & Cowie, 1971). It is generally felt, however, that genetic influences are dramatically shaped and molded by the forces of the environment acting on the genetic foundations of the individual. The specific mechanisms by which the environment acts to shape genetic undergirdings is unclear at this time however.

Prenatal Maternal Factors. Considering prenatal development and its effects on personality development of the child, Millon (1969) states, "It is well known that fetal development can be adversely affected by various pregnancy complications or the poor health and nutritional status of the mother" (p. 96). There is evidence, for example, that caffeine consumed by the mother will stimulate the nervous system of the fetus; alcohol consumption by the mother may lead to temporary reductions in fetal cerebral blood flow as well as mental retardation and fetal alcohol syndrome in the child; alcohol is also thought to depress fetal cerebral neural propagation temporarily; a mother's cigarette smoking may lead to premature delivery and low birth weight; cortisone taken by the mother may lead to placental abnormalities and stillbirth; and, maternal malnutrition may lead to mental retardation and dental caries in the child (Brown & Wallace, 1980; Diagram Group, 1977; Marx, 1973). The specific mechanisms by which prenatal maternal factors may affect the personality development of the child are currently unclear. Yet, many personologists agree that such factors do, indeed, influence the formation of healthy personalities as well as various personality disorders. It may well be that the phenomenon of temperament described earlier is greatly affected by prenatal maternal factors. Perhaps limbic structure and function in the fetus is affected by not only exogenous chemicals that the mother may consume, but by endogenous enzymes, polypeptides, and hormones produced within the mother (Brown & Wallace, 1980; Weil, 1974).

Bioenvironmental Factors

Although basic biological mechanisms can be shown to have influence on human personality development, biological factors are most likely shaped to their final form of expression by environmental factors. Yet, before addressing the nature of primary environmental factors, we should discuss those factors that themselves represent an interaction of biological and environmental processes—bioenvironmental factors.

    In some instances, biological factors become so intertwined with environmental factors that their interaction comes to create another set of factors capable of influencing personality development. Those factors are referred to as bioenvironmental factors. The most obvious and cogent of these environmental factors is represented by neuropsychological developmental processes.

Neuropsychological Development. The process of neuropsychological development is really a process of neurological maturation. Maturation refers to that sequence of developmental processes in which structures of the body unfold into functional units. It was once believed that neural maturation was affected solely by prenatal influences. This view is no longer tenable however. Furthermore, maturation simply fails to progress in a genetically determined sequence without alteration. Rather, neural maturation is now thought to be shaped through postnatal environmental factors as well as prenatal factors (Brown & Wallace, 1980; Simmel, 1970).

One answer to why early postnatal experiences are crucial to human development, including personality formation, derives from the fact that human neurological development is incomplete at birth. The greatest growth spurts in the human neurological system have been identified as occurring from prenatal periods through the first 5 years of life. Furthermore, there is evidence (Bayley, 1970; Child, 1941; McGraw, 1943) that environmental stimuli can exert dramatic influences on development during such neurological growth spurts and yet have little effect on development if applied after these periods of neurological sensitivity have passed. In the final analysis, both prenatal and postnatal development depend on nutrition.

To understand this issue more fully, however, we must view nutrition from a broader perspective than just protein, fats, carbohydrates, vitamins, and other metabolic factors. Rather, we must recognize that neurological development depends on experiential nutrition as well. Rapaport (1958) coined the term stimulus nutriment to refer to the process by which environmental stimuli can exert an influence on the biochemical composition and functional anatomy of neurological patterns within the brain. The belief that the maturing organism must receive adequate stimulus nutriment at appropriate periods of growth for proper development has been well documented (Harlow, 1963; Kovach, 1970; Thompson & Grusec, 1970).

Numerous developmental theorists such as Heinz Werner (1940) and Jean Piaget (1956) and even Sigmund Freud (1957) and Erik Erikson (1950), have based their theories of development on the notion of "sensitive" periods of growth and maturation. Based on such foundations, Millon (1969) has developed a theory of neurological growth stages that focus on development as shaped through stimulus nutriment during important stages of neurological growth (see Millon, 1969, 1981).

The notion that there exist "sensitive" periods of neurological development argues that there exist limited time periods during which particular stimuli are necessary for full maturational development. Furthermore, if these stimuli are experienced before or after those sensitive periods or if the stimulus nutriment is inadequate or excessive, developmental inadequacies or dysfunctions are likely to occur.

Three neuropsychological stages of development may be delineated based on three major sensitive periods in the developmental process (see Table 1.1):

1. The *sensory-attachment* stage is the first stage in this schema. It ranges from birth to about 18 months of age. The processes that dominate this stage are fundamental sensory processes that serve to aid in neurological development and attachment processes that merely reflect the degree to which the newborn child is dependent on others for its very survival. Stimulus impoverishment during this stage results in apathy, deficits in social attachment, social alienation, and depression. Extreme sensory impoverishment is likely to result in sensory retardation as well. Excessive stimulus nutriment during this stage is likely to result in hypersensitivities; stimulus-seeking, highly demanding hyperactive behavior; and abnormal interpersonal dependencies.

2. *Sensorimotor-autonomy* is the second stage in the present neuropsychological growth model. This stage begins at roughly 12 months and may range through 6 years. This stage is characterized by the refinement of what were gross muscular activities into finer motor-controlled behavior. As the abilities for verbalization, locomotion, and fine motor manipulation increase, the child becomes more autonomous. Stimulus impoverishment is likely to result in a lack of exploratory and competitive behavior, and the stifling of such behavior is likely to result in timidity, passivity, and submissiveness. Excessive stimulus nutriment, on the other hand, is likely to result in uncontrolled self-expression, social irresponsibility, and narcissism.

3. The third stage in the present model is called the *intracortical-initiative* stage. This stage ranges from about 4 years of age through adolescence. During this stage, we observe a rapid

Table 1.1 Stages of Neuropsychological Development

Stage	Age Range	Dominant Processes	Effects of Stimulus Impoverishment	Effects of Excessive Stimulus Nutriment
Sensory-Attachment	Birth through 18 months	Sensory neurological development. Psychological attachment.	Sensory retardation. Apathy. Social alienation.	Abnormal dependency. Hyperactivity.
Sensorimotor-Autonomy	12 months through 6 years	Refinement of verbal, locomotive, and fine motor skills. A process of increasing autonomy and exploratory behavior.	Lack of exploratory behavior. Development of passive behaviors.	Social irresponsibility. Narcissism.
Intracortical-Initiative	4 years through adolescence	Rapid neocortical growth. Development of abstract mental abilities.	Lack of abstract cognitive ability. Inability to plan and organize. Impulsive behavior.	Rigidity. Compulsivity.

growth in higher cortical brain function. The child can plan, organize, and act in his/her own behalf. Thought processes evolve beyond the limitations of concrete thought into the domain of abstract thought. Abstract thought processes allow the child to develop both an internal base and an introspective ability to attempt to act upon his/her environment. Stimulus impoverishment at this stage is likely to result in an inability to find direction in one's life, a lack of discipline, and an impulsive behavior pattern. Furthermore, the individual tends to demonstrate the inability to mobilize and direct resources in a productive manner, often behaving in irresponsible and "immature" ways. Excessive stimulus nutriment during this stage is likely to result in suppressed spontaneity, flexibility, and creativity. The result is a rigid, restrained individual.

In considering these three neuropsychological stages, we should mention that each stage reflects an interaction of biological and environmental influences. Each stage sets the basis for the subsequent stage. If the processes at one stage are incomplete or dysfunctional, the subsequent stages are likely to be adversely affected as well.

In summarizing the origins of personality to this point, we see that the ultimate biological potentials of each organism may be defined by genetic factors. However, the rate and ultimate level to which these potentials are achieved will be shaped by environmental factors that influence the biochemical composition and functional anatomy of the biological substrates themselves.

Environmental Factors

As implied above, normal psychological development and function depend on an orderly substrate of neuronal connections. It can be argued that although the basic foundation for these biological networks is laid through genetic programming, these networks are then modified through environmental experience, or stimulus nutriment. These processes collectively shape the biological foundations for personality development. In this section, we will discuss an additional role that environmental factors play in the development of personality. This role is best conceived in the context of learning.

Learning may be thought of as the acquisition of various cognitive, affective, and overt behavioral responses that the organism did not initially possess. Because these cognitive, affective, and overt behavioral responses become the manifestation of personality itself, we should make note of how the majority of such responses are acquired. Most learning relevant to personality development may be categorized under three headings: contiguous learning, instrumental learning, and vicarious learning.

Contiguous Learning. Contiguous learning represents the simplest method of acquiring new cognitions, affect, and overt behavioral patterns. Simply stated, the principle of contiguity learning is "that any set of environmental elements which occurs either simultaneously or in close temporal order will become associated with each other" (Millon & Millon, 1974, p. 158). Contiguous learning helps explain the heterogeneous nature of many stimulus complexes that seem to be characteristic of many learning paradigms.

Instrumental Learning. Perhaps the most powerful method of acquisition yet demonstrated, however, is instrumental learning. Instrumental learning principles have grown primarily out of the work of two researchers: Edward Thorndike (1935), beginning in the 1890s, followed by B. F. Skinner (1953). The bases of instrumental learning can be best summarized in Thorndike's law of effect. This states that behavior that is followed by consequences that are satisfying, or rewarding, to the individual will be repeated; on the other hand, behavior that is followed by consequences that the individual finds punishing, or unpleasant, will be reduced. Skinner applied the work of Thorndike to a wide range of human endeavors. Skinner has gone so far as to argue that all behavior is determined by reinforcement or punishment, that is, the consequences provided by the social environment. Later writers, such as Albert Ellis (1962) and Richard Lazarus (1966, 1976), argue that the same learning principles that undergird overt behavior govern covert (cognitive-affective) behavior. This new field has been referred to as cognitive behaviorism.

Vicarious Learning. Finally, we must consider the process of vicarious learning. According to Bandura (1974), "As social beings, [people] observe the conduct of others and the occasions on which it is rewarded, disregarded, or punished. They can therefore profit from observed consequences as well as their own direct experiences" (p. 861). In other words, humans can learn by observing as well as by doing. This is an extremely efficient and necessary process and one that accounts for the remarkably rapid rate at which a child becomes "civilized." This form of learning may be referred to as vicarious learning. Bandura (1974) argues that vicarious learning introduces another perspective into the overall learning model—cognitive evaluation of observed phenomena. He concludes, "Human conduct is better explained by the relational influence of observed and direct consequences rather than by either factor alone" (p. 861).

Pathogenic Learning. We see, then, that there are three types of behavior acquisition particularly relevant to personality development: contiguous learning, instrumental learning, and vicarious learning. It seems reasonable to believe that all three combine ultimately to shape the formation of a normal, healthy personality. Similarly, however, these same forces must somehow act to shape the abnormal, unhealthy personality. "Popular psychology has it that most forms of psychopathology can be traced to a single, very severe experience, the residues of which account for the manifest disorder. Current thinking [,however,] indicates that most pathological behaviors accrue gradually through repetitive learning experiences" (Millon, 1981, p. 97). Using this perspective, we can identify three major processes of pathogenic learning (see Table 1.2).

1. Positive reinforcement of maladaptive, self-defeating behavior patterns.
2. Negative reinforcement of maladaptive, self-defeating behavior patterns.
3. Underlearning.

Recalling Thorndike's law of effect will assist us in understanding the first two processes of pathogenic learning. Thorndike demonstrated that behavior that is followed by a reward will tend to increase. Using this perspective, we can understand why people behave in maladaptive, self-defeating ways: because such behavior (albeit obviously self-defeating in the long run) is somehow rewarding to the individual, usually in the immediate short-run. In some instances, maladaptive behavior directly results in some positive reinforcement (defined as the addition of a rewarding stimulus). For example, cheating on an exam may increase a student's grade on a specific exam, but it will not help that student ultimately learn the desired knowledge. This behavior is maladaptive because although the short-term goal has been served, the long-term goal has been eroded. In other instances, some maladap-

Table 1.2 Major Processes of Pathogenic Learning

1. Positive reinforcement of maladaptive, self-defeating behavior.
2. Negative reinforcement of maladaptive, self-defeating behavior.
3. Underlearning.

tive behavior may provide negative reinforcement (defined as the removal of an undesirable stimulus). For example, lying about, or denying responsibility for, one's own actions may temporarily avoid punishment but may tend to inhibit the individual from learning how to accept "adult" responsibilities. In either case, the maladaptive behavior will increase because it has resulted in a desired outcome (the addition of a reward or the removal of an undesired stimulus).

The final category of pathogenic learning involves underlearning. Underlearning refers to a sheer insufficiency of knowledge or skills necessary for the development of adaptive behavior patterns. Underlearning may be found in the form of inadequate or incomplete learning experiences, contradictory communications, or imitation of defective/dysfunctional models.

To summarize, we see that personality development is a function of biological factors interacting with learning in response to environmental factors. The interaction of biological and environmental factors is clearly complex and will vary from person to person. However, we believe that biological factors serve to set the foundation for personality development and that environmental factors, through processes of bioenvironmental interaction and learning, serve to shape the final nature of human personality. This explanation helps us understand not only the normal personality, but also the abnormal personality as well. Through processes of inadequate genetic transmission, insufficient prenatal or postnatal metabolic and stimulus nutrition, and, finally, through pathogenic learning, the normal personality may be transformed into an abnormal, unhealthy personality.

EARLY PROCESSES AND PERSONALITY DEVELOPMENT

It is a basic premise of this text that early developmental processes are more significant in the formation of personality than are later experiences. According to Millon (1981), "Early experiences are not only ingrained more pervasively and forcefully, but their effects tend to persist and are more difficult to modify than the effects of later experiences" (p. 97). This conclusion is based on two assumptions: (1) that the biological foundations of personality are constructed early in life and are difficult to modify in later life and (2) that the environmental influences on personality that are learned in early life are also more difficult to modify compared to other learned experience.

Part of the continuity that we see from childhood to adulthood may, indeed, be a form of underlying biological substrate. Although some of that biological constitution may be genetic, we reviewed in the previous section the notion that neuronal maturation may also be shaped from environmental influences through a process involving what Rapaport (1958) called stimulus nutriment. Once constructed, the underlying biological substrates of personality may be very difficult to alter.

Although the biological substrates may define the boundaries of personality development in the gross sense, learning must assume the responsibility for the definitive shaping of human personality as we know it. McClelland (1951) has argued that the early learning experiences of childhood are unique when compared to later learning experiences. He argues that the events of early life are experienced in such a manner as to make them difficult to reproduce and, therefore, resistant to extinction.

Thus, because early influences on personality development (1) may occur during the prenatal and postnatal stages of neuronal development and serve to construct a network of neuronal substrates and (2) may occur under unique learning conditions that cannot be replicated in later life, we may conclude that the first years of life are perhaps the most important for the formation of personality development. Perhaps owing to this fact, we further believe that personality tends to be both stable and consistent.

The term stability is applied when a trait endures over time, whereas the term consistency is applied when behavior that is displayed in one situation is exhibited in other situations. "Temporal stability and cross-situational consistency are fundamental to the concept of personality. If individuals fail to exhibit reasonably stable and consistent behaviors, then the very notion of personality itself may be in jeopardy" (Millon, 1981, pp. 20–21). Earlier in this chapter, we defined personality patterns as being deeply rooted, persistent over time, and resistant to extinction. Inherent in the use of those descriptors is the belief that personality patterns are, indeed, stable and consistent.

That is *not* to say that all individuals show agreement in which aspects of behavior are consistent. Research has shown that individuals differ in the degree to which their behavior is stable and consistent (Endler & Magnusson, 1976; Epstein, 1979). Evidence indicates that individuals display stability and consistency only in certain characteristics, that is, some traits will be extremely resistant to change, whereas others may not. Furthermore, these traits will vary among individuals. Therefore, we must conclude that each individual possesses a small and distinct group of primary traits that persist and endure. These stable and consistent traits are what we mean when we speak of personality. In addition, "personality pathology comprises those stable and consistent traits that persist inflexibly, are exhibited inappropriately, and foster vicious circles that perpetuate and intensify already present difficulties (Millon, 1981, p. 23).

Despite our present conclusions, we in no way believe that personality (or personality disorder) is unalterable. Rather, we merely see it as being deeply embedded and, therefore, difficult to alter. True alteration of personality will usually result: (1) naturally, through a process of learning that contradicts previous learning experiences (probably combined with cognitive introspection) or through a process of extreme physical or psychological trauma or (2) somewhat artificially, through a process of planned professional intervention, for example, psychotherapy.

Summary

It has been the purpose of this chapter to introduce the reader to the nature of human personality. Let us review some of the main points.

1. Personality may be thought of as a *pattern* of deeply embedded and broadly exhibited cognitive, affective, and overt behavioral traits that persist over extended periods of time.

2. A normal and healthy personality may be conceived of as "the capacity to function autonomously and competently, a tendency to adjust to one's social environment effectively and efficiently, a subjective sense of contentment and satisfaction, and the ability to self-actualize or to fulfill one's potentials" (Millon, 1981, p. 8).

3. Normality and abnormality are best conceived of as relative concepts. They may be thought of as representing points along a continuum rather than as discrete categories.

4. An abnormal, or unhealthy, personality pattern is characterized by adaptive inflexibility; a tendency to foster vicious, self-defeating cycles; and tenuous stability that is fragile and lacks resiliency. All of these factors inhibit the individual's ability to cope and function in an autonomous, self-satisfying manner.

5. The origins of personality may be traced to three primary sets of factors: basic biological factors, bioenvironmental factors, and environmental factors.

   a. Basic biological factors include heredity and prenatal maternal factors.

   b. Bioenvironmental factors are factors that represent a combination of biological and environmental factors that are so enmeshed in one another that no one component takes dominance as the primary component. Neuropsychological development represents the epitome of a bioenvironmental determinant of personality.

   c. Environmental factors include contiguous, instrumental, and vicarious learning.

6. Early developmental processes are more significant in the formation of personality than are later life experiences. This conclusion is based on two assumptions:

a. Early life experiences are intertwined in biological undergirdings.

b. Early life experiences set the structure and tone for subsequent learning throughout life.

7. Personality is both stable and consistent.

a. Stability refers to the endurance of a trait over time.

b. Consistency refers to the replication of behavior across various situations.

8. Regardless of the assumptions that personality is both stable and consistent, personality and personality disorders are amenable to change.

CHAPTER 2

Personality Types and Their Disorders

In Chapter 1, we described the nature and origins of human personality. In this chapter, we will address the classification of personality and its disorders.

THE CLASSIFICATION DILEMMA

Before addressing the issue of classification with regards to personality and its disorders, let us address a more fundamental issue—the issue of classification itself.

A classification or diagnostic label may be thought of as a symbol used by clinicians to summarize the particular cognitions, emotions, and overt behavior patterns that somehow characterize the individual. During the 1960s and 1970s, there was considerable reluctance on the part of many mental health professionals to use classification schemata or diagnostic labels. Three major objections to the use of such systems emerged:

1. The act of labeling individuals often leads those individuals to adopt a role that reflects society's expectation of someone possessing that particular label; therefore, labels may be seen as a form of a *self-fulfilling prophecy* (Goffman, 1973; Scheff, 1973).

2. Rather than being used as descriptions, labels become explanations of the very behaviors they were intended to simply summarize; for example, it is an inappropriate use of a diagnostic label to submit that a patient experiences delusional thinking *because* he/she is paranoid. Rather, the term paranoid has validity only as a description of the patient's behavior. When diagnostic labels are used to explain behavior, a form of erroneous *circular logic* has been employed (Millon, 1969).

3. The classification of an individual may be viewed as a justification for depriving that individual of his/her individuality (Stuart, 1970) and perhaps even his/her humanity (Sarbin & Mancuso, 1970). Such *externally imposed homogeneity* leads clinicians and others to view all individuals with the same diagnostic label, not as individuals, but as one in a group. This approach propagates the traditional syndromal discontinuity model of mental disorders and at the same time denies the person his/her individuality.

Despite these three potential problems with the use of classification schemata and diagnostic labels, we must continue to support their use. We believe that a classification system serves to simplify the search for relevant characteristics. Categorization and labeling can serve as a valuable starting point for the clinician. They can serve to enable the clinician to deduce characteristics of the person's psychological development that may not otherwise be readily obtainable. They may guide the clinician to various treatment options or alert him/her to potential resistences or complications.

In conclusion, classification systems and diagnostic labels can serve both the clinician and the patient well if used appropriately. The problems of *self-fulfilling prophecy, circular logic,* and *externally imposed homogeneity,* although legitimate concerns, seem to us to be no justification for throwing the baby out with the bathwater. The resolution of the classification/labeling dilemma will be found in (1) the refinement of classification systems, (2) the proper use of such systems, and (3) the realization by clinicians that classifications or labels can never be ends unto themselves.

HISTORY OF PERSONALITY CLASSIFICATION

As far as written records can document, Hippocrates, writing in the 5th century B.C., was the first to formulate typologies of personality. It was Hippocrates who postulated that every individual possessed four bodily humors. These humors were yellow bile, black bile, blood, and phlegm. These humors, or fluids, were thought to be the embodiment of earth, water, fire, and air, which were declared to be the four basic elements of the universe by the philosopher Empedocles. To Hippocrates, normal personality was represented by a functional, quantitative balance among the four humors. Psychopathology, however, was thought to arise from a dysfunctional, quantitative imbalance of these humors. The specific psychopathology an individual would experience was postulated to be the result of one pathologically dominant humor. Excessive yellow bile resulted in a choleric, or irascible, personality. Excessive black bile resulted in a melancholic, or sad, personality. Excessive blood resulted in a sanguine, or hopeful, personality. Finally, excessive phlegm resulted in a phlegmatic, or apathetic, personality.

The humoral typologies of Hippocrates are reflected both in the work of Plato, Aristotle, and Galen, and in that of Caelius Aurelianus who translated the Hippocratic formulations into Latin around the 5th century A.D.

As the Roman Empire fell, so did the revised and extended work of Hippocrates. It was not until the late 18th century that systematic efforts to analyze the basic elements of personality were reborn.

Franz Joseph Gall (1758–1828) made what was an honest and serious attempt to construct a science of personology. Gall based his typologies on phrenology. This was a personology based on the measured variations of the skull. The rationale that Gall presented for the use of skull-contour variations as a basis for understanding personality was logical for the science of his day. Gall felt that mental processes would be reflected in the morphological structure of the brain, which would ultimately be reflected in the contours of the skull. Although obviously invalid, his model did serve as a precursor for the morphological typologies of Ernst Kretschmer (1888–1964) and William Sheldon.

In the late 19th century, psychiatrists Pierre Janet (1859–1947) and Emil Kraepelin (1856–1926) promulgated personality typologies limited to the mentally ill. Janet's work focused on what was then termed neurotic processes, whereas Kraepelin is noted for nosology surrounding what was termed manic-depressive psychosis and dementia praecox.

In his text *Physique and Character* (1925), Kretschmer synthesized Gall's notion relating body structure to personality and Carl Jung's (1875–1961) characterization of extravert and introvert personalities. Kretschmer observed that schizophrenics possessed elongated physiques and that manic-depressives possessed rounded and soft physiques; he extended this into a theory connecting body build to normal personality. In a series of studies, he demonstrated that tall and slender individuals tended to be more introversive, whereas heavier, more rotund individuals tended to be more extraversive.

Sheldon (Sheldon, 1940; Sheldon & Stevens, 1942), a disciple of Kretschmer, developed an extensive series of hypotheses concerning the relationship between body build, personality, and psychopathology. He identified three basic morphological dimensions, called somatotypes. These were endomorphy, characterized by a soft and round physical appearance; mesomorphy, characterized by a solid and muscular physical appearance; and ectomorphy, characterized by a fragile and lean physical appearance. The personality temperaments of these three body builds were identified as viscerotonia (comfort loving, people oriented), somatotonia (assertive, competitive, action oriented), and cerebrotonia (emotionally restrained, apprehensive, solitude oriented), respectively. Sheldon argued that the viscerotonic temperament had the potential to deteriorate into affectively oriented (fluctuations from elation to depression) mental disorders, the somatotonic temperament had the potential to deteriorate into paranoid mental disorders, and finally that the cerebrotonic temperament had the potential to deteriorate into the heboid disorders (characterized by withdrawal and autistic fantasy).

Advances in mathematics in the late 19th century led to a reawakened interest in identifying the "basic units" of personality. Mathematically derived factors (i.e., a set of independent elements derived from behavioral samples) are statistically combined according to their common aspects and then used to create typologies. This factor-analytic method was applied to personality research by Cyril Burt, Lloyd Thurstone, J. P. Guilford and most recently by Hans Eysenck and Raymond Cattell. The goal of such research was to identify statistically based personality factors that may serve as the basis for personality typologies.

Gordon Allport (1897–1967) was highly critical of factor-analytic approaches to personality typology. He stated that factors were statistical fictions devoid of intrinsic psychological meaning. He also took exception to the notion that personality factors must be independent of one another. In his classic text, *Personality: A Psychological Interpretation* (1937), he argued that personality typologies should be based on trait concepts, that is, relatively enduring personality dispositions that underlie overt behavior. Allport supported the growing trend that personality is best conceived of as a unique and highly integrated, or holistic, system.

An integrated systems view of personality argues that personality is a function of an integrated, interactive unity between biological and environmental factors. This view was first fostered by the early Gestalt psychologists and later expanded by Kurt Goldstein (1876–1965) and Kurt Lewin (1890–1947).

Goldstein (1939, 1959) argued that personality could not be understood by isolating behaviors because the organism operated as a whole unit that could not be fully understood by only analyzing its parts. Based on his experience as a neurosurgeon, Goldstein offered considerable evidence that the human organism operates as an integrated, interactive whole, not as an aggregation of parts.

Lewin (1935, 1936), following a similar philosophy, portrayed personality as a structure composed of interdependent and communicating regions interacting in a dynamic equilibrium with a psychological environment. Of particular importance is Lewin's notion that the environment affects the individual on the basis of how that individual perceives and consciously interprets the environment, *not* on the basis of the environment's objective reality.

The system's perspective of personality was significantly extended by Henry Murray (1938), Gardner Murphy (1947), and Theodore Millon (1969, 1981). To these authors, personality can only be understood through an appreciation of the intrinsic unity between biological factors and environmental stimulation. Intrinsic and pervasive, personality represents an individual's distinctive pattern of thinking, feeling, and coping; this pattern represents the epitome of biological and environmental integration.

The personality typology presented in this text is based on the work of Millon (1969, 1981) and has played a large role in forming the theoretical basis for the classification schema for personality disorders employed in DSM-III, Axis II.[1]

The present classification system for personality and its disorders grew out of a dissatisfaction with the personality classification systems employed by the previous manuals (DSM-I and DSM-II). The ma-

----

[1]Unlike its predecessor, DSM-II, the DSM-III offers a multiaxial diagnostic system that includes "Clinical Syndromes" (Axis I), "Personality Disorders" (Axis II), "Physical Disorders and Conditions" (Axis III), "Severity of Psychosocial Stressors" (Axis IV), and "Highest Level of Adaptive Functioning Past Year" (Axis V). This format now places the consideration of personality disorders in a prominent position when developing a psychiatric diagnosis.

jor shortcomings in the previous nosologies included, according to Millon (1969):

1. The lack of a coherent theoretical foundation for the classification of personality disorders.
2. The tendency to present personality disorders as discrete, pathological entities but failing to recognize potential interrelationships among such disorders.
3. An emphasis on "dramatic" symptomatology but neglecting less dramatic, more typical and clinically relevant "everyday" symptoms and behaviors.
4. The formulation of classifications based on tradition and "clinical impression" rather than more rigorous empirical bases.
5. The tendency to view all of the personality disorders as being equally severe.
6. The disregard for the wide *range* of symptoms that exist within *each* personality disorder and the value of seeing these symptoms as existing in variable intensities along numerous descriptive continua within each disorder. (This is still a major shortcoming of the current DSM-III.)

CLASSIFYING PERSONALITY AND ITS DISORDERS: A BIOSOCIAL LEARNING SYSTEM

The present classification system, referred to as a biosocial learning approach, was developed by Millon as an attempt at improving the shortcomings inherent in the previous DSM systems for personality disorders. Aspects of this system have been incorporated in, and serve as the basis for, the present DSM's classification schema for personality disorders (Axis II).

More specifically, the present classification system:

1. Builds on a coherent and integrating theory of personality development and psychopathology (Millon, 1969).
2. Recognizes the natural covariation or clustering that occurs between various aspects of specific personalities or personality disorders.
3. Sensitizes the clinician to the typical "everyday" symptoms of personality disorders, while noting their more dramatic symptoms.
4. Employs empirically generated evidence as well as theoretical

formulations in support of its typologies (see Millon, 1981, for a review; Millon, 1982; see also Millon & Klerman, in press).

5. Allows for the differentiation of personality disorders according to their severity.

6. Recognizes the value of describing personality and its disorders by using sets of descriptive criteria placed along graduated descriptive continua that are collectively reflective of a potentially wide range of symptoms and variable symptom intensities rather than using discrete symptom states to describe personality disorders (as is the case in the current DSM-III).

Any classification system oversimplifies its subject. The present classification system is no different. However, we cannot condemn a classification system for failing to account for the unique characteristics of individual cases. Inevitably, innumerable differences and subtle variations of behavior will be found among individuals who are classified together no matter what classification system is used. This loss of individuality is inherent in any process that attempts to group individuals together. Despite this inevitable problem, a classification system becomes of value when its unifying theme is capable of: (1) highlighting *salient* and *clinically relevant* features of the subject it is attempting to categorize and (2) accurately grouping individuals possessing these features in common. We believe that the present classificaton meets these criteria.

A Reinforcement Matrix

In attempting to develop a coherent model of human personality, it is of value to search for unifying themes or undergirdings that may be used as a conceptual basis from which subsequent descriptions of personality variations may extract some meaning or relevance. It is interesting to note that when one reviews the personality patterns described by theorists such as Freud (1957), Fromm (1955), Heymans and Wiersma (1906), Horney (1939), Kollarits (1912) as well as by researchers such as Leary (1957), Lorr (Lorr, Klett, & McNair, 1963), McDougall (1908), and Millon (1969), one finds considerable overlap as to the salient types of interaction/coping strategies used by the individuals. In the case of the present model for personality and personality disorders, we will use the notion of reinforcement as the unifying theme around which the model will be constructed. Therefore, these reinforcement strategies may be thought of as the core elements of personality, as noted in Chapter 1.

The term reinforcement has been used synonymously with the terms reward, satisfaction, and even pleasure throughout relevant literature. The notion of reinforcement lies at the core of the present model. We are interested in examining the process by which individuals seek to obtain their reinforcements, that is, their pleasures in life.

The process of seeking reinforcement can be analyzed from two broad, interacting perspectives, or *polarities:* (1) an analysis of the *instrumental* behaviors utilized to obtain reinforcement, that is, *how* the individual seeks reinforcement and (2) an analysis of the *sources* of reinforcement, that is, *where* the individual seeks reinforcement.

The *instrumental polarity* helps us define in what manner the individual will seek reinforcement and has two discrete points: (1) the active pursuit of reinforcement and (2) the passive pursuit of reinforcement.

Individuals who pursue reinforcement actively are proactive individuals. They are characterized by alertness, vigilance, persistence, ambition, and goal-directed behavior. "They are firmly committed to secure what they want; they plan strategies, scan alternatives, manipulative events and circumvent obstacles, all to the end of eliciting pleasure and rewards or evading the distress of punishment and anxiety" (Millon, 1969, p. 195). These individuals are energetic and enterprising, and they demonstrate a need to control their environment.

Juxtaposed to the active individuals are the passive individuals. Individuals who seek reinforcement passively are reactive individuals. They initiate few strategies. Rather, they seem content to wait for their environment to provide them with reinforcement. They display varying degrees of inertness and tend to acquiesce quickly to others' needs. Some individuals may be temperamentally ill equipped to assert themselves. According to Millon (1969), "past experience has deprived them of an opportunity to acquire a sense of competence, a confidence in their ability to master the events of their environment; equally possible is a naive confidence that things will come their way with little or no effort on their part" (p. 195). In some cases, passive individuals may seem suspended, immobile, restrained, or even listless. They seldom act on their own behalf, being content to wait for the environment to act on them; only then will they choose to react to those events.

The *source polarity* helps us define the source from which the individual's reinforcements will be sought. Within this polar dimension, we find four discrete points: independent, dependent, ambivalent, and detached.

The person who seeks reinforcement independently, seeks reinforcement from himself/herself. This individual has learned that self-reliance is the most effective way to gain reinforcement and avoid punishment. It is possible that a need for control coupled with disappointed expectations in others have helped shape aspects of this pattern.

Persons who seek reinforcement dependently seek reinforcement from others. They have learned that to maximize reinforcement, they should depend on others. Interpersonal attention, affection, and support are important for these individuals.

The person who seeks reinforcement ambivalently is unsure of where to seek reinforcement. Unlike the independent and dependent styles, which are characterized by a definite preference, the ambivalent has learned that reinforcement can be obtained by acting both independently and dependently. Unable to resolve this dilemma, the ambivalent individual is often trapped in a vacillating pattern between dependence and conformity on the one hand and independence, autonomy, and even aggression on the other hand. The result is that these individuals often become plagued by feelings of dissonance and self-doubt. They may develop rigid self-protective controls. Trapped in conflict, they may develop feelings of guilt, self-deprecation, and pessimism.

Finally, the person who seeks reinforcement from a detached perspective fails, in reality, to seek reinforcement at all. These individuals seem unwilling or unable to achieve reinforcement from self of others. This deficit appears to present itself in the individual's lack of drive to achieve pleasure or avoid punishment.

A combination of the two polarities just discussed yields a 2×4 matrix (instrumental behavior $\times$ source) that may be used to define the unifying central theme, or core, of our personality model: reinforcement. The matrix that is formed through the interaction of our two polarities yields eight cells. Each cell will contain a basic personality pattern (see Table 2.1).

Normal Personality Patterns

By utilizing the matrix that was created from the interaction of the reinforcement polarities, we have a tool that allows us to define the generic aspects of normal personality functioning (see Table 2.2).

The following represents brief descriptions of the eight basic normal personality patterns derived from the 2×4 reinforcement matrix. In describing these personality patterns, we have elected to utilize five standardized criteria:

Table 2.1 A Reinforcement Matrix

Instrumental Behavior Pattern	Source of Reinforcement			
	Independent (Self)	Dependent (Others)	Ambivalent (Confused)	Detached (Neither Self Nor Others)
Active (proactive)	1	3	5	7
Passive (reactive)	2	4	6	8

Table 2.2   Normal Personality Patterns

Instrumental Behavior Pattern	Source of Reinforcement			
	Independent	*Dependent*	*Ambivalent*	*Detached*
Active (Proactive)	Forceful personality	Sociable personality	Sensitive personality	Inhibited personality
Passive (Reactive)	Confident personality	Cooperative personality	Respectful personality	Introversive personality

1. Behavioral appearance (i.e., how the individual appears to others).
2. Interpersonal conduct (i.e., how the individual interacts with others).
3. Cognitive style (i.e., the characteristic nature of the individual's thought processes).
4. Affective expression (i.e., how the individual displays emotion).
5. Self-perception (i.e., the manner in which the individual sees himself/herself).

The eight basic normal personality patterns derived from the reinforcement matrix are:

1. The forceful personality pattern (active-independent) is characterized by:
   a. an adventurous, risk-taking behavioral appearance.
   b. intimidating interpersonal conduct.
   c. a subjective cognitive style.
   d. angry affective expressions.
   e. an assertive self-perception.
2. The confident personality pattern (passive-independent) is characterized by:
   a. a poised behavioral appearance.
   b. unempathic interpersonal conduct.
   c. an imaginative cognitive style.
   d. a serene affective disposition.
   e. a confident self-perception.

3. The sociable personality pattern (active-dependent) is characterized by:
   a. an animated behavioral appearance.
   b. demonstrative interpersonal conduct.
   c. a superficial cognitive style.
   d. a dramatic affective disposition.
   e. a charming self-perception.

4. The cooperative personality pattern (passive-dependent) is characterized by:
   a. a docile behavioral appearance.
   b. compliant interpersonal conduct.
   c. an open cognitive style.
   d. tender affective expression.
   e. a weak self-perception.

5. The sensitive personality pattern (active-ambivalent) is characterized by:
   a. an erratic behavioral appearance.
   b. unpredictable interpersonal conduct.
   c. a divergent cognitive style.
   d. pessimistic affective expression.
   e. an unappreciated self-perception.

6. The respectful personality pattern (passive-ambivalent) is characterized by:
   a. a highly organized behavioral appearance.
   b. polite interpersonal conduct.
   c. a circumspect cognitive style.
   d. restrained affective expression.
   e. a reliable self-perception.

7. The inhibited personality pattern (active-detached) is characterized by:
   a. a watchful behavioral appearance.
   b. shy interpersonal conduct.
   c. a preoccupied cognitive style.
   d. uneasy affective expression.
   e. a lonely self-perception.

8. The introverted personality pattern (passive-detached) is characterized by:
   a. a passive behavioral appearance.
   b. unobtrusive interpersonal conduct.
   c. a vague cognitive style.
   d. bland affective expression.
   e. a placid self-perception.

The basic personality patterns just described are graphically summarized in Table 2.3. It is important to note that, in reality, it would be unlikely to find an individual whose personality conforms to any one of the eight theoretically "pure" patterns described. Rather, individuals' personality patterns more commonly tend to be "clusters," or combinations, of two or three of the patterns we have delineated.

The Syndromal Continuity Issue

Having described the characteristics of the eight basic normal personality patterns to emerge from the 2 × 4 reinforcement matrix and the biosocial learning theory on which that matrix is built, we will now turn our discussion to personality disorders. Before that, however, we must return our attention to a brief discussion of the relationship between normal personality and the pathological personality disorder. This section will address that topic and at the same time serve as a segue for the discussion of basic personality disorders.

If you believe that personality disorders represent *qualitatively* distinct mental processes when compared to normal personality patterns, you would probably support the notion of what has been called *syndromal discontinuity*. On the other hand, if you believe that personality disorders merely represent *quantitatively* pathological extensions, or elaborations, of normal personality patterns, then you would probably support the notion of what is called *syndromal continuity*. According to Millon (1981), "The notion of syndromal discontinuity is an outgrowth of the belief that all psychopathologies are qualitatively distinct disease entities. Syndromal continuity reflects the view that all psychological abnormalities are quantitative deviations from the average on a distribution of traits. Discontinuity implies that some unusual process has intruded upon the individual's functioning" (pp. 18–19).

We would support the notion of syndromal continuity. In other words, as the concept relates to this discussion, personality disorders may be seen as representing exaggerated and pathologically distorted deviations emanating from a normal and healthy distribution of traits and *not* as the intrusion of some alien external force upon the individual's personality. This concept can be shown through the use of a continuum.

In Figure 2.1, we see the dependent behavioral pattern represented as a relatively homogeneous distribution of traits dispersed along a continuum according to their functional value. In other words, the pattern of behaviors generally defined as being indicative of depen-

Table 2.3 Multidimensional Criterion List for Normal Personality Patterns

Personality Pattern	Dimension				
	Behavioral Appearance	Interpersonal Conduct	Cognitive Style	Affective Expression	Self-Perception
Forceful	Adventurous	Intimidating	Subjective	Anger	Assertive
Confident	Poised	Unempathic	Imaginative	Serene	Confident
Sociable	Animated	Demonstrative	Superficial	Dramatic	Charming
Cooperative	Docile	Compliant	Open	Tender	Weak
Sensitive	Erratic	Unpredictable	Divergent	Pessimistic	Unappreciated
Respectful	Organized	Polite	Circumspect	Restrained	Reliable
Inhibited	Watchful	Shy	Preoccupied	Uneasy	Lonely
Introversive	Passive	Unobtrusive	Vague	Bland	Placid

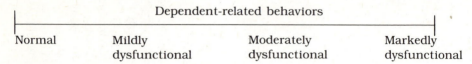

Figure 2.1 Syndromal continuity.

dency is represented on a continuum ranging from normal, healthy, and commonly encountered dependent behaviors, on the left, to increasingly dysfunctional and pathological dependent behaviors as one moves to the right along the continuum. The continuum is but a graphic device used to demonstrate that psychopathological conditions represent but quantitative extensions of normal and quite functional behavioral traits. Although in our example we used only the dependent-related behaviors, we feel that the concept of syndromal continuity applies for all of the eight basic personality patterns and their dysfunctional elaborations: the eight basic personality disorders.

Table 2.4 serves as a graphic representation of how the syndromal continuity hypothesis relates to the DSM-III, Axis II personality disorders. Using Table 2.4, the dependent personality disorder, for example, may be seen as a more severe syndromal variant of the cooperative personality pattern, discussed earlier, but as a less severe variant of the borderline personality disorder—and so throughout the matrix.

Historically, the concept of syndromal continuity can be traced back some 2,500 years to the personality typologies of Hippocrates (described earlier). It will be recalled that Hippocrates believed psychopathology resulted from quantitative imbalances among the four basic humors and not from the intrusion of some alien substances. The notion of syndromal continuity can be found again two centuries later in the work of another Greek physician, Aretaeus, who practiced medicine in ancient Rome. Aretaeus is reported to have believed that psychopathology was but an extreme of normal personality functioning. So, we see that the syndromal continuity hypothesis dates back some 2,500 years to Hippocrates, yet still survives in one form or another in the modern-day writing of theorists such as Sheldon (1940), Szasz (1960), Beck (1967), and Millon (1969, 1981).

It should be noted at this point, however, that the syndromal continuity hypothesis has yet to be fully accepted throughout psychiatric and psychological literature.

Personality Disorders—DSM-III, Axis II

Let us now examine the nature of personality disorders according to the present theory and model. We will begin by reminding the reader

Table 2.4 From Personality to Personality Disorder

Instrumental Behavior Pattern	Source of Reinforcement			
	Independent	*Dependent*	*Ambivalent*	*Detached*
Active (proactive)	Forceful personality → Antisocial personality disorder / Paranoid personality disorder	Sociable personality → Histrionic personality disorder / Borderline personality disorder	Sensitive personality → Passive-aggressive personality disorder / Borderline personality disorder	Inhibited personality → Avoidant personality disorder / Schizotypal personality disorder
Passive (reactive)	Confident personality → Narcissistic personality disorder / Paranoid personality disorder	Cooperative personality → Dependent personality disorder / Borderline personality disorder	Respectful personality → Compulsive personality disorder / Paranoid personality disorder	Introversive personality → Schizoid personality disorder / Schizotypal personality disorder

that it is our belief that the personality disorders to be discussed are considered to be *pathological extensions* of the personality patterns just described. That is to say, the personality disorders are thought to emerge out of normal personality patterns as a result of a complex interaction of biological dispositions, maladaptive learning, and especially challenging environmental stressors. From such a perspective, the reader will find that the personality disorder described herein parallel the DSM-III, Axis II disorders but are generally *broader* in their formulations and less restrictive in their clinical criteria. This is due to the nature of the syndromal continuity hypothesis and the continua upon which those traits reside (compared to the discrete clinical criteria use by the DSM-III).

Our discussion of the 11 DSM-III personality disorders will be in two stages. First, we will summarize the eight personality disorders that we feel constitute mildly severe pathological conditions. These are summarized by way of the matrix in Table 2.5, and they are then described briefly within the text, using the same standardized criteria used to describe the normal personality patterns. Second, we will describe the 3 remaining DSM-III personality disorders, which we believe to be of moderate to marked severity.

Mildly Severe Personality Disorders:

1. The antisocial (active-independent) personality disorder is characterized by:

Table 2.5   Eight Mildly Severe Personality Disorders[a]

Instrumental Behavior Pattern	Source of Reinforcement			
	Independent	*Dependent*	*Ambivalent*	*Detached*
Active (proactive)	Antisocial	Histrionic	Passive-aggressive	Avoidant
Passive (reactive)	Narcissistic	Dependent	Compulsive	Schizoid

[a]The terms used to identify the 8 personality disorders adheres to the DSM-III nomenclature.

a. a behavioral appearance that ranges from fearless to reckless.
b. interpersonal conduct that ranges from antagonistic to belligerent.
c. a cognitive style that ranges from personalistic to bigoted.
d. affective expression that ranges from hostile to malevolent.
e. a self-perception that ranges from competitive to domineering.

2. The narcissistic (passive-independent) personality disorder is characterized by:
a. a behavioral appearance that ranges from arrogant to pompous.
b. interpersonal conduct that ranges from exploitive to shameless.
c. a cognitive style that ranges from expansive to undisciplined.
d. affective expression that ranges from insouciant to exuberant.
e. a self-perception that ranges from being admirable to wonderful.

3. The histrionic (active-dependent) personality disorder is characterized by:
a. a behavioral appearance that ranges from affected to theatrical.
b. interpersonal conduct that ranges from flirtatious to seductive.
c. a cognitive style that ranges from flighty to scattered.
d. affective expression that ranges from fickle to impetuous.
e. a self-perception that ranges from being sociable to hedonistic.

4. The dependent (passive-dependent) personality disorder is characterized by:
a. a behavioral appearance that ranges from incompetent to helpless.
b. interpersonal conduct that ranges from submissive to clinging.
c. a cognitive style that ranges from naive to gullible.
d. affective expression that ranges from pacific to timid.
e. a self-perception that ranges from inept to inadequate.

5. The passive-aggressive (active-ambivalent) personality disorder is characterized by:

    a. a behavioral appearance that ranges from stubborn to contrary.

    b. interpersonal conduct that ranges from ambivalent to uncooperative.

    c. a cognitive style that ranges from inconsistent to disorienting.

    d. affective expression that ranges from irritable to agitated.

    e. a self-perception that ranges from being discontented to mistreated.

6. The compulsive (passive-ambivalent) personality disorder is characterized by:

    a. a behavioral appearance that ranges from being disciplined to perfectionistic.

    b. interpersonal conduct that ranges from respectful to ingratiating.

    c. a cognitive style that ranges from constricted to blocked.

    d. affective expression that ranges from being solemn to grave.

    e. a self-perception that ranges from being conscientious to righteous.

7. The avoidant (active-detached) personality disorder is characterized by:

    a. a behavioral appearance that ranges from guarded to alarmed.

    b. interpersonal conduct that ranges from being aversive to withdrawn.

    c. a cognitive style that ranges from distracted to perplexed.

    d. affective expression that ranges from being anguished to overwrought.

    e. a self-perception that ranges from being alienated to rejected.

8. The schizoid (passive-detached) personality disorder is characterized by:

    a. a behavioral appearance that ranges from lethargic to sluggish.

    b. interpersonal conduct that ranges from being aloof to remote.

    c. a cognitive style that ranges from being impoverished to barren.

    d. affective expression that ranges from being flat to bleak.

    e. a self-perception that ranges from being complacent to lifeless.

Moderately to Markedly Severe Personality Disorders:

9. The schizotypal personality disorder, which can be seen to emerge from a deterioration of the schizoid or avoidant disorders, is characterized by:
   a. a behavioral appearance that ranges from being eccentric and aberrant to bizarre.
   b. interpersonal conduct that ranges from being detached and secretive to inaccessible.
   c. a cognitive style that ranges from being ruminative and autistic to deranged.
   d. affective expression that ranges from being apprehensive to distraught and frantic in the case of active schizotypal variant or ranges from being apathetic to insentient and deadened in the case of the passive schizotypal variant.
   e. a self-perception that ranges from being forlorn to estranged and vacant.

10. The borderline personality disorder, which can be seen to emerge from a deterioration of the dependent, histrionic, or passive-aggressive disorders, is characterized by:
    a. a behavioral appearance that ranges from being spontaneous to precipitous and even chaotic.
    b. interpersonal conduct that ranges from being oppositional to paradoxical and mercurial.
    c. a cognitive style that ranges from being inconstant to capricious and disorganized.
    d. affective expression that ranges from being temperamental to labile and even volatile.
    e. a self-perception that ranges from being troubled to uncertain and at times conflicted.

11. The paranoid personality disorder, which can be seen to emerge from a deterioration of the narcissistic, antisocial, or compulsive disorders, is characterized by:
    a. a behavioral appearance that ranges from being wary and defensive to vigilant.
    b. interpersonal conduct that ranges from being quarrelsome and provocative to acrimonious.
    c. a cognitive style that ranges from being incredulous to suspicious and conspirative.
    d. affective expression that ranges from sullen to irascible and fractious.

Table 2.6 Multidimensional Criterion List for Personality Disorders

	Dimension				
Disorders	Behavioral Appearance	Interpersonal Conduct	Cognitive Style	Affective Expression	Self-Perception
Antisocial	Fearless to reckless	Antagonistic to belligerent	Personalistic to bigoted	Hostile to malevolent	Competitive to domineering
Narcissistic	Arrogant to pompous	Exploitive to shameless	Expansive to undisciplined	Insouciant to exuberant	Admirable to wonderful
Histrionic	Affected to theatrical	Flirtatious to seductive	Flighty to scattered	Fickle to impetuous	Sociable to hedonistic
Dependent	Incompetent to helpless	Submissive to clinging	Naive to gullible	Pacific to timid	Inept to inadequate
Passive-aggressive	Stubborn to contrary	Ambivalent to uncooperative	Inconsistent to disorienting	Irritable to agitated	Discontented to mistreated
Compulsive	Disciplined to perfectionistic	Respectful to ingratiating	Constricted to blocked	Solemn to grave	Conscientious to righteous
Avoidant	Guarded to alarmed	Aversive to withdrawn	Distracted to perplexed	Anguished to overwrought	Alienated to rejected
Schizoid	Lethargic to sluggish	Aloof to remote	Impoverished to barren	Flat to bleak	Complacent to lifeless
Schizotypal	Eccentric and aberrant to bizarre	Detached and secretive to inaccessible	Ruminative and autistic to deranged	Apprehensive to distraught and frantic / Apathetic to insentient and deadened	Forlorn to estranged and vacant
Borderline	Spontaneous to precipitous and chaotic	Oppositional to paradoxical and mercurial	Inconstant to capricious and disorganized	Temperamental to labile and volatile	Troubled to uncertain and conflicted
Paranoid	Wary and defensive to vigilant	Quarrelsome and provocative to acrimonious	Incredulous to suspicious and conspirative	Sullen to irascible and fractious	Formidable to inviolable and embittered

     e. a self-perception that ranges from being formidable to inviolable and embittered.

These, then are the 11 DSM-III, Axis II personality disorders defined from the perspective of the reinforcement matrix described earlier and the biosocial learning theory upon which that matrix is built. They are graphically summarized in Table 2.6.

Once again, it is important to note that, in reality, it would be unlikely to find an individual who conforms to any one of the eight theoretically "pure" personality disorders described. Rather, personality disorders are more likely to be expressed in the form of combinations, or clusters, of two or three of these pathological patterns.

Having provided the basic groundwork for understanding the nature and classification of personality and its disorders, let us now turn our attention to a detailed examination of the 11 basic personality disorders.

Summary

In this chapter, we have addressed the generic concept of classification and, more specifically, the classification of personality and its disorders. Let us take this opportunity to review some of the main points:
1. A classification or diagnostic label may be thought of as no more than a symbol used by clinicians to summarize a set of conditions.
2. Objections to diagnostic labels include:
    a. The label may become a self-fulfilling prophecy for the person labeled.
    b. Labels may become explanations rather than descriptions of behavior.
    c. Diagnostic labels may serve as a rationale for dehumanizing individuals.
3. The value of classifications and diagnostic labels include that they serve to help refine diagnoses, prognoses, and treatment.
4. The history of personality classification dates back 2,500 years to the writings of Hippocrates.
5. This text presents a classification system for healthy personality patterns as well as personality disorders.
    a. The present classification system is built upon a biosocial learning theory of personality.
    b. The central, or unifying, theme of this theory is reinforcement.
    c. A 2 × 4 reinforcement matrix may be constructed by intersecting the two basic instrumental behaviors used to seek reinforcement (active vs. passive) with the four major sources of reinforcement (self, others, self vs. others, neither self nor others).
6. Eight theory/matrix-derived healthy personality patterns are summarized in Tables 2.2 and 2.3.

7. A useful way of viewing personality disorders is as quantitative syndromal extensions, or elaborations, of normal and healthy personality patterns. Table 2.4 summarizes this perspective, called syndromal continuity, as it relates to DSM-III, Axis II.

8. The 11 DSM-III, Axis II personality disorders are summarized in terms of the biosocial learning theory in Tables 2.5 and 2.6.

Two

THE INDEPENDENT
PERSONALITY DISORDERS

In the preceding chapters, we discussed the nature and the classification of human personality and its disorders. In the remaining chapters we will address the 11 personality disorders recognized in the nosology of the American Psychiatric Association—DSM-III. We have grouped the remaining chapters according to the biosocial learning theory and reinforcement matrix described in Chapter 2.

In Part Two, we will describe first the antisocial personality disorder and then the narcissistic personality disorder. According to our reinforcement matrix and the biosocial learning theory upon which it is built, these personality disorders represent *independent* patterns. That is to say, individuals who possess these basic personality patterns turn inward for gratification and reinforcement. They rely on themselves for safety, security, and comfort. Weakness, inferiority, and dependency are threatening to them. They tend to be overly

concerned with issues of power and prestige;
and they feel that these things must, virtually
always, be in their favor. A fear common to
independent personalities is losing self-
determination. In short, it is what they can
provide for themselves, not what others say or
can provide for them, that serves as the
cornerstone for their satisfaction and security—
this is the essence of their personalities.

Having described what independent
personalities share, we turn to an overview of
how they are different. Independent personalities
may be usefully divided into two subdivisions:
active-independent and *passive-independent.*

Individuals who possess the antisocial
personality disorder would be examples of
individuals manifesting an active-independent
personality disorder. These people struggle to
"prove" themselves. They insist on achieving
their "rights," even if it means usurping the
rights of others. At times, they will be ruthless
and cunning to exert power over others. Active-
independent antisocial individuals are driven, or
motivated by, a general distrust of others and a
fear that others will try to exploit or humiliate
them. Thus, self-determination and autonomy
may be seen as protective mechanisms. They are
a means of countering, with the person's own
power and prestige, the hostility, deception, and
victimization they expect from others.

Individuals who possess the narcissistic
personality would be categorized as passive-
independent individuals. These individuals
possess an inflated sense of confidence and self-
worth. They feel that they need merely be
themselves to be secure and content. Their self-
esteem is based on a blind assumption of
superiority. Their behavior is often motivated by
a desire to achieve the things they feel they
deserve because of their "superiority."

Although both active-independents and

passive-independents devalue others and find gratification only within themselves, they are quite different. Let us take a closer look at the antisocial and narcissistic personality disorders, that is, the basic independent personality disorders.

CHAPTER

3

The Antisocial Personality Disorder

Let us now examine, in detail, the first of the independent personality disorders—the active-independent antisocial personality disorder.

We will begin with a case example of the antisocial personality disorder. As you read the opening case about John W. make note of any major examples of these descriptive criteria:

1. Behavioral appearance (i.e., how the individual appears to others).
2. Interpersonal conduct (i.e., how the individual interacts with others).
3. Cognitive style (i.e., the characteristic nature of the individual's thought processes).
4. Affective expression (i.e., how the individual displays emotion).
5. Self-perception (i.e., the manner in which the individual sees himself/herself.
6. Primary defense mechanism.

CASE 3.1

The Antisocial Personality Disorder

John W., Age 42, Production Supervisor, Married, Two Children

The company for whom Mr. W. worked recently contracted with a management consulting firm to have their middle and senior level executives "talk over their personal problems" on a regular basis with visiting psychologists. Mr. W. was advised to take advantage of the arrangement because of repetitive difficulties with his subordinates. He had been accused of being "rough" with his secretaries, and excessively demanding of engineers and technicians directly responsible to him. The validity of these accusations was attested to by a rapid turnover in his department, and the frequent requests for transfer on the part of his professional staff.

Mr. W. was seen as a tall, broad-shouldered, muscular, but slightly paunchy, man with a leathery, large-featured face, large hands and brusque manner. He was the third child in a family of four. The oldest child was a girl, the others were boys. He recalled that his mother spoke of him as a strong-willed and energetic baby, one who fought to have his way right from the start. Until he left for college at 18 he lived with his family on a small ranch in Montana. His father struggled to "make a go of things" through the depression, and died just as he was "starting to make ends meet." Mr. W. spoke of his father as a tough, God-fearing man. He dominated the household, was a "mean" disciplinarian and showed no warmth or gentility. Toward the end of his life, while Mr. W. was in his teens, his father "got drunk three or four times a week," and often would come home and try to "beat up the kids and mom." He hated his father, but recognized that he served as a model for his own toughness and hardheaded outlook.

Mother was a background figure. She cooked, cleaned and helped out on the ranch when father asked her to do so. She never interfered with her husband's wishes and demands, turning over all decisions and responsibilities to him. Mr. W.'s older sister was quiet like his mother. They both "sort of faded into the wall." The three brothers were quite different. They fought "tooth and nail" ever since they were young. Mr. W. proudly boasted, "I could beat up my older brother when I was ten and he was 12." He remained the dominant sibling from then on.

Mr. W. was given a "paid scholarship" to play college football, but was drafted into the Army between his freshman and sophomore years. He served in the final European phase of World War II and recalled his harrowing experiences with considerable pride. He currently is an active member of a veterans organization. Upon returning home, he continued his education on the G.I. Bill of Rights, played football for two seasons and majored in business economics. Upon graduation he joined, as field production assistant, the oil firm in which he is currently employed, married a girl he "picked up" some months before and moved about from one field location to another as assigned by his company.

On the job, Mr. W. was known as a "hard boss"; he was respected by the field hands, but got on rather poorly with the higher level technicians because of his "insistence that not a penny be wasted, and that nobody shirk their job." He was an indefatigable worker himself, and demanded that everyone within his purview be likewise. At times he would be severely critical of other production chiefs who were, as he saw it, "lax with their men." Mr. W. "couldn't stand lazy, cheating people"; "softness and kindness were for social workers"; "there's a job that's to be done and easygoing people can't get it done the way it should be." Mr. W. feared "the socialists" who were going to ruin the country." He had a similar distaste for "lazy and cheating" minority and racial groups.

Mr. W. was assigned to the central office of his company on the basis of his profitable production record. For the first time in his occupational life he had a "desk job." His immediate superior liked the way Mr. W. "tackled problems" but was concerned that he alienated others in the office by his gruffness and directedness. It was only after considerable dissension within his department that Mr. W. was advised, as he put it, "to unload on someone other than my secretaries and my pussy-footing engineers."

(From T. Millon, *Modern Psychopathology: A Biosocial Approach to Maladaptive Learning and Functioning.* Philadelphia: Saunders, 1969. Used with permission of the author.)

The case of John W. represents one variation of the antisocial personality disorder. We will now discuss the nature and development of this disorder.

CLINICAL PICTURE

The antisocial personality disorder represents an active-independent personality disorder in terms of the reinforcement matrix discussed in Chapter 2. This simply means that individuals who possess the antisocial disorder proactively seek reinforcement through self-reliance. This personality disorder is characterized by ambition, persistence, goal-directed behavior, an apparent need to control the environment, and an unwillingness to trust the abilities of others.

The antisocial personality may be thought of as a syndromal extension of the nonpathological forceful personality (discussed in Chapter 2)—as such, this definition is far broader than the current DSM-III formulation of this disorder. The antisocial personality is best conceived of as an aggressive personality type, ranging in varying degrees along a symptomatological continuum from mild forms to extremely severe forms. In its mildest forms, the antisocial personality, as a rule. frequently fits into the mainstream of our society. These milder manifestations are often not only commended, but they are endorsed and cultivated in our competitive society where tough, hard-headed realism is an admired attribute. Such personality characteristics are often considered necessary for survival in the cold, cruel business world, in political arenas, and in military and quasi-military organizations, such as police departments.

The antisocial personality, by current and more narrow DSM-III definition, begins to manifest itself prior to age 15. The personality disorder is more common among the lower socioeconomic classes and is over three times more prevalent among men than women. In its extreme forms, about 3% of American men show such personality

Table 3.1   A Multidimensional Appraisal of the Antisocial Personality Disorder

1. Behavioral appearance: fearless to reckless.
2. Interpersonal conduct: antagonistic to belligerent.
3. Cognitive style: personalistic to bigoted.
4. Affective expression: hostile to malevolent.
5. Self-perception: competitive to domineering.
6. Defense mechanism: acting-out.
7. Differential personality diagnosis: paranoid personality disorder.

characteristics and less than 1% of American women show such personality characteristics (American Psychiatric Association, 1980).

In our presentation of the clinical picture for each of the 11 personality disorders we are addressing, we have elected to employ a standardized seven-section format: (1) behavioral appearance, (2) interpersonal conduct, (3) cognitive style, (4) affective expression, (5) self-perception, (6) primary defense mechanism, and (7) differential personality diagnosis. This standardized format is used to facilitate comparisons among the various personality disorders on selected clinical criteria. Table 3.1 summarizes these criteria as they relate to the antisocial personality disorder.

Behavioral Appearance

Behavioral appearance may be thought of as how individuals are characteristically perceived through the eyes of others. The behavioral appearance of those with an antisocial personality disorder ranges from being perceived as fearless in milder forms of the disorder to being perceived as reckless in the more severe forms of the disorder.

Antisocials tend to be impulsive and forceful in their activities. They are seldom inhibited by danger or fear of punishment and can be seen characteristically to take risks. Risk-taking behavior often provides an exhiliration. Yet, such behavior may also be considered by others to be aggressive and irresponsible, owing to the antisocials' apparent lack of consideration for the rights of others.

In the case of John W., he enjoyed taking risks. He enjoyed fighting, whether it was with his brothers or in World War II. He enjoyed the physical aggression that characterized football. He was seen by his coworkers as a vigorous, energetic, and domineering man. These characteristics won the respect of his field hands but drew the contempt and resentment of his engineers and secretaries.

In extreme variations of the antisocial disorder, risk-taking behavior becomes a reckless disregard for the rights and welfare of self and others. Social rules, ethics, and customs are grossly disregarded in what may become a tirade of aggressive, irresponsible behavior, which may include numerous confrontations with the law and the acquisition of a criminal record.

Interpersonal Conduct

Interpersonal conduct may be thought of as the manner in which antisocials relate to, and interact with, other individuals. The interpersonal conduct of the antisocial personality ranges from being antagonistic in its milder forms to being belligerant in its more severe forms. Antisocial personalities have learned to rely on themselves and to distrust others. They have few feelings of interpersonal loyalty and feel little remorse in using others to achieve desired goals.

At times, antisocial individuals appear to be coarse, cold, and interpersonally imperceptive, even antagonistic. As a result, many people shy away from them, feeling intimidated by their aggressive and sometimes arrogant manner. People often sense that the antisocial individual is cold, callous, and insensitive to the feelings of others. In reality, however, most are perceptually alert and are finely attuned to the elements of human interaction. They simply choose to project such an image to take advantage of that perception in order to be intentionally callous should the need arise.

Antisocial individuals almost invariably have difficulty keeping responsible or intimate relationships over an extended period of time with coworkers, friends, sexual partners, and even family members because of their antagonistic behavior. This point is clearly brought out in the case of John W. He "fought 'tooth and nail'" with his brothers, ultimately to become the dominant sibling. He dominated his secretaries and engineers, resented his peers, and generally alienated other office personnel. In general, antisocial personalities are distrusting of others, fearing that they will harm them in some way.

Individuals who possess the antisocial personality tend to be interpersonally aggressive. They can be argumentative, abusive, and cruel. They often insist on being "right." They are highly competitive and tend to be poor losers. Underlying these interpersonal behaviors is a need to control. It seems to serve as a mechanism to defend themselves. Their active-independent style of seeking reinforcement stems not so much from a belief in self-worth as from a general fear and distrust of others. Thus, they are interpersonally insecure. These individuals are secure only when they are in control of the situation and are independent of the will of others who may threaten their security.

In extreme cases, antisocial personalities are interpersonally belligerent and vindictive. They may seem to derive satisfaction from the failure and humiliation of others, particularly if those individuals represent a potential threat or competition or if those individuals have in some way harmed them in the past. In many, the vengeful, punitive approach to others may stem from an abusive childhood. Extreme antisocial individuals lack interpersonal compassion and humanistic qualities. They are often contemptuous of appeasement and compromise, equating such interpersonal strategies as signs of weakness. As John W. indicated, only through toughness will the job get done.

It is not uncommon to see these individuals adopt a jungle mentality where might makes right, and their behavior reflects such an attitude. The rights of others are characteristically ignored or usurped through deception and forceful aggression. This behavior is rationalized through an end-justifies-the-means attitude. Extreme cases of the antisocial personality are highly resistant to authority. Anticipation of punishment tends not to deter their behavior. This attitude is what often leads to numerous confrontations with the law and the possible development of a criminal record.

Cognitive Style

Here we address the nature and structure of the characteristic cognitive processes displayed within the antisocial personality disorder. The cognitive style of the antisocial personality ranges from personalistic in its milder forms to bigoted in its more severe forms.

Antisocial personalities usually exhibit rigid, inflexible cognitive patterns that are externally oriented. Cognitive flexibility and introspection tend to be avoided because they represent inconsistency and wasted effort, respectively. These externally directed cognitive patterns are usually characterized by a controlling nature and devious manner.

In milder forms of the antisocial personality, the cognitive style may be thought of as hard-nosed and very realistic. Such characteristics are often desirable in the industrial and business worlds.

In the case of John W., we find an individual who has accrued an effective production record, presumably because of hard-nosed attitudes. He proclaimed that "there's a job that's to be done and easygoing people can't get it done the way it should be."

In extreme cases, antisocial personalities are characterized by an externalized and often bigoted cognitive style. They commonly perceive the external environment as threatening and, therefore, remain vigilant. They attribute their own hostility and vengeful characteristics to the actions of others. They consider others to be even more devious and punishing than themselves. Thus, they are simply acting according to the norm and in self-defense. John W. resented minority racial and ethnic groups because he felt that they were going to ruin the country.

Affective Expression

The term affective expression refers to the manner in which individuals display, or express, felt emotion. The affective expressions that characterize the antisocial personality may range from hostility to malevolence.

In general, antisocial personalities tend to guard their emotions carefully when it comes to the "softer" emotions. Sentimentality, warmth, and intimacy are usually avoided as signs of weakness. In many cases, antisocial personalities will tend to be suspicious of compassion and altruism in others. Humanistic emotions are often viewed as liabilities and barriers to success. As John W. has stated, "softness and kindness were for social workers." For the antisocial individual, denying such emotions protects him/her against painful memories, usually of childhood.

As individuals who possess the antisocial personality are prone to guard their "softer" emotions, they are just as prone to display their more aggressive emotions, ranging from anger to hostility. When matters go their way, antisocial personalities may seem affable, courteous, and even gracious. When matters do not go their way, however, or when they become frustrated (generally indicative of a perceived loss of control), they tend to become angry. If the problem is severe enough, they are quick to become furious, resentful, and revengeful. Antisocial personalities can display an irascible temper that flares in verbal arguments and, on occasion, physical violence. All in all, antisocial personalities have a very low tolerance for frustration and tend to be easily provoked to attack, demean, humiliate, and dominate others with little or no display of remorse regarding their actions.

Self-Perception

Self-perception may be thought of as how antisocial individuals characteristically view themselves. The self-perception of the antisocial disorder ranges from competitive in its milder forms to domineering in its more severe forms.

The antisocial personalities typically view themselves as being competitive, energetic, self-reliant, and even hard-nosed—all traits that they hold in high regard. The self-concept of antisocial individuals is built around seeing themselves as strong, realistic, and tough. This point is exemplified in the case of John W. who relates his combative childhood, war experiences, and rigid managerial style with considerable pride. It is clear that antisocial personalities value competition and power-oriented lifestyles. There are few feelings as rewarding as the thrill of victory and few feelings as painful as the agony of defeat.

In extreme cases, antisocials tend to see themselves as being a dominating force. This is clear in the case of John W. who dominates his family, secretaries, and subordinate engineers. Not only does the antisocial individual desire to dominate people, but events as well. This aspect of the antisocial personality may be seen as an extension of the need to be in control of the environment. Also, in extreme cases, we see these individuals as considering themselves above rules, regulations, and even laws.

Primary Defense Mechanism

Under persistent or extraordinary stress, individuals may be forced to deceive themselves or to distort reality to reduce the tension or anxiety that is actually experienced. To some degree all of us avoid conflicts, kid ourselves, and attempt to soften blows to our egos to maintain our self-image. The mechanisms we select are often called ego-defense mechanisms. Sometimes the mechanisms we choose to accomplish these goals may be maladaptive.

Although many defense mechanisms may be employed by individuals with various personality disorders, our discussions throughout the book will focus on the primary one utilized by individuals possessing the personality discussed in each respective chapter.

The defense mechanism most commonly employed by aggressive, antisocial individuals is *acting out.*

Acting out refers to the tendency impulsively to display socially offensive thoughts, emotions, and overt actions. For example, a temper tantrum is a characteristic example of acting out. The desired goal of such behavior is to relieve, through ventilation, any inner tension of turmoil that has arisen and that might continue to grow if it is not discharged. Rather than refashion socially undesirable behavior into socially acceptable forms, these tensions are discharged directly and often indiscriminately with little or no concern for the interpersonal consequences of such a discharge. There are seldom any feelings of guilt or remorse should others be injured by these ventilations.

In the case of John W., it will be recalled that he was recommended for counseling because of tendencies to be " 'rough' with his secretaries and excessively demanding" on his other subordinates. A review of John's case reveals a history that is filled with verbal and physical violence, starting in his childhood. Sibling confrontations would commonly end up in physical violence. At age 10 John became the dominant sibling by demonstrating his physical superiority. Throughout his developmental history, John gravitated to activities that not only allowed, but promoted, impulsive, violent behavior, for example, football and the armed services.

When John W. was confronted with his tendencies to be overly aggressive, he was devoid of any guilt or remorse; he even resented the suggestion that he should act less aggressively towards his secretaries and "pussy-footing engineers." So, we see John W. as a person who throughout his life frequently and impulsively acted out his frustrations and hostilities not only in verbal, but physical forms as well. This acting out served as a defense mechanism because it prevented the build-up of tensions or turmoil that would have been intolerable to John.

Differential Personality Diagnosis

Throughout the book, we will briefly discuss the personality disorders that are clinically most similar to—therefore, most likely to be confused with—the disorder under discussion in each respective chapter.

Pragmatically, it should be noted that the issue of differential diagnosis is no longer the clinical problem that it has been historically. The DSM-III not only allows for multiaxial diagnosis, but it also allows for multiple diagnoses within axes. Therefore, it is possible to list multiple personality disorders when, indeed, disorders appear to overlap or co-exist within the same individual. Therefore, subsequent discussions on differential personality diagnosis are provided as much for pedagogical purposes as for clinical purposes.

As we will see later, the antisocial personality can often be found to blend with or mix in coexistent fashion with the paranoid personality disorder. As a result, there is often a tendency to confuse the two disorders. Let us take a moment to briefly describe the most prominent differences.

The antisocial personality disorder may be considered a less severe syndromal variant of the paranoid disorder. Similarly, the paranoid disorder may be considered a more severe continuation of the anti-social disorder. In general, the aggressive antisocial patient exhibits greater emotional controls and is less inclined to irrational behavior than the paranoid. Antisocial patients tend to be less vigilant and less suspicious when compared to paranoid patients. Paranoids expect to be tricked and deceived by others. This tense, edgy, and extremely suspicious quality is usually lacking in aggressive antisocials who tend to be more arrogant and self-assured, despite their vigilance and mis-trust. Finally, full-blown antisocials are far more inclined to engage in obviously illegal behavior when compared to paranoid patients.

ETIOLOGY AND DEVELOPMENT

Biogenic Factors

There exists a high frequency of antisocial personalities within the same familial constellation, suggesting the presence of hereditary fac-tors in the etiology of this personality disorder. Of course, observed similarities in family behavior is just as likely to be a function of learn-ing as it is to be a function of heredity. However, it has been noted that "studies attempting to separate genetic from environmental influences within the family suggest that both are important because there seems to be inheritance from biological fathers separated from their offspring early in life and a social influence from adoptive fathers" (American Psychiatric Association, 1980, p. 319). Therefore, there seems to be some evidence that aspects of the antisocial personality may be biolog-ically based and genetically transmitted. Low thresholds for limbic sys-tem stimulation, especially amygdalar nuclei, have been implicated in related behavioral patterns (Weil, 1974). Similarly, inefficient limbic inhibitory centers may account for parallel behavior (Weil, 1974).

Environmental Factors

Although antisocial behaviors, especially hostility, can be traced back, in part, to biogenic factors, environmental factors will tend to shape the content and direction of these dispositions. Furthermore, we be-lieve that the environmental factors listed below may be, in and of themselves, sufficient to result in the manifestation of the antisocial disorder.

Parental Hostility. The developmental history of the antisocial person-ality may be characterized by parental hostility. A child sometimes becomes the target for parental hostility. Such hostility may result from the fact that the child was disruptive to the relationship of the mother and the father. It may result from the fact that the child was disruptive to one or both of the parents or even other children in the family. Hostility directed towards a child may also result from the perception that the child is ill-tempered. Finally, parental hostility may be directed towards a child if the child can be used as a scapegoat for the frustrations of the parents or the family in general. Whatever the initial source, a major cause for the development of the antisocial personality disorder is exposure to parental hostility, cruelty, or domination.

It is clear that hostility breeds hostility. Not only does hostility breed hostility in the child because of the anger and resentment that the child probably develops as a result of being the recipient of parental hostility and abuse, but a child learns to be hostile by simply observing the parental models. Therefore, impulsive or hostile parents have the potential to arouse and release strong feelings of hostility in their children by initiating a hostile response from the target of hostility (in this case, the child), by serving as a model, or by simply acting in such a manner as to sanction hostile behavior on the part of the child. In the case of John W., his father not only sanctioned violent behavior, but served as a role model as well.

Children who are exposed to parental hostility are likely to acquire such traits themselves. Yet, this developmental factor, although among the most common developmental factors, is not the only environmental factor that may contribute to the development of the antisocial personality.

Deficient Parental Models. Another environmental factor that is conducive to the development of the antisocial personality is a lack of an appropriate parental model. In cases of deficient parental models, there is either little or no parental guidance for the child. As a result, the child is left to find whatever models he/she can. Broken families, especially those in which the father or other authority figure has abandoned the family, characterize this environmental condition.

Without an authority figure and often feeling rejected or abandoned, these children frequently become hardened to the world around them. They tend to become streetwise and engage in socially deviant behavior as a means of survival. Under conditions such as these, the children learn to employ rationalizations, such as "It's a dog-eat-dog world," "Only the strong survive," and "The end justifies the means." Such deviant behavior usually draws social condemnation that tends to further harden the individual and reinforces the need to be self-reliant, as is characteristic of the antisocial personality.

Learned Vindictive Behavior. Conditions such as being the target of parental hostility; the perception of being abandoned, figuratively or literally; and social condemnation for socially deviant behavior are likely to have dramatic impact on most individuals. The most common result is that they learn not to trust others for fear that others will exploit and humiliate them. It is similarly common to see the emergence of a vengeful, vindictive pattern of interpersonal interaction. In effect, such behavior can be seen as a means of not only protecting oneself, but as a means of getting even with the individuals, system, or society-at-large that mistreated them.

Bioenvironmental Factors

It seems clear that biogenic factors and environmental factors can exert direct effects on the development of the antisocial personality. However, it is also likely that biogenic and environmental factors interact to contribute to the development of the antisocial personality. To examine how biogenic factors and environmental factors interact, we will analyze the effects of a hostile environment on neuropsychological development. We will use the three stages of neuropsychological development delineated by Millon (1969) and described in Chapter 1:

1. The sensory-attachment stage of neuropsychological development of the antisocial personality is probably characterized not so much by the amount of stimulation received, but by the quality of the stimulation received by the child. It will be recalled that the sensory-attachment stage (birth to 18 months) is characterized by significant growth spurts within the child's sensory neurological systems and is also important for laying the psychological foundations for attachment behaviors. Rough, harsh treatment during this stage certainly provides adequate stimulation, if not excessive stimulation. Harsh treatment, although providing adequate stimulation, also communicates a tone, or "feeling," to the child that the world is an unkind, painful, and potentially dangerous place. The child quickly learns that the environment cannot be trusted and that the world should be viewed with suspicion.

2. Having learned that the world is going to treat the child harshly, he/she enters the sensorimotor-autonomy stage. This stage ranges from about 12 months to 4 to 6 years. Here the child's verbal, locomotive, and fine motor skills are refined. Similarly, as these skills are developing, the child is reaching out, exploring the environment and developing a

sense of autonomy. Yet, for the antisocial child, he/she is learning to mistrust, to doubt, and to be self-reliant because no one else appears to care.

3. Being both suspicious of others and reliant only upon themselves, these youngsters enter the intracortical-initiative stage. This stage ranges from age 4 years through adolescence and is the era in which higher mental abilities are developed. Antisocial youngsters have become determined to reject parental and social directives and restraints. These individuals are now convinced in their ability to survive and see no need to have to depend on others; especially if all others cannot be trusted. Thus, the distrust and contempt of others cultivated in the sensorimotor-autonomy stage combines with the refinement of self-reliant and autonomous behavior that occurs in the intracortical-initiative stage and lays the personological foundations for the distrusting, vindictive, aggressive, and self-reliant personality that we refer to as the antisocial personality.

In cases where the interaction of biogenic and environmental factors shape the development of the antisocial personality, we see children who have learned to question, oppose, and often reject many of the values of the society-at-large. Having done so, the individual embarks on a course of independence and mistrust with a need to shape his/her own destiny through intrapersonal, interpersonal, and environmental control. This need for control motivates the antisocial individual to be rigidly realistic, callous, and aggressive in defense of maintaining control. Should the individual perceive a loss of control coming about, extreme variations of the basic antisocial personality may emerge, characterized by extreme psychopathology.

SELF-PERPETUATION OF THE ANTISOCIAL PERSONALITY DISORDER

We have described the clinical picture of the antisocial personality and the processes relevant to understanding etiological and developmental aspects of this personality. Now we will discuss the major processes by which the antisocial personality acts to perpetuate his/her own pathological pattern.

Perceptual and Cognitive Distortions

Much of what we understand about our environment is based on fragmented information. We take bits and pieces of information and fit them together into a reality that we can understand. Frequently, we tend to fill in missing pieces of information based on our expectations of how we believe things are. Thus, our perceptions of reality consist of data, that is, pieces of information from the environment, plus our own inferences, that is, filler about how we expect the environment to be.

In the active-independent antisocial personalities, there is an ever-present undertone of anger and resentment. There is a persistent suspicion that others are devious and hostile. Because of this expectation of the environment and the people around them, antisocial personalities have learned to distort the incidental remarks and actions of others so that they appear to be intended to injure them. They misinterpret what they see and hear and magnify minor incidents into major insults and slanders.

By perceiving hostility where none exists, antisocial personalities are prevented from recognizing the objective good will of others, even when it actually occurs. Therefore, we see that for the antisocial personality, reality is truly in the eye of the beholder, not necessarily what factually exists.

Demeaning of Affection and Cooperative Behavior

The antisocial personalities are suspicious of sentimentality, tenderness, and cooperative behavior. They lack sympathy for the weak and oppressed. As John once noted, "kindness is for social workers."

By denying tender feelings, these individuals protect themselves from the pain of parental or societal rejection. Furthermore, such feelings as well as cooperative behavior are likely to be viewed as forms of weakness. To the antisocial personality, only through strength will they survive. John W. genuinely believed that being tough and hard-nosed was the only way to survive.

Creation of Real Antagonists

Antisocial personalities evoke hostility in others. Their aggressive, callous, and vindictive behavior incidentally evokes hostility in others; at the same time, they may intentionally provoke anger in other individuals. They often appear to be arrogant and carry a chip on their shoulders. This tendency to antagonize other people often results in aggressive behavior being returned to the antisocial individual. Therefore, what emerges is objective validation for their assumption that the world is a hostile and dangerous place. In effect, we see the creation of a self-fulfilling prophecy—if one expects the world to be hostile and acts towards the world as if it is hostile, it is likely to become hostile.

Operant Conditioning

According to learning theorists, such as E. L. Thorndike (1935), behaviors that are maintained, or perpetuated, must, in some way, be reinforcing to the individuals displaying those behaviors. This has been referred to as the law of effect. In the case of personality disorders, the overtly displayed behaviors may be but symptoms of more fundamental covert dysfunctions and can be best understood in the context of the reinforcement that they provide.

How is hostile, vengeful, antagonistic, fearless, and distrusting behavior reinforcing? The answer lies in the fact that such behaviors are negatively reinforcing. Negative reinforcement is defined as the removal of threatening, punishing, or otherwise aversive stimuli. Therefore, antisocial behaviors must serve to reduce the probability that antisocial individuals will experience something aversive. Antisocial individuals commonly experience a chronic fear of being used by others, publicly humiliated, taken advantage of, or otherwise degraded. It is this fear that motivates most antisocials. When examined in this context, antisocial behavior becomes a powerful source of negative reinforcement, that is, a way of avoiding that which the antisocials so desperately fear. To look at the world through the eyes of the antisocial individual and see "a place fraught with frustration and danger, a place where he must be on guard against the malevolence and cruelty of others" (Millon, 1969, p. 273) gives us a far better understanding of why the characteristics of the antisocial personality are self-perpetuated.

In summary, through cognitive distortions, a contempt for affection, a tendency to provoke others to anger, and the negatively reinforcing aspects of the antisocial behavior itself, the antisocial personality acts to perpetuate his/her own pathological disorder.

ASSOCIATED DISORDERS

The major personality disorders addressed in this volume have been described in their theoretically "pure" and discrete forms according to the biosocial learning theory discussed earlier. Yet, we do not believe that one frequently encounters personality disorders in discrete nor theoretically pure forms. Rather, we would expect to see various personality disorders covary, combine, and otherwise overlap with other personality disorders as well as with the major clinical syndromes (DSM-III, Axis I). Based on the work of Millon (1969; 1982), it has been found that certain personality disorders do, indeed, seem commonly to combine, coexist, or overlap with other psychopathological conditions within the same individual.

In our discussion on associated disorders (here and in each of the remaining chaters), we will briefly describe: (1) other personality disorders that frequently seem to mix with the personality disorder under discussion (although there can be combinations in addition to those described) and (2) the DSM-III, Axis I disorders that most commonly coexist with the personality disorder under discussion.

There are several rationales for including these sections in the book:

1. We would expect to find personality disorders manifesting themselves in combinations rather than in discrete and theoretically "pure" forms.

2. It is a contention of this volume that a *full* understanding of the major clinical syndromes (Axis I of the DSM-III) requires the study of basic personality disorders (Axis II of the DSM-III). Symptom disorders, as they appear on Axis I, are best regarded as an outgrowth of deeply rooted sensitivities and coping strategies that reflect interwoven biogenic and psychogenic factors that have also formed the person's basic personality pattern. According to Millon (1982), Axis I clinical syndrome disorders are "best seen as extensions or distortions of the patient's basic personality patterns. However, these syndromes differ in that they are relatively distinct or transient states, waxing and waning over time. Most typically, they caricature or accentuate the basic personality style" (p. 34).

3. Finally, and most important, these discussions are provided in an attempt to help the reader relate the concept of personality disorders back to what is usually the focus of most discussions of psychopathology, that is, the major clinical syndromes (Axis I). Thus, it is hoped that inclusion of these discussions will help bridge the gap between personality disorders and the major psychopathological symptom disorders.

Mixed Personality Disorders

In the case of the antisocial personality disorder, we are likely to see combinations with the narcissistic, histrionic and paranoid personalities. Later chapters will illustrate the first two mixtures.

Antisocial-Paranoid Mixed Personality Disorder. The antisocial-paranoid combination disorder is the epitome of the extreme and least attractive features of antisocial disorders. These individuals are hostile and vindictive. They are highly impulsive and display a hateful and defiant pattern of behavior targeted against conventional social rules, mores, ethics, and even laws.

Antisocial-paranoid individuals are distrusting of others. They anticipate betrayal and punishment. They have usually accrued a cold-blooded ruthlessness and an intense desire to achieve revenge for the real or imagined mistreatment they feel they were subjected to during some aspect of their life, usually childhood.

These individuals dread the thought that others may view them as weak or that others may manipulate them. As a result, antisocial-paranoid individuals rigidly maintain an image of hard-boiled strength, acting tough, callous, and fearless. To "prove" their courage they place themselves in high-risk, antisocial situations that often lead to punishment. But punishment, should it occur, fails to act as a deterrent for such future behavior. Rather, it serves to verify their expectations of "unjust" treatment and further serves to reinforce further rebelliousness and desires to get even.

When these individuals find themselves in positions of power, they tend to dominate and even brutalize those over whom they have control. They usually display an arrogant contempt for the rights of others and will be devoid of any guilt or remorse for injuring others.

In sum, the antisocial-paranoid mixed personality may be viewed as a more severe syndromal continuation of the antisocial disorder, moving towards the full-blown paranoid personality disorder to be discussed later.

Associated Axis I Disorders

The antisocial personality disorder is characterized by a tendency impulsively to discharge psychologic discomfort. As a result, decompensation into associated Axis I disorders is not that prevalent. The two that do appear with some frequency are anxiety disorders and paranoid disorders.

Anxiety Disorders. Despite their general infrequency, the aggressive personalities do, indeed, experience brief periods of anxiety prior to their discharging or acting-out behavior. Usually, the major cause of this anxiety is a fear of losing control or of being controlled. Thus, generalized, or free-floating, anxiety is seldom encountered; rather, the anxiety is closely tied to a particular person, place, or thing. Similarly, chronic anxiety is seldom encountered. The reason is that anxiety is seldom allowed to build up over an extended period of time. It is the nature of these individuals to release tensions; discharge hostility; and to act assertively, if not domineeringly, so as to avoid the prolonged psychologic pain of anxiety and the fear of losing control.

Paranoid Disorders. Under prolonged or extreme environmental pressure, it is common to see the appearance of paranoid symptoms emerging from aggressive, antisocial personalities. According to the DSM-III, the essential features of the paranoid disorders are "persistent persecutory delusions or delusional jealousy, not due to any other mental disorder. . . The persecutory delusions may be simple or elaborate and usually involve a single theme or series of connected themes, such as being conspired against, cheated, spied upon, followed, poisoned or drugged, maliciously maligned, harassed or obstructed in the pursuit of long-term goals" (American Psychiatric Association, 1980, p. 195). At times, verbal or physical abusiveness towards others may occur.

The antisocial personalities are particularly prone to these disorders as a result of a decompensation of the basic antisocial pattern. The Axis I paranoid disorders, when they do occur, represent among the most severe decompensated variant of the basic antisocial pattern. Once fully developed, these episodes can be characterized by wild, violent, and delusional rages.

Summary

In this chapter, we have described the nature and development of the antisocial personality disorder. Let us review the main points:

1. The clinical picture of the active independent antisocial personality disorder may be summarized as follows:
   a. Behaviorally, antisocials appear to range from fearless to reckless in the eyes of others. They are thick-skinned, impulsive, and power oriented.
   b. Interpersonally, antisocials typically conduct themselves in a manner that ranges from antagonistic to belligerant. They mistrust, often intimidate and derogate others, and they lack social compassion.
   c. Cognitively, these individuals range from being personalistic to bigoted. They are egocentric, seeing the world in relation to their own needs only.
   d. Affectively, they range from being hostile to malevolent with a labile temper.
   e. Antisocials perceive themselves ranging from competitive to domineering. They see themselves as tough-minded, action-oriented, independent, and self-reliant individuals.
   f. Acting out is the most commonly used defense mechanism for these individuals.
   g. Differential personality diagnoses to be considered would be the paranoid, histrionic, and narcissistic personality disorders.

2. Parental hostility, deficient parental models, and operant conditioning of vindictive behavior contribute to the development of the antisocial personality, as may low limbic system thresholds.

3. The antisocial personality is self-perpetuated through consistent perceptual distortions, a demeaning attitude towards affection and interpersonal cooperation, antagonistic behavior towards others that breeds antagonism in return, the negative reinforcement of the antisocial behavior itself, and, finally, a fear of being used and put in an inferior, dominated position.

4. Among the most common mixed personality disorders that are anchored to the antisocial pattern is the antisocial-paranoid mixed personality disorder.

5. Common DSM-III, Axis I disorders that are associated with the antisocial personality disorder are anxiety disorders and paranoid disorders.

CHAPTER 4

The Narcissistic Personality Disorder

We begin with a case example of the personality disorder to be presented. In this chapter, we will examine the narcissistic personality disorder. As you read the opening case about Steven F., make note of any major examples of these descriptive criteria:

1. Behavioral appearance.
2. Interpersonal conduct.
3. Cognitive style.
4. Affective expression.
5. Self-perception.
6. Primary defense mechanism.

CASE 4.1

The Narcissistic Personality Disorder

Steven F., Age 30, Artist, Married, One Child

Steven came to the attention of a therapist when his wife insisted that they seek marital counseling: According to her, Steve was "selfish, ungiving and preoccupied with his work." Everything at home had to "revolve about him, his comfort, moods and desires, no one else's." She claimed that he contributed nothing to the marriage, except a rather meager income. He shirked all "normal" responsibilities and kept "throwing chores in her lap," and she was "getting fed up with being the chief cook and bottlewasher tired of being his mother and sleep-in maid."

On the positive side, Steve's wife felt that he was basically a "gentle and good-natured guy with talent and intelligence." But this wasn't enough. She wanted a husband, someone with whom she could share things. In contrast, he wanted, according to her, "a mother, not a wife"; he didn't want "to grow up he didn't know how to give affection, only to take it when he felt like it, nothing more, nothing less."

Steve presented a picture of an affable, self-satisfied and somewhat disdainful young man. He was employed as a commercial artist, but looked forward to his evenings and weekends when he could turn his attention to serious painting. He claimed that he had to devote all of his spare time and energies to "fulfill himself," to achieve expression in his creative work. His wife knew of his preoccupation well before they were married; in fact, it was his self-dedication and promise as a painter that initially attracted her to him. As Steve put it "what is she complaining about . . . isn't this what she wanted, what she married me for?"

Exploration of Steve's early history provided the following. Steve was an only child, born after his mother had suffered many miscarriages; his parents had given up hope of every having a child until he came along, "much to their surprise and pleasure." His parents doted upon him. He never assumed any household or personal responsibilities. He was given music and art lessons, discovered to have considerable talent in both and given free rein to indulge these talents to the exclusion of everything else. He was an excellent student, won several scholarships and received much praise for his academic and artistic aptitudes. To his family he was "a genius at work." Life at home revolved entirely around him.

Socially, Steve recalled being "pretty much of an isolate," staying home "drawing and reading, rather than going outside with the other kids." He felt he was well liked by his peers, but they may have thought him to be a "bit pompous and superior." He liked being thought of this way, and felt that he was "more talented and brighter" than most. He remained a "loner" until he met his wife.

His relationships with his present co-workers and social acquaintances were pleasant and satisfying, but he did admit that most people viewed him as a "bit self-centered, cold and snobbish." He recognized that he did not know how to share his thoughts and feelings with others, that he was much more interested in himself than in them and that perhaps he always had "preferred the pleasure" of his own company to that of others.

(From T. Millon, *Modern Psychopathology: A Biosocial Approach to Maladaptive Learning and Functioning.* Philadelphia: Saunders, 1969. Used with permission of the author.)

CLINICAL PICTURE

The narcissistic personality disorder represents a passive-independent personality in terms of the reinforcement matrix discussed in Chapter 2. This means that narcissists are capable of self-reinforcement, but rather than actively pursuing reinforcement through ambitious, persistent, goal-directed behaviors, as do antisocials, narcissists feel no need to prove themselves. To narcissists, simply "being" gives them the right to receive reinforcement.

The label narcissistic connotes more than mere egocentricity. Narcissism signifies, more specifically, that these individuals overvalue their personal worth, direct their affections towards themselves rather than others, and expect that others will recognize their unique and special value.

The narcissistic personality disorder ranges from mildly severe forms, which are but minimally dysfunctional, to more severe forms, which can be markedly dysfunctional. The narcissistic personality disorder, by current DSM-III standards, is characterized by a need for constant attention, a belief in entitlement, fantasies, exploitiveness, and grandiose feelings of self-importance (American Psychiatric Association, 1980). As such, the DSM-III conceptualization represents a more severe variation of the overall narcissistic disorder as conceived in this volume. Let us now take a closer look at the narcissistic personality disorder using the standardized format described and utilized in the last chapter. Table 4.1 summarizes these criteria as they relate to the narcissistic personality disorder.

Behavioral Appearance

Recall that the term behavioral appearance, as used in the present text, refers to how individuals are perceived by others.

The behavioral appearance of the narcissistic personality disorder characteristically ranges from being perceived as arrogant in its milder variations to pompous in its more severe variations. In many instances, narcissists display a benign form of arrogance. They believe themselves to be "above" the conventions and ethics of their cultural group—and they act accordingly. Narcissists feel they are exempt from the responsibilities that govern society. Other individuals are simply expected to submerge their own desires in favor of the whims of the narcissist. As a result, narcissists are commonly viewed as lacking humility, being highly conceited, boastful, snobbish, self-centered, spoiled, and disdainful.

Narcissists flout the conventional rules of shared living. They consistently disregard, and appear indifferent to, the rights of others. In short, narcissists possess illusions of an inherent superiority. They move through life with the irrational belief that their inalienable rights are greater than those of others.

Table 4.1   A Multidimensional Appraisal of the Narcissistic Personality Disorder

1. Behavioral appearance: arrogant to pompous.
2. Interpersonal conduct: exploitive to shameless.
3. Cognitive style: expansive to undisciplined.
4. Affective expression: insouciant to exuberant.
5. Self-perception: admirable to wonderful.
6. Defense mechanism: rationalization.
7. Differential personality diagnosis: histrionic personality disorder.

In the case of Steven F., he was perceived by his wife as being "selfish, ungiving and preoccupied with his work." She complained that the home environment was centered around his comforts and his desires, with an apparent disregard for her rights and feelings. Steven's descriptions of his own behavior included references to the fact that most people viewed him as a "bit self-centered, cold and snobbish." It became clear that he liked to be thought of as "'more talented and brighter' than most," even "a bit pompous and superior."

In extreme cases, narcissists may be viewed as pompous, living in a delusion of personal grandeur. In such instances, these individuals may become consumed with their own importance as they literally reside at the center of their own universe.

Interpersonal Conduct

We are using the term interpersonal conduct to refer to the manner in which individuals interact with others. Narcissists range from being interpersonally exploitive in milder variants to shameless in their disregard for others in more severe variations. Narcissists tend to take others for granted. They may exploit others to enhance themselves or indulge their own desires. Narcissists often feel entitled to express themselves in ways denied to others. They are interpersonally unempathic and tend to expect special favors or consideration for others without feeling a need to reciprocate. In short, the narcissist tends to have little patience with, or concern for, the rights, feelings, and desires of others. They are more than ready to take from others but see no reason to give in return. It is not uncommon for those who live or work with narcissists to feel as if they are being used, or taken advantage of.

Steven, exemplifies the benignly exploitive narcissist. Steven's wife complained that he shirked all normal household and marital responsibilities. He constantly kept "throwing chores in her lap." In her opinion, Steven often acted like a spoiled brat who never wanted to grow up. She felt as if he viewed her more as a mother than as a wife. In her opinion, Steven did not know how to give affection, only how to take it. In sum, Steven's wife declared that she was "getting fed up with being the chief cook and bottle-washer. . . tired of being his mother and sleep-in maid."

In extreme variations, interpersonal conduct might be considered as manifesting a shameless disregard for the rights and welfare of others. According to the DSM-III, "Interpersonal exploitiveness, in which others are taken advantage of in order to indulge one's own desires or for self-aggrandizement, is common" (American Psychiatric Association, 1980, p. 316).

Cognitive Style

The cognitive style of narcissists may range from expansive in milder variants of the disorders to undisciplined in the more extreme forms of the disorder. Narcissists place few limits on their fantasies. Their imagination runs free of the constraints that restrict others. They tend to exaggerate their abilities, they freely transform failure into success, and they employ extensive rationalizations to inflate their self-worth, justify what they feel is their due, and depreciate those who refuse to accept or enhance their self-image. Narcissists are often preoccupied with immature fantasies.

The case of Steven provides us with an example of a young man who "'preferred the pleasure' of his own company," not because he necessarily felt a need to withdraw interpersonally but because it gave him the opportunity to let his mind wander, unrestricted by the influences of others. Indeed, Steven noted that he looked forward to the evenings and weekends when his mind could turn to true artistic creativity.

In extreme cases of the narcissistic disorder, cognitive expansion turns to undisciplined thinking. Daydreams may turn into elaborate fantasies or nonpsychlistic delusions of success, glory, beauty, love, or wealth. Individuals may also resort to lies, or fabrications, to maintain, or redeem, their illusions of self-esteem.

Affective Expression

The affective expression of the narcissist may range from being insouciant in milder forms to being exuberant in more severe instances.

Spurred on by the unrestricted workings of their expansive imaginations, narcissists experience a pervasive sense of well-being. They manifest a general air of nonchalance and imperturbability. They often appear to be cooly unimpressionable, even buoyantly optimistic. At times, when the narcissist's confidence is shaken, he/she may experience brief displays of ventilated rage, shame, or emptiness and depression. These periods are usually short-lived however, owing to the tendency of most narcissists to use rationalizations as a protective defense mechanism. The use of such a mechanism quickly turns defeats into victorys and awkward, humiliating behavior into gallant efforts.

Steven F., from an emotional perspective, would be considered calm, almost imperturbable. He projected an air of cool nonchalance, even in the face of his wife's marital complaints. When confronted, he coolly responded "what is she complaining about . . . isn't this what she wanted. . . ?"

Self-Perception

The self-perception of most narcissistic individuals ranges from seeing themselves as being admirable to the more severe variations who see themselves as being wonderful. Clearly, narcissists view themselves as superior persons, individuals who are extra special, individuals entitled to unusual rights and privileges. This self-concept is so firmly anchored in their minds that they rarely question whether this quantum assumption is, indeed, valid. As a result, anyone who challenges this self-concept is looked on with contempt and scorn. So special do narcissists perceive themselves, they believe they are "above" the rules, mores, ethics, and customs that govern their society. It was noted earlier that narcissists are commonly perceived as being self-centered. This observation is an accurate one, yet narcissists see nothing wrong with being self-centered or conceited when one is as wonderful or desirable as most narcissists see themselves.

Steven recognized his self-centeredness, but only within the context of his extraordinary talents. Thus, his egocentric behavior was nothing for him to be criticized but rather should be understood and nurtured by those of lesser abilities, namely his wife.

In extreme variations of this disorder, individuals may view themselves as being not only admirable, gifted, and unique, but also wonderful—capable of being all things to all people.

Primary Defense Mechanism

The narcissistic personality is built on inflated self-esteem, feelings of superiority, and unrealistically high notions of ability. It is not surprising, then, to see the primary defense mechanism employed by narcissistic individuals to be *rationalization.*

Rationalization is the most commonly employed mechanism of reality distortion. It represents an unconscious process of self-deception in which the individual creates an alibi, an excuse, or a justification for disappointments, failures, or socially unacceptable acts. It is important to keep in mind that these excuses or justifications may be plausible, yet they are not true. Rationalization is a process of creating explanations to conceal the real reasons for the disappointment or the socially unacceptable motive. In effect, rationalization is a deceptive maneuver designed to place oneself in the best possible light, despite shortcomings, failures, or socially unacceptable behavior that would actually serve to diminish self-esteem.

In the case of Steven F., rationalization was used frequently and effectively. Steven dismissed his shortcomings as a spouse by rationalizing that his need for artistic expression did not allow for familial concerns. Similarly, the majority of Steven's interpersonal relationships were somewhat impersonal, cold, and even formal at times. He rationalized this by stating he enjoyed being thought of as a "bit pompous and superior" and had always "'preferred the pleasure' of his own company." Thus, we see Steven used rationalization as a way of making excuses for his familial and interpersonal shortcomings, which is an example of a defense mechanism, Steven defending his narcissistic ego from the realities of inadequacy.

Differential Personality Diagnosis

The narcissistic personality shares some superficial similarities with the histrionic personality. As a result, they are likely to be confused. Let us discuss the similarities as well as the differences in these disorders.

Both narcissists and histrionics desire to be the center of attention. They both behave exhibitionistically, and both are emotionally labile. Because of these similarities, there is a tendency to confuse the two disorders.

The major differences between the two disorders appear to be centered around the issue of dependency. It may be argued that narcissists are inclined to avoid having to depend on others. They tend to view themselves as independent, cool, and "above" many aspects of social responsibility. They are exploitive. In contrast, histrionic personalities are extremely dependent on others for approval and feelings of self-worth. They can be warm and expressive rather than cool and egocentric. They are seductive rather than exploitive. Finally, histrionic personalities can be very conforming to social convention, especially if such behavior yields the reinforcement they require from others. Narcissists recoil from meaningless conformity—their concept of self is built on their unique superiorities.

ETIOLOGY AND DEVELOPMENT

Having described the overall clinical picture of the narcissistic personality, let us now examine factors that may give rise to such a personality disorder.

Biogenic Factors

The role of biogenic factors in all personality disorders remains speculative. The role of biogenic factors in the narcissistic personality is especially unclear. Owing to the fact that no distinctive biogenic characteristics have emerged, we have no basis for even reasonable speculation, therefore, no such factors will be proposed.

Environmental Factors

Because there is virtually no promising biogenic evidence to point to for the initiation or development of the narcissistic personality disorder, we must place particular emphasis on environmental factors. We will describe three such potential factors: parental indulgence and overevaluation, learned exploitive behavior, and only-child status.

Parental Indulgence and Overevaluation. For many reasons, some parents view their children as God's gift to humankind. They tend to pamper and indulge these children. In the case of Steve, his mother had suffered many miscarriages and had given up hope until he came along "much to their surprise and pleasure." His parents virtually spoiled him, never insisting that he assume any household responsibilities. To his family, Steve could do no wrong; he was "a genius at work." Children such as Steve are likely to learn several things quickly:

1. that they *deserve* to be treated with distinction without having to do anything to *earn* such treatment.
2. that they are special, superior people.
3. that they can expect compliance and even subservience from other not-so-special people.

4. that they can expect commendation and praise for virtually everything they do.

Having accepted such expectations from the family, these children are unlikely further to develop appropriate social behaviors. For example, they are unlikely to learn:

1. how to cooperate with others.
2. how to consider the rights, interests, and well-being of others.
3. how to express interpersonal responsibility.

In effect, these children who have been overindulged learn to believe that the world revolves around their whims and wishes. It is not surprising to find such children becoming extremely egotistical in their perspectives and narcissistic in their expressions of love and emotion.

So, having been raised receiving such special treatment from their families, these children often learn to expect the same from others outside their families. When such special treatment is not readily forthcoming, these children begin to experiment with demanding and exploitive tactics designed to receive the special treatment they have learned to enjoy, expect, and virtually require. This manifests itself in the passive-independent, narcissistic pattern.

Learned Exploitive Behaviors. As noted previously, narcissistic children become accustomed to the special, favored treatment they receive from their families. When they move outside the family sphere, they carry with them expectations to be treated in similarly special ways. If such special treatment is not rendered to them, these children, through a process of trial-and-error learning, develop considerable skill in manipulating and exploiting others so as to receive the special attention and consideration they feel they deserve. Thus, they learn what individuals and under what circumstances they can extract the special consideration that is so important to them.

In summary, we must remember that narcissists have learned to think of, and treat, themselves kindly because of their status as "special people." They have learned to admire their own prowess, intelligence, physical attributes, or special talents. They have, in effect, learned that they need to depend on no one but themselves for reinforcement.

At the same time that the narcissist is learning to admire himself/herself, he/she is also learning that most other people are inferior, weak, and can be exploited. So, although it is clearly satisfying to reinforce oneself, the narcissist learns that it is even more reinforcing to use the people and systems in the environment to provide further reinforcements. In contrast to the dependent personalities who must perform and be seductive (in the case of the active-dependent, histrionic personality disorder), the passive-independent style of the narcissist involves exploiting the environment so as to derive passively the special consideration and treatment narcissists genuinely feel they so justly deserve. Sometimes this goal may be achieved by developing a following of admirers (e.g., passive-dependent personalities) who are quickly trained by the narcissist to be solicitous and subservient. In many cases, narcissists will marry a passive-dependent person who will serve as chief cheerleader and subservient admirer without expecting anything in return but strength and support. It seems that Steve holds just such an expectation for his wife, expecting her to play the roles of "chief cook and bottlewasher, mother and sleep-in maid."

The process of learning to exploit others may begin in childhood (as is usually the case), adolescence, or even adulthood. Regardless of when the behavior is learned, exploitation of others seems to be powerfully reinforcing and, therefore, difficult to bring to extinction.

Only-Child Status. Brief mention should be made of the high frequency with which parental overindulgence and the opportunity to learn exploitive behavior occurs in only children. Obviously, it is often the case that such children are viewed quite literally as "gifts"—beings of special value. In such circumstances, these children seldom encounter many restrictions and seldom acquire the same sense of social responsibility that can be obtained through sharing with siblings. This condition is exemplified in the case of Steve, an only child who encountered few restrictions and was given free rein to develop his artistic and musical talents.

Thus, the stage is set for the development of narcissistic characteristics as described earlier. Obviously, such events are not restricted to only children nor are all only children destined to live out such scenarios.

These three factors, then, represent major environmental determinants of the narcissistic personality. They may act singly or in combination to shape the narcissistic personality disorder.

Neuropsychological Development

There is a clear potential for environmental factors to interact with biological development to shape personality configuration. We will describe the effects of parental overindulgence and overevaluation on the stages of neuropsychological development as proposed by Millon (1969) and used throughout the text:

1. The effects of parental overindulgence and overevaluation do not seem to effect the child's sensory-attachment stage dramatically, where the primary neuropsychological developmental processes involve basic neurological sensory development and psychological attachment. Therefore, we must move to the next stage of development to see the foundations of the narcissistic personality disorder.

2. Certain feelings of omnipotence can be easily communicated through parental overevaluation. These feelings are likely to take hold during the child's sensorimotor-autonomy stage. In this stage, the child's verbal, locomotive, and fine motor skills are developing most rapidly. The quest for psychological autonomy is the result of such neurological development. As the sensorimotor-autonomy stage evolves, parental overevaluation may lead to the child developing a deluded sense of self-competence—even omnipotence.

3. The failure of adequate parental direction that usually accompanies parental overindulgence seems to exert a significant influence on the next stage of development—the intracortical-initiative stage. During this stage, the child's cognitive abilities are rapidly shaped. Under conditions of parental overindulgence, one is likely to see a child imagining, exploring, and generally behaving without useful, constructive parental constraints. This situation breeds a delusion of power and self-worth that is not grounded in other relevant environmental interactions. The narcissist, then, having been deprived of sufficient parental discipline and unexposed to the constraints of socially based fear, guilt, or shame fails to develop any regulatory mechanisms of self-control.

SELF-PERPETUATION OF THE NARCISSISTIC PERSONALITY DISORDER

The narcissistic personality pattern is characterized by persistence and inflexibility. This persistent and inflexible pattern is maintained through a self-perpetuating process. We will describe four major mechanisms that serve to maintain the narcissistic personality disorder: (1) self-reinforcing illusions of competence, (2) lack of self-control, (3) deficient social responsibility, and (4) operant conditioning of narcissistic behavior.

Self-Reinforcing Illusions of Competence

Narcissists act as though a belief in their superiority will suffice as proof of its existence. Steve readily believed this and was considered a snob for doing so. Most narcissists view themselves as already competent at virtually everything they do, so, there is no perceived need to seek education or training to become competent. In fact, to do so might undermine the illusion of competence in the first place. Therefore, they can retain their illusion of superiority without fear of finding out that they may not actually be superior by simply avoiding formal training.

Unwilling to expend any significant effort to develop various competencies, the narcissist may begin to slip increasingly behind others in realistic attainment. Before long, such deficits are likely to become pronounced, making such shortcomings visible to all. Because the narcissist's belief in *intrinsic* superiority is the foundation of psychological existence and the core aspect of environmental coping strategies, they will resort to even more pronounced narcissistic behavior as demands increase. Thus, the pattern is perpetuated.

Any disparity between the illusional self-perception of competence and reality becomes increasingly painful. Over time, the illusion of competence requires greater and greater effort to maintain. At some point, it is possible that such sustained effort may result in the emergence of severe pathological disturbances, particularly as a result of decompensation under increasing environmental pressure.

Lack of Self-Control

The narcissist's illusion of competence is only one aspect of what appears to be a more generalized disdain for reality. Based on what approaches unrestrained parental acceptance and indulgence combined with a lack of parental discipline, the narcissist takes liberties with the rules of reality and fantasizes at will. He/she seems to be in no way inclined to consider objective facts if such facts are in opposition to his/her preferences or illusions. Furthermore, there seem to exist a disdain for social custom and rules that govern cooperative living. Steve felt no need to help his wife around the house. He had no sense of cooperative living.

Given this apparent disdain for reality, the narcissist's imagination is free to wander uncontrolled in a world of fiction. In extreme cases, these individuals may genuinely lose touch with reality. In effect, many narcissists may simply lack the necessary self-control mechanisms to keep their fantasies in check. As a result, their fantasies take flight as the individual slips further and further from objective reality. Thus, the disorder is perpetuated. In Steve's case, he clearly enjoyed being by himself rather than having to share his reality with others.

Deficient Social Responsibility

If narcissists could learn to respect other people, respect others' opinions, and develop a sense of empathy, they would stand a good chance of controlling their tendencies toward illusion and unreality. But narcissistic personalities have learned not to trust others and generally to devalue others' opinions and their abilities. These tendencies are characteristic of both independent patterns—the antisocial and narcissist. However, in the case of narcissists, these tendencies are rooted in their sublime self-confidence and belief in themselves as superior beings. In the case of the antisocial personality, these feelings of distrust for others are rooted not in feelings of self-worth, but in feelings of insecurity and fear of being harmed by others.

Narcissists, then, usually feel they have no social responsibility to people of less ability than themselves. Steve felt household chores were beneath him. When in conflict with others, narcissists are prone to consistently believe the fault is with the other person. The more they find themselves in disagreement with others, the greater their belief that most people are basically inferior. This tendency further feeds their superiority illusion and further decreases any sense of social responsibility. Thus, once again, the disorder is perpetuated.

Operant Conditioning

As we search for sustaining factors in the narcissistic disorder, we must include perhaps the most powerful of all such factors: the fact that the behaviors associated with the narcissistic disorder are themselves reinforcing. It would certainly not be too great of an assertion that the behaviors and attitudes that constitute the narcissistic disorder are positively reinforcing. Being skilful at manipulating others, having unrestricted cognitive boundaries, being cool, calm, and collected, and being the center of one's own universe all have their positively reinforcing qualities. More important, however, lying at the core of these symptoms is a deeply embedded belief in the unique superiority of self. Thus, most of the reinforcements for which we must look to others, the narcissist provides for himself/herself—little wonder that the narcissistic personality is self-perpetuating.

In summary, the narcissistic personality disorder is self-perpetuated through several factors: (1) the narcissist's illusion of competence, when distilled, assumes that a belief in superiority is sufficient as proof of its existence; (2) a lack of self-controls that appear to be manifest as a general disdain for objective reality that does not support the views held by the narcissist; (3) deficient social responsibility based on the assumption that the narcissist owes nothing to those inferior to him/her; and, (4) the operant conditioning of narcissistic behavior itself.

ASSOCIATED DISORDERS

We will now discuss the personality disorders that frequently combine with the narcissistic personality as well as the Axis I disorders that commonly emerge from it.

Mixed Personality Disorders

The two most common coexisting personality disorders that blend with the narcissistic personality are the histrionic and antisocial patterns.

Narcissistic-Histrionic Mixed Personality Disorder. The most common narcissistically centered mixed personality disorder is the narcissistic-histrionic pattern. Data (Millon, 1982) indicate that the narcissistic-histrionic disorder appears frequently in settings such as youth service bureaus, drug treatment programs, and marital counseling clinics.

Narcissistic-histrionic individuals tend to be clever, charming, flippant, and seductive. They tend to be impulsive, immature, and driven by a need for excitement. These people are often thrill-seekers who are easily but temporarily infatuated by a myriad of people, places, and things. They generally lack social dependability; they are irresponsible and lack self-discipline. According to Millon (1981) "There may be a capricious disregard for agreements hastily assumed, and a trail may be left of broken promises and contracts, squandered funds, distraught employers, and so on" (p. 147).

Narcissistic-Antisocial Mixed Personality Disorder. The second most prevalent blending of narcissistically oriented personality disorders is found in the form of the narcissistic-antisocial mixed pattern. This disorder, as with the narcissistic-histrionic disorder, can be found in great frequency in drug rehabilitation programs, centers for youth offenders, and in jails and prisons—it is less commonly found in marital counseling centers.

The primary feature of note in this blend of disorders is an indifferent conscience, an aloofness to the truth, social irresponsibility, and a tendency to deceive others. These individuals will commonly engage in sexual excesses, fraud, pathological lying, and the blatant exploitation of others. Yet, these transgressions are often "neither hostile nor malicious in intent" (Millon, 1981, p. 172). Rather, these antisocial characteristics seem to emerge from feelings of egocenteredness, omnipotence, and privilege—in effect, a sense that the rules and ethics of society do not apply to them. Criticism and punishment are of little value in altering the behavior of these individuals, in that they are likely to dismiss them as the product of jealous and inferior others.

Case 4.2 is an example of the narcissistic-antisocial mixed personality disorder.

CASE 4.2

The Narcissistic-Antisocial Mixed Personality Disorder

A Psychological Test Report on a 20 Year-Old Man Arrested for Fraud

The patient's behavior is characterized by an arrogant sense of self-worth, an indifference to the welfare of others, and a mixed seductive and intimidating social manner. There is a tendency to exploit others, expecting special recognition and consideration without assuming reciprocal responsibilities. A deficient social conscience is evident in his tendency to flout conventions, engage in actions that raise questions of personal integrity, and to disregard the rights of others. Achievement deficits and social irresponsibilities are justified by expansive fantasies and frank prevarications.

There is pride in self-reliance, unsentimentality, and hard-boiled competitive values. He evidences a rash willingness to risk harm and is notably fearless in the face of threats and punitive action. Malicious tendencies are projected outward, precipitating frequent personal and family difficulties, as well as occasional legal entanglements. Vindictive gratification is often obtained by humiliating and dominating others. When matters are well under control, the patient is successful in attracting attention and enjoying a rapid-paced social life with short-lived periods of dramatic acting out. More characteristically, he evidences a jealousy of others, being wary and suspicious of their motives, feeling unfairly treated, and easily provoked to irritability and authority; and he appears to feel secure only when possessing control and power over others. The thin facade of sociability gives way readily to quick antagonisms and caustic comments. Antisocial tendencies, alcoholism, or drug problems may be prominent.

The patient displays an indifference to truth that, if brought to his attention, is likely to elicit an attitude of nonchalant indifference. He is skillful in the ways of social influence, is capable of feigning an air of justified innocence, and is adept in deceiving others with charm and glibness. Lacking any deep feelings of loyalty, he may successfully scheme beneath a veneer of politeness and civility. His principal orientation is that of outwitting others, getting power and exploiting them "before they do it to you." He often carries a chip-on-the-shoulder attitude, a readiness to attack those who are distrusted or who can be used as scapegoats.

This patient attempts to maintain an image of cool strength, acting tough, arrogant, and fearless. To prove his courage, he may invite danger and punishment. But punishment only verifies his expectation of unjust treatment. Rather than having a deterrent effect, it only reinforces his suspiciousness and rebelliousness. If unsuccessful in channeling these ever-present aggressive impulses, resentments may mount into overt acts of hostility.

(From T. Millon, *Millon Clinical Multiaxial Inventory (MCMI) Manual.* Minneapolis: National Computer Systems, 1982. Used with permission of the author.)

Associated Axis I Disorders

There are four commonly encountered Axis I disorders that appear to be associated with the narcissistic personality disorder. They are the dysthymic affective disorder, acute anxiety reactions, somatoform disorders, and paranoid disorders.

Dysthymic Affective Disorder (Depressive Neurosis). The dysthymic affective disorder is among the more common Axis I disorder encountered among narcissists. It is defined as a "depressed mood, or loss of interest or pleasure in all, or almost all, usual activities" (American Psychiatric Association, 1980, p. 221). This disorder is less severe than a major depressive disorder. When narcissists are confronted with their inability to live up to their inflated self-image, they tend to revert to feelings of self-doubt, uncertainty, and a general dissatisfaction with themselves. They exhibit a process of self-disillusionment that leads to a depressed state. Yet, prolonged severe depression (major depression) is seldom encountered in narcissists. They are usually successful at using rationalization to reduce the significance of their past failures. At times, however, a major decompensation process may result in a severe depressive episode.

Acute Anxiety Reactions. Narcissistic personalities do not characteristically exhibit prolonged anxiety disorders. However, the narcissist is prone to acute anxious episodes when his/her inflated image of self is challenged by environmental realities of incompetence. Yet, prolonged anxiety is unlikely in these personalities because of their aversion to appearing weak, and anxiety is a symptom of weakness for most narcissists. Therefore, prolonged bouts with anxiety are avoided by these individuals' tendency to transform anxiety into irritability or anger. Such emotions are far more acceptable to these individuals, in that they may be portrayed as displays of superiority and dominance.

Somatoform Disorders. *Hypochondriacal symptoms* (i.e., preoccupations with, or unwarranted concerns for, physical illness) are the most likely somatoform symptoms to arise among narcissists. It may be argued that these symptoms serve as an excuse that these individuals can hide behind to explain their defeats, setbacks, or failures. In effect, it is a way of maintaining their inflated self-image in the face of failure.

Paranoid Disorders. Under conditions of prolonged adversity, one is likely to see the narcissist decompensate into a *paranoid disorder.* Because these individuals are unwilling to accept the facts that they may be personally inadequate or incompetent, they may begin to allow their imaginations to run wild searching for reasons for their failures. Delusions of persecution may emerge after major failures or setbacks. According to Millon (1981) "Here we may see the rapid unfolding of persecutory delusions and an arrogant grandiosity characterized by verbal abuse and bombast [as well as] a flow of irrational and caustic comments in which others are upbraided and denounced as stupid and beneath contempt" (p. 172).

Summary

In this chapter, we have described the nature and development of the narcissistic personality disorder. Let us review the main points:

1. The clinical picture of the passive-independent narcissistic personality disorder may be summarized as follows:
  a. Behaviorally, narcissists appear to range from being arrogant to pompous. They tend to disregard the rights of others.
  b. Interpersonally, they range from being exploitive in milder variations to shameless in more severe forms. They take others for granted, using or exploiting them.
  c. Cognitively, narcissists range from being expansive to being undisciplined. They tend to stretch the truth and overtly lie to enhance or redeem self-illusions.
  d. Affectively, these individuals range from being insouciant to exuberant. They can be nonchalant or seem cooly imperturbable, except when self-confidence is eroded.

    e. Narcissists perceive themselves as self-assured, superior individuals. They commonly see themselves as special, "entitled" people.

    f. Rationalization is a defense mechanism commonly employed by narcissists.

    g. A differential personality diagnosis might be the histrionic personality disorder.

2. Parental overevaluation and indulgence may play significant roles in the etiology and development of the narcissistic personality disorder. No major biological factors have been identified.

3. The narcissistic disorder is self-perpetuated through self-reinforcing illusions of competence, a lack of self-control, a deficient sense of social responsibility and positive reinforcement of the narcissistic behavior itself. A primary motive is their "need" to be seen as "special."

4. The two most common mixed personality disorders anchored in the narcissistic disorder are the narcissistic-histrionic mixed personality disorder and the narcissistic-antisocial mixed personality disorder.

5. Common DSM-III, Axis I disorders that are associated with the narcissistic personality disorder are the dysthymic affective disorder, acute anxiety reactions, somatoform disorders, and paranoid disorders.

PART Three

THE DEPENDENT PERSONALITY DISORDERS

In the preceding section, we described the antisocial and narcissistic personality disorders as examples of basic independent patterns.

In this section, we will describe the histrionic personality disorder and the dependent personality disorder. According to the biosocial learning theory presented in Chapter 2, these personality disorders are examples of *dependent* personality patterns.

Dependent personalities are characterized by their marked need for social approval, support, and affection. In contrast to the independent personalities, who look towards themselves for reinforcement, dependent personalities literally depend on others for reinforcement. They are noted for their willingness to make significant alterations in their lifestyles to establish or maintain interpersonal harmony with others. Dependent individuals tend to be sensitive and vulnerable to disapproval. Criticism can be devastating. They tend to devalue themselves, and their self-esteem is usually determined by the comments and actions of others. Protectively, then, dependent individuals must make themselves so pleasing and attractive to others that no one would want to abandon them *or* they must submit to, and comply with, the wishes of others. Loneliness and abandonment are the greatest fears of dependent personalities.

Dependent personalities, congruent with the biosocial learning theory, may be dichotomized into two categories: *active-dependent* individuals and *passive-dependent* individuals.

Histrionic individuals can be regarded as active-dependent personalities. Their strategy for obtaining protection and approval is to captivate or entice others. Their devious manipulations tend to fascinate and seduce those from whom they seek support. Rather than passively submitting to the whims of others, they actively seek to use their own cleverness and charm to manipulate the approval and support they need.

Dependent individuals, on the other hand, would be regarded as passive-dependent personalities. Rather than actively charm and seduce those from whom they seek support, these dependents submit themselves to the demands and desires of others. They tend to be docile, self-effacing, and basically passive in their need for nurturance.

CHAPTER 5

The Histrionic Personality Disorder

We now turn our attention to the first of two dependent patterns—the active-dependent, histrionic personality disorder. As you read the opening case about Suzanne D., make note of any major examples of these descriptive criteria:

1. Behavioral appearance.
2. Interpersonal conduct.
3. Cognitive style.
4. Affective expression.
5. Self-perception.
6. Primary defense mechanism.

CASE 5.1

The Histrionic Personality Disorder

Suzanne D., Age 34, Twice Divorced, Married, One Child

Suzanne, an attractive and vivacious woman, sought therapy in the hope that she might prevent the disintegration of her third marriage. The problem she faced was a recurrent one, her tendency to become "bored" with her husband and increasingly interested in going out with other men. She was on the brink of "another affair" and decided that before "giving way to her impulses again" she had "better stop and take a good look" at herself. The following history unfolded over a series of therapeutic interviews.

Suzanne was four years older than her sister, her only sibling. Her father was a successful and wealthy business executive for whom children were "display pieces," nice chattels to show off to his friends and to round out his "family life," but "not to be troubled with." Her mother was an emotional but charming woman who took great pains to make her children "beautiful and talented." The girls vied for their parents' approval. Although Suzanne was the more successful, she constantly had to "live up" to her parents' expectations in order to secure their commendation and esteem.

Suzanne was quite popular during her adolescent years, had lots of dates and boyfriends and was never short of attention and affection from the opposite sex. She sang with the high school band and was an artist on the school newspaper, a cheerleader, and so on.

Rather than going on to college, Suzanne attended art school where she met and married a fellow student—a "handsome, wealthy ne'er-do-well." Both she and her husband began "sleeping around" by the end of the first year, and she "wasn't certain" that her husband was the father of her daughter. A divorce took place several months after the birth of this child.

Soon thereafter she met and married a man in his forties who gave both Suzanne and her daughter a "comfortable home, and scads of attention and love." It was a "good life" for the four years that the marriage lasted. Her husband was wealthy and had interesting friends. Suzanne attended a dramatic school, took ballet lessons, began to do free-lance artwork and, in general, basked in the pleasure of being the "center of attention" wherever she went. In the third year of this marriage she became attracted to a young man, a fellow dancing student. The affair was brief, but was followed by a quick succession of several others. Her husband learned of her exploits, but accepted her regrets and assurances that they would not continue. They did continue, and the marriage was terminated after a stormy court settlement.

Suzanne "knocked about" on her own for the next two years until she met her present husband, a talented writer who "knew the scoop" about her past. He "holds no strings" around her; she is free to do as she wishes. Surprisingly, at least to Suzanne, she had no inclination to venture afield for the next three years. She enjoyed the titillation of "playing games" with other men, but she remained loyal to her husband, even though he was away on reportorial assignments for periods of one or two months. The last trip, however, brought forth the "old urge" to start an affair. It was at this point that she sought therapy.

Suzanne felt that she had attained what she wanted in life and did not want to spoil it. Her husband was a strong, mature man who "knew how to keep her in check." She herself had an interesting position as an art director in an advertising agency, and her daughter seemed finally to have "settled down" after a difficult early period. Suzanne feared that she would not be able to control her tendency to "get involved" and turned to therapy for assistance.

(From T. Millon, *Modern Psychopathology: A Biosocial Approach to Maladaptive Learning and Functioning.* Philadelphia: Saunders, 1969. Used with permission of the author.)

On superficial examination, the case of Suzanne D. demonstrates what our society tends to admire and foster in its members: to be well liked, successful, attractive, and sociable. On closer examination, however, the case of Suzanne D. represents one variation of the histrionic personality disorder.

CLINICAL PICTURE

The histrionic personality disorder represents an active-dependent disorder according to the biosocial learning theory of Millon (1969, 1981). This designation simply refers to the observation that these individuals proactively seek their reinforcements from others. They must behave in a charming, gregarious, and seductive manner to "earn" reinforcement from others.

This histrionic disorder may be thought of as a pathological syndromal extension of the sociable personality pattern discussed in Chapter 2. The histrionic personality presents itself in variations that range from mildly dysfunctional to more severely pathological. In its milder forms, histrionics are well disguised by a veneer of flirtatious sociability and interpersonal charm. In its more severe forms, this disorder is characterized by overly dramatic behavior, exaggerated and labile affect, and overtly dysfunctional interpersonal relationships characterized by immaturity, seductiveness, and obvious manipulation.

This disorder is diagnosed far more frequently among women and is more frequently found clustering among family members. Let us now take a closer look at the clinical picture of this disorder through the use of our seven standardized criteria. Table 5.1 summarizes the clinical picture of the histrionic personality disorder.

Behavioral Appearance

How are histrionic individuals characteristically seen by others? At first, one is typically impressed by the ease in which histrionics express their thoughts and their feelings. One is also usually struck by their flair for the dramatic and by their apparent natural ability to become the center of attention. In general, the behavioral appearances of histrionics will range from affected in milder variations to theatrical in the more severely pathological forms.

These gregarious individuals are highly labile and capricious. Women usually appear seductive and men often appear charming. Histrionics are generally overreactive and seem to have a penchant for

Table 5.1   A Multidimensional Appraisal of the Histronic Personality Disorder

---

1. Behavioral appearance: affected to theatrical.
2. Interpersonal conduct: flirtatious to seductive.
3. Cognitive style: flighty to scattered.
4. Affective expression: fickle to impetuous.
5. Self-perception: sociable to hedonistic.
6. Primary defense mechanism: dissociation.
7. Differential personality diagnosis: narcissistic personality disorder.

---

excitement. As a result, they can be seen to engage in a series of stimulating "adventures." They often seem to be impulsive. Once the momentary excitement has worn off, they characteristically move on in search of more thrills, be they interpersonal or materialistic.

In the case of Suzanne D., we see a good example of an attractive gregarious woman who is in constant search for stimulation. Not only did Suzanne seem to become quickly bored with her avocations, but she exhausted her marital relationships almost as rapidly.

Characteristically, histrionics, even in mild variations, are unable to maintain the favorable initial impression that others usually have of them. Impressions of sophistication, sociability, and perceptiveness quickly fade in the eyes of those who come to know these individuals. Images of these individuals as superficial, shallow, unempathic, and manipulative soon prevail.

In extreme cases of the histrionic personality disorder, these individuals are perceived as being exhibitionistic, immature, insecure, exploitive, flirtatious, and even promiscuous. These individuals are quickly recognized as being vain, demanding, inconsiderate, and quite dependent on others.

Interpersonal Conduct

Histrionic individuals are clearly dependent on others for there reinforcements. Their insecurities can only be resolved by the nurturance, warmth, and support of others. In general, the interpersonal conduct of the histrionic personality will range from flirtatious to seductive.

These gregarious individuals are more than just friendly and helpful to others. They are actively solicitous of praise, nurturance, support, and well-being. To secure these things, histrionics utilize their abilities to be entertaining, sociable, charming, seductive, and even interpersonally exploitive. In the sphere of sexuality, for example, they are quite good at "playing the game," but become immature and even apprehensive as things get more serious.

Interpersonally, histrionics appear to be remarkably sensitive to the thoughts or moods of those from whom they seek approval and support. This allows them to minimize disappointments and to be effective at interpersonal manipulation. In mild variations of the histrionic disorder, these individuals are often flirtatious as they seek approval and support. Suzanne D. proved to be extremely seductive when in search of stimulation as well as approval. In more severe cases, the histrionics become interpersonally dishonest, manipulative, and egocentric, yet remain extremely dependent on others.

In sum, perhaps the most cogent aspect of the histrionic personality disorder within the domain of interpersonal conduct must be the observation that the sociable, alluring, charming, gregarious, and, seductive behavior is actively designed to acquire, or secure, the interpersonal affection, support, nurturance, and approval that histrionic individuals literally crave.

Cognitive Style

The cognitive style of histrionic individuals can be seen to range from flighty in mild variations of the disorder to scattered in more severe forms of the disorder.

Histrionics clearly demonstrate what can be inferred to be an external cognitive orientation. This external, or exteroceptive, orientation leads to a fleeting, impressionistic, and in severe cases, a scattered and diffuse cognitive pattern. Such a pattern accounts for the histrionic's scattered attention to details, susceptibility to distraction, and apparent superficial cognitive processing. They seem to have a genuine inability to concentrate on difficult or involved cognitive tasks. They lack curiousity. Habits of superficiality also may represent an intellectual evasiveness. Thus, until her recent marriage, Suzanne D. rarely digested anything she had learned, and simply picked up and left whenever she was bothered or bored. Part of the flighty behavior of the histrionic individual derives, therefore, from an avoidance of potentially disruptive ideas and urges, especially those that might bring to awareness their deeply hidden dependency needs. For these and other reasons, histrionics keep running and steer clear of too much self-knowledge and too much depth in interpersonal relationships. In effect, they dissociate themselves from inner thoughts as well as people and activities that might upset their strategy of superficiality.

Affective Expression

To many, the domain of affective expression is what distinguishes histrionics from other personality disorders. Clearly it is the most salient feature of this disorder. The affective expression for the histrionic pattern ranges from fickle to impetuous.

In milder variations, the fickle affect of histrionic individuals is displayed in the form of short-lived dramatic and superficial moods. These individuals can vacillate between displays of enthusiasm, boredom, joy, and anger, much to the confusion and dismay of those who interact with them. This highly labile affectivity seems more uncontrolled than of conscious choice.

The case of Suzanne D. represents a mild variation of the histrionic disorder in terms of its affective expression. We must, therefore, deduce from her behavior that underlying her desires to be sexually adventurous are tendencies to become easily bored and to experience vacillations between contentment and distress.

In the more severe variations of the histrionic disorder, we find much more obvious affective displays than in the case of Suzanne D. We find, for example, conspicuous self-dramatization expressed through attention-getting clothing or direct behavioral displays. Similarly, more extreme histrionic variations tend to overreact impulsively to minor stimulation. At times, these individuals may display extremely irrational expressions of affect, which may persist or vacillate between contrasting affective states.

Self-Perception

Histrionic individuals characteristically lack self-insight. They usually fail to recognize, or admit recognizing, any signs of turmoil, weakness, depression, or hostility. Their preoccupation with their external world and the rewards that it presents has left these individuals bereft of an identity apart from others—apart from those from whom they seek their needed reinforcement. They describe themselves not in terms of their own intrinsic traits, but in terms of their social relationships and their effects on others. As a result, their self-perception tends to range from sociable in mild variations to hedonistic in more severe variations.

Suzanne D. was characteristic of the histrionic pattern in her earlier years. Now, however, she appears to be ready to "stop and take a good look" at herself. She is becoming cognizant of her "old urge" to have extramarital affairs. She appears ready to explore some of what may be at the root of her flighty, flirtatious, and fickle behavior.

Primary Defense Mechanism

The histrionic personality disorder has been depicted as a sociable, charming, seductive, yet labile and superficial pattern. The characteristic superficiality of this pattern lends itself to the adoption of *dissociation* as a defense mechanism.

Dissociation refers to the tendency of individuals to separate, or dissociate, their "real" selves from their "public" selves. Histrionics characteristically alter their public presentations of self to create a succession of changing and socially acceptable images, or facades. Dissociation serves as a mechanism for distracting others from the unpleasant realities that may constitute the "real" histrionic individual. Perhaps more important, dissociation represents a self-distracting process that allows the individual to avoid formulating and reflecting on unpleasant thoughts and emotions. Thus, the charming, dramatic, and even seductive facade of the histrionic prevents him/her from dwelling on the inadequacies that he/she may really possess.

The case of Suzanne D., is the case of a 34-year-old woman whose whole life appears to be a facade. From her childhood through her second divorce, she carefully manipulated her "public" image to achieve approval and support from others. Yet, her "real" self remained a mystery not only to others, but also to Suzanne herself. Finally, through therapy, Suzanne decided she needed to "'take a good look' at herself." Thus, dissociation was a defense mechanism for Suzanne because it protected her from dwelling on unpleasant thoughts or emotions, and perhaps the unpleasant or unacceptable aspects of her own personality and lifestyle.

Differential Personality Diagnosis

As described in Chapter 4, the histrionic personality disorder is most likely to be confused with the narcissistic personality disorder. The essential difference between the two disorders lies in the tendencies to seek reinforcement dependently (from others) or independently (from self). Histrionics seek out others from whom to derive their reinforcement. Narcissists, on the other hand, disdain dependency. Although the histrionic behaves seductively, the narcissist behaves in a nonchalant, ego-centered, and coolly superior manner. The narcissist's level of interpersonal exploitation is far greater when compared to that of the histrionic.

ETIOLOGY AND DEVELOPMENT

Given this clinical picture of the histrionic personality disorder, we will discuss the potential factors that may initiate and perpetuate the disorder as we have described it.

Biogenic Factors

The very nature of the histrionic disorder suggests biogenic temperamental foundations. The high energy levels and the apparent low thresholds for emotional and autonomic reactivity (presumably sympathetic in nature) seem to suggest low excitability thresholds for limbic and posterior hypothalamic nuclei (see Weil, 1974). Low thresholds for ascending reticular system activation should be considered as playing an interactive role as well.

The role of heredity cannot be underestimated in searching for the origins of the histrionic disorder, but it is clear that behavioral influences may foster such autonomic excitability as well (Gellhorn, 1957). In either case, it would seem reasonable to expect that histrionic adults would have displayed a high degree of emotional lability and responsiveness in their infancy and early childhood.

Given a potential role for biogenic influences in the formation and development of the histrionic personality, it would be too extreme of an inference to suggest that biogenic influences alone shape the histrionic disorder. We must turn, therefore, to environmental factors to further explain the etiology and development of the histrionic disorder.

Environmental Factors

We have stated that it is likely that biogenic temperamental factors may undergird the histrionic personality disorder. Yet, these factors alone seem insufficient to shape the development of this condition. More likely, environmental factors overlay biogenic factors to shape much of what we know as the histrionic personality. The following are some of the more common environmental conditions likely to foster the development of the histrionic personality disorder.

Parental Reinforcement of Histrionic Behaviors. The active-dependent child apparently learns to engage in certain behaviors in order to meet parental expectations or satisfy certain parental desires. Should these expectations and desires be met, the child has learned that parental attention and affection are likely to be forthcoming. For example, Suzanne D. learned that parental approval was contingent on looking pretty or showing them her latest artistic masterpiece or the fancy ballet steps she had just learned in dancing school. In Suzanne's quest for parental attention and approval, she slowly acquired a set of behaviors we refer to as histrionic.

We can look more specifically at the nature of parental reinforcement. In doing so, we uncover three tendencies that seem common to the active-dependent histrionic pattern:

1. Minimal punishment, for example, Suzanne D.'s parents rarely criticized or punished her.
2. Positive reinforcement contingent on "performance" that met parental expectations or was otherwise pleasing to them, for example, Suzanne D.'s parents seemed to reward her only when she looked pretty or "performed."
3. Inconsistent positive reinforcement, for example, Suzanne D.'s parents failed consistently to reward her for expected or desired behavior—even when she especially attempted to extract praise from her parents. This variable ratio schedule of reinforcement was perceived as frustrating by Suzanne D., and, by definition, such reinforcement schedules are very difficult to extinguish.

These three characteristics of parental reinforcement often result in three predictable outcomes:

1. Children who have the tendency to attempt to relate freely and openly to others and indiscriminately seek positive reinforcement without a sense of overdoing it, that is, excessive efforts to seek approval, showing-off, etc.
2. Children whose feelings of competence and self-worth are solely dependent on the approval of others.
3. Children who are reinforced on an irregular or variable ratio reinforcement schedule and, thus, are likely to fail to grasp exactly what behavior is being reinforced. The tendency, then, is to expand the search for approval to include as many behaviors and people as possible until the child behaves as if he/she

is constantly on stage seeking approval, constantly showing-off to gain attention.

Histrionic Parental Models. There is little question that children learn, often unconsciously, to mimic what they feel are desired behaviors. Parents serve as strong models for such learning. Therefore, it is quite common to observe children imitating parental behavior. This form of vicarious learning is made especially easy for the child if the parental behavior is particularly pronounced or dramatic. Thus, when parents go out of their way to draw attention to themselves, as is the case with the histrionic parent, the child cannot help but acquire some of those same behaviors. It is not surprising, then, to note that Suzanne D. stated she was just like her mother. Not coincidentally, Suzanne D.'s mother "was an emotional but charming woman" who Suzanne D. further described as flirtatious with men and often bored to tears with the routines of home life. Given such a parental model, it is easy to see why Suzanne acquired at least some histrionic traits.

Learned Manipulative Behavior. People can learn to manipulate others at virtually any age. In the case of the histrionic personality, the origins of such learned manipulative behavior can often be traced back to child-hood sibling rivalries.

Children who struggled long and hard to capture the attention and love of their parents under conditions of competition from siblings, usually have such manipulative behaviors quickly engrained. They tend to utilize such attention-seeking and manipulative behavior long after the need (sibling rivalry) has passed. In effect, these children have learned to employ cuteness, charm, attractiveness, and seduction to secure parental reinforcement, as did Suzanne D. Furthermore, these behaviors are likely to become a long-term active-dependent pattern, as they did in Suzanne D.'s case.

We see, then, that histrionics develop skill in the manipulation of others. They learn to sell themselves, that is, use their charm to elicit approval. They present an attractive front by seductive pretensions, apparent sophistication, exhibitionistic displays, clever stories, and shocking clothes. These things are *not* designed to be expressions of self, but rather are designed to draw attention to themselves. All of these attributes are superficial and remarkably short-lived to those who get to know these individuals.

Although learned manipulative, attention-seeking behavior is usually spawned in childhood, it can develop in adolescence and, al-though unlikely, even later.

In summary, we see that patterns of parental reinforcement, histrionic models and learned manipulative behavior are common environmental factors that may give rise to the histrionic personality disorder.

Neuropsychological Development

The reader will recall that, in terms of the model of neuropsychological development proposed in Chapter 1, the first stage of such development is the sensory-attachment stage. This stage ranges from birth to about 18 months of age. The dominant processes of this stage are sensory neurological development and psychological attachment. It is this stage of development that appears to play the primary role in the bioenvironmental shaping of the histrionic personality.

Excessive stimulus nutriment during this stage is likely to result in low stimulus thresholds and resultant hypersensitivity as well as increased psychological attachment. Both of these developments are characteristic of the histrionic. It appears, then, that as a consequence of early stimulus bombardment, these children tend to look outward for gratification rather than inward—into themselves. But such an external orientation is characteristic of the passive-dependent, dependent personality disorder as well. The primary difference appears to be that the active-dependent, histrionic pattern emerges from conditions where the early stimulus bombardment originated from multiple and diverse sources. In contrast, the passive-dependent, dependent pattern appears to emerge from conditions where the early stimulus bombardment originated from a single, perhaps exclusive, source.

SELF-PERPETUATION OF THE HISTRIONIC PERSONALITY DISORDER

Virtually all of us seek approval and other forms of reinforcement from others. The process of seeking approval represents a normal system of social feedback. The histrionic is literally dependent on such approval, however,—pathologically dependent. This pathological dependence tends to persist beyond a point of any social utility and tends to lead into self-defeating, vicious cycles of continued dependency. What aspects of the histrionic pattern contribute to the continued existence of this personality disorder? Here, we will highlight four such factors.

Preoccupation with External Stimuli

We have noted that the histrionic has an attentional orientation to the external world. Furthermore, perceptions tend to be fleeting, impres-

sionistic, and superficial. This scattered preoccupation with incidental and superficial details prevents the histrionic from fully understanding and appreciating many aspects of the environment. There is
little chance for reflection and introspection.

Although the histrionic is sharply attuned to the outside world,
the disadvantages of such hyperalertness outweigh any advantages.
Unless external stimuli are digested and integrated, they cannot be
fully appreciated nor effectively utilized. In effect, by being preoccupied
with fleeting external stimulation, the histrionic fails to extract anything of lasting value from such stimulus encounters. The result is
that the quest for further, superficial stimuli goes on. The histrionic
goes through external stimulus encounters much the same as water
goes through a sieve. Thus, the disorder goes on. In Suzanne D.'s case,
multiple and diverse hobbies and relationships were her stimulation,
but none proved lasting or meaningful—so, her search went on.

Fleeting Social Relationships

Characteristic of the histrionic pattern are fleeting, superficial social
relationships. Suzanne D.'s social history clearly demonstrates such
tendencies: her series of marriages and affairs as well as her own self-
disclosures indicate the fleeting nature of her interpersonal relationships. One consequence of such erratic relationships is that histrionic individuals can never be sure of securing the affection and
support they crave. Moving from one relationship to another, actively
extracting whatever approval they can, and then moving on to another
relationship is the characteristic pattern of histrionic personalities.
This behavior places them in emotional jeopardy as they lack the social
support to fall back on between relationships. They risk finding themselves high and dry, left alone, virtually abandoned with no one to love
as a result of their own exploitive behavior. Therefore, such fears lead
these histrionic individuals to consume affection and approval almost
ravenously from whatever sources are available and then to search
frantically, sometimes indiscriminately, for new affective stimulation.
Thus, the pattern perpetuates itself.

Massive Repression

Another self-perpetuating mechanism of the histrionic personality disorder involves massive repression. The histrionic has a tendency to
seal off and repress aspects of his/her inner world. By insulating emotions and introspective cognitions from everyday life, the histrionic
denies himself/herself any opportunities to grow in a psychological

sense. This condition aggravates the already-existing dependence, and the individual matures little beyond childhood—hence, the immature childish behaviors of the histrionic. Without the opportunity to grow, the pattern simply perpetuates itself. Examination of Suzanne D.'s case indicates patterns of childish immaturity throughout her adult life. Even in her marriages, she led a pampered life, never having to behave in a truly mature manner.

Operant Conditioning

Another self-perpetuating mechanism of the histrionic personality disorder involves the positively reinforcing qualities of the histrionic behavior pattern itself. Once again, according to the law of effect, we know that behavior that is perpetuated is in some way reinforcing. The histrionic behavior pattern can be seen to be positively reinforcing, that is, the pattern of behavior that we are calling histrionic provides the individuals who employ it with outcome that they consider rewarding. What is rewarding about the histrionic pattern? The answer lies in the fact that histrionic individuals *need* to derive support, attention, affection, and approval from others. The histrionic behavior pattern represents a constellation of behaviors that are ideally designed to achieve those goals, at least in the short run. Thus, the histrionic pattern is perpetuated.

Earlier we asked the question: What aspects of the histrionic pattern contribute to the continued existence of this personality disorder? The answer, in sum, appears to be the tendency on the part of histrionics: (1) to have a preoccupation with external stimulation, thus, virtually excluding any meaningful introspection or internalization of external stimuli; (2) to engage in fleeting, superficial social relationships that, by their very nature, stimulate an almost frantic search for similar relationships; (3) to utilize massive repression as a defense mechanism; such repression inhibits psychological maturation and, thus, perpetuates the tendency to behave histrionically; and (4) operant conditioning of the histrionic behavior pattern itself. Thus, when considered in combination, the histrionic individual has a powerful aggregation of self-perpetuating mechanisms at work—so, the disorder goes on.

ASSOCIATED DISORDERS

Having described the nature and development of the histrionic disorder, let us now turn to a discussion of the disorders that are closely associated with it.

Mixed Personality Disorders

When we examine the histrionic personality disorder as a basis for other personality disorders with which it blends, we find the antisocial and borderline disorders emerging rather frequently.

Histrionic-Antisocial Mixed Personality Disorder. A commonly encountered fusion of personality disorders is represented by the histrionic-antisocial mixed personality disorder. This combination is most commonly found in delinquent and prison populations. It is also encountered in drug rehabilitation settings. Case 5.2 represents a useful example of these personality combination.

CASE 5.2

The Histrionic-Antisocial Mixed Personality Disorder

27 Year-Old Man Currently in Drug Rehabilitation Program, with Criminal Record Dating Back to Age 16

This patient's behavior is typified by a veneer of friendliness and sociability. Although making a superficially good impression upon acquaintances, his more characteristic unreliability, impulsive tendencies, and deep resentments and moodiness are seen frequently among family members and other close associates. The socially facile life-style may be noted in a persistent seeking of attention and excitement, often expressed in seductive and self-dramatizing behaviors. Relationships are shallow and fleeting, frequently disrupted by caustic comments and hostile outbursts. Impulses are acted upon with insufficient deliberation and poor judgment.

The patient is frequently seen as irresponsible and undependable, exhibiting short-lived enthusiasms and immature stimulus-seeking behaviors. Not likely to admit responsibility for personal or family difficulties, he manifests a testy defensiveness and vigorous denial of psychological tensions or conflicts. Interpersonal difficulties are rationalized and blame is projected upon others. Although egocentrically self-indulgent and insistent on attention, he provides others with minimal loyalty and reciprocal affection.

The patient is fearful lest others see him as indecisive or soft-hearted, and antagonism is often expressed toward those upon whom there is dependence. Tendencies to act out antisocially may be present. When mildly crossed, subject to minor pressures, or faced with potential embarrassment, this patient may be quickly provoked to anger, often expressed in a revengeful or vindictive way. A characteristic undercurrent of defensive vigilance and hostility rarely subsides. The air of superficial affability is extremely precarious and he is ready to depreciate anyone whose attitudes touch a sensitive theme. Temper outbursts may reach intense proportions and sudden, unanticipated violence may be expressed. Although infrequent, when the thin veneer of sociability is eroded there may be momentary upsurges of abuse and uncontrollable rage.

(From T. Millon, *Millon Clinical Multiaxial Inventory (MCMI) Manual.* Minneapolis: National Computer Systems, 1982. Used with permission of the author.)

Important features of the case provided above include the patient's history of shallow and fleeting interpersonal relationships, the patterns of social irresponsibility and undependable behavior, as well as, the impulsive, caustic, and hostile outbursts. Although this patient is superficially affable, he is fearful of others seeing him as weak or softhearted. Displays of temper and violent behavior also characterize this seemingly paradoxical behavior pattern.

Histrionic-Borderline Mixed Personality Disorder. The histrionic-borderline combination disorder is another commonly encountered fusion. This disorder is characterized by infantile behavior and labile and diffuse emotions as well as sometimes crude and direct sexual provocativeness. This personality disorder may be viewed, in general, as a decompensated histrionic disorder.

CASE 5.3

The Histrionic-Borderline Mixed Personality Disorder

34 Year-Old Woman, Divorced

This patient's behavior is typified by a veneer of sociability, maturity, and independence. Beneath this veneer is a fear of genuine autonomy, a need to present a good public front, and a deeply conflictful submission to the expectancies of others. Her front of social propriety and self-assurance cloaks deep and increasingly intense but suppressed antagonisms. To control these oppositional tendencies, she struggles to maintain a disciplined self-restraint and a socially agreeable affability, perhaps with moments of dramatic conviviality. This patient engages in a wide variety of interpersonal maneuvers designed to elicit favorable attention and social approval. There is a longstanding pattern of being deferential and ingratiating with superiors, going out of the way to impress them with efficiency and seriousmindedness [*sic*].

Recent failures to evoke authority approval have led to depressive periods and chronic anxiety. She is now high-strung and moody, straining to express attitudes contrary to her inner feelings of tension, anger, and dejection. To avoid these discomforts, she has become increasingly sensitive to the moods and expectations of others. Although she views herself as prudent and disciplined the extreme other-directedness utilized in the service of achieving approval has resulted in a life-style characterized by its high adaptability. She has also learned to be alert to signs of potential hostility and rejection. By paying close attention to the signals that others transmit, the patient usually avoids disapproval, adapting all behaviors to conform with their desires. This pattern has been central to her life-style, that is, doing that which corresponds to the wishes of others. Moreover, by identifying with the views of authorities and adhering to the rules of bureaucracies, she has acquired a feeling of importance and significance. This preoccupation with external approval, however, has resulted in a growing sense of personal impotence and social dependency.

This patient denies awareness of her inner deficiencies since it would point up the fraudulence that exists between the overt impressions she seeks to create and her personally felt sterility and emotional poverty. This tendency to seal off and deny the elements of inner life further intensifies her dependence on others. Increasingly, deep resentments toward those to whom she conforms and depends on have begun to emerge. These antagonisms have periodically broken through surface constraints, erupting in outbursts of guilt and contrition. These vacillations in behavior between periods of submissive compliance and testy negativism compound her discomforts. Such public displays of inconsistency and impulse expression contrast markedly with her self-image. There are bitter complaints about being treated unfairly, of expecting to be disappointed and disapproved by others, and of no longer being appreciated for her diligence, sociability, and respectability. With the persistence of these ambivalent feelings, she has begun to suffer somatic discomforts, voicing growing distress about a wide range of physical symptoms.

(From T. Millon, *Millon Clinical Multiaxial Inventory (MCMI) Manual.* Minneapolis: National Computer Systems, 1982. Used with permission of the author.)

Case 5.3 illustrates a syndromal continuation of the histrionic pattern that has decompensated under recent failures.

Associated Axis I Disorders

Our discussion now turns to an examination of the Axis I disorders to which the histrionic personality is most susceptible.

Anxiety Disorders. We find that the histrionic personality is especially vulnerable to *separation anxiety.* Unlike dependent personalities, to be examined in Chapter 6, histrionics promote their own anxiety by their tendency to seek diverse sources of stimulation and support in order to serve an insatiable appetite for those reinforcements. Histrionics set themselves up for interpersonal isolation owing to their tendency to become quickly bored with their identified sources of stimulation and support. When the histrionics are alone (in between sources of reinforcement), they suffer genuine feelings of isolation and emptiness. As a result, they learn to fear such periods—hence, the fear of separation from current support personnel. Although their separation anxiety is real, they also have a tendency to overdramatize its adversity. The probable motive would be to seek the attention and support they crave. It should be noted that phobias, especially *agoraphobia,* is prevalent among histrionics.

Obsessive Compulsive Disorders. *Obsessional symptoms* defined as recurrent, persistent thoughts or ideas occur frequently among histrionics. Yet, as a result of their lack of cohesive cognitive organization, these obsessional symptoms may lack a specific focus, as do those experienced by compulsive personalities. Histrionics are prone to experience free-floating sexual impulses, hostility, and general emotional lability. These feelings are seldom anchored to a specific person, place, or thing.

Somatoform Disorders. *Conversion reactions* are the most prevalent of the somatoform disorders likely to be seen among histrionic personalities. Conversion reactions are best described as "a loss of or alteration in physical functioning that suggests physical disorder but which instead is apparently an expression of psychological conflict or need. . . The disturbance is not under voluntary control, and after appropriate investigation cannot be explained by any physical disorder or known pathophysiological mechanism" (American Psychiatric Association, 1980, p. 244). The open and dramatic display of these symptoms is apparently an attempt to seek support from those around them. Conversion reactions are excellent "choices" for the histrionic owing to their eye-catching and dramatic characteristics.

Of similar value to histrionics are the utilization of *hypochondriacal symptoms.* Once again, their value arises from their ability to generate attention, sympathy, and support. According to Millon (1981), "To be fussed over with care and concern is rewarding for most individuals. In histrionics, it is 'like a drug' that is needed to sustain them. When histrionics feel a sense of emptiness and isolation, they desparately seek a diet of constant concern and approval. To be ill is a simple solution since it requires little effort yet produces guaranteed attention" (pp. 144–145).

Dissociative Disorders. During periods of strain and adversity, it is not uncommon to see histrionics lose what little cognitive organization they do possess. The result may very well be the Axis I dissociative disorder *psychogenic fugue.* This disorder is characterized by "sudden unexpected travel away from one's home or customary place of work, with inability to recall one's past" (American Psychiatric Association, 1980, p. 257). This fugue state results without the presence of an organic mental disorder. When they do occur, these symptoms usually result from the histrionics need to acquire new forms of stimulation or support. Most commonly, this need arises when the patient feels unwanted or deprived.

Affective Disorders. *Dysthymic disorders* are the most common affective disorders experienced by histrionic personalities. These relatively mild episodes of depression tend to be manifest through typical histrionic behaviors, for example, dramatic and eye-catching displays. This exhibitionistic display is a natural manifestation of the histrionic's basic style of actively seeking attention and approval. Dysthymic disorders arise, most often, in these individuals when they are anticipating or actually feeling isolated, abandoned, or stranded.

It is not uncommon for histrionics to philosophize about their existential anxiety or the alienation that we all share in this age of anxiety or this impersonal society. Thus, they tend to engage in pseudosophisticated discussions, career counseling, or other activities in an attempt to rationalize their own lack of identity or lack of personal or professional direction. Their interpersonal and work histories usually reflect a series of short-lived relationships and occupations. They purport to be in search of meaningful relationships, careers, and self-identity.

Should histrionic individuals fail to establish the support they need, they may decompensate into other Axis I affective disorders, such as *major depression, hypomanic symptoms* or *bipolar episodes.*

Summary

In this chapter we have described the nature and development of the histrionic personality disorder. We have found it to be a pattern characterized by sociability, charm, emotional lability, and superficiality. Let us review the main points that should be kept in mind when considering this disorder:

1. The clinical picture of the histrionic personality disorder may be summarized as follows:
   a. Behaviorally, histrionics appear to range from affected to theatrical. They tend to overreact and act impulsively with a penchant for excitement.
   b. Interpersonally, they range from being flirtatious to seductive. They commonly solicit praise and manipulate others to gain attention.
   c. The cognitive style of histrionics appears to range from flighty to scattered. They resist introspection and tend to exhibit poor judgment.
   d. The affective expression of the individuals ranges from fickle to impet-

uous. They exhibit dramatic displays of emotion and the tendency to become easily excited, as well as bored.

e. The self-perception of these individuals ranges from sociable to hedonistic. They see themselves as outgoing and gregarious.

f. Their primary defense mechanism is dissociation.

g. A probable differential personality diagnosis would be the narcissistic personality disorder.

2. Although there is some evidence for biogenic factors in the histrionic personality disorder, primary environmental factors include parental reinforcement of attention-seeking behavior, histrionic parental role models, and operant conditioning of interpersonally manipulative behavior.

3. The histrionic personality is self-perpetuated through four basic mechanisms:

a. Preoccupation with external stimuli.

b. Short-lived social relationships.

c. Massive repression.

d. Operant conditioning of the histrionic behavior pattern itself, which appears to satisfy a need for interpersonal affiliation, affection, approval, and support.

4. In addition to the narcissistic personality mix, the most commonly encountered mixed personality disorders that are anchored to the histrionic disorder are the histrionic-antisocial mixed personality disorder and the histrionic-borderline mixed personality disorder.

5. Common DSM-III, Axis I disorders that are associated with the histrionic personality disorder include anxiety disorders, obsessive compulsive disorders, somatoform disorders, dissociative disorders, and affective disorders.

CHAPTER 6

The Dependent Personality Disorder

In the previous chapter, we examined the active-dependent histrionic personality disorder. In this chapter, we will address the passive-dependent variation—the dependent personality disorder.

As you read the case of Harry G., make note of any major examples of these descriptive criteria:

1. Behavioral appearance.
2. Interpersonal conduct.
3. Cognitive style.
4. Affective expression.
5. Self-perception.
6. Primary defense mechanism.

CASE 6.1

The Dependent Personality Disorder

Harry G., Age 57, Married, Four Children

Mr. G. was a rather short, thin and nicely featured but somewhat haggard man who displayed a hesitant and tense manner when first seen by his physician. His place of employment for the past 15 years had recently closed and he had been without work for several weeks. He appeared less dejected about the loss of his job than about his wife's increasing displeasure with his decision to "stay at home until something came up." She thought he "must be sick" and insisted that he see a doctor; the following picture emerged in the course of several interviews.

Mr. G. was born in Europe, the oldest child and only son of a family of six children. As was customary of his ethnic group, the eldest son was pampered and overprotected. His mother kept a careful watch over him, prevented him from engaging in undue exertions and limited his responsbilities; in effect, she precluded his developing many of the ordinary physical skills and competencies that most youngsters learn in the course of growth. He was treated as if he were a treasured family heirloom, a fragile statue to be placed on the mantlepiece and never to be touched for fear he might break. Being small and unassertive by nature, he accepted the comforts of his role in a quiet and unassuming manner.

His life was uneventful and inconspicious until he was called to serve in the army. Despite all kinds of maneuvers on the part of his mother, he was physically removed from his home and trundled off to a training camp. No more than a week elapsed, during which time he experienced considerable anguish, than his eldest sister bribed her way into the camp and spirited him to the home of a distant relative. The records of the government whose army he was to serve were so ill kept that he was able to return to his home several months thereafter with no awareness on the part of local officials that he had failed to fulfill his service obligations.

A marriage was arranged by his parents. His wife was a sturdy woman who worked as a seamstress, took care of his home and bore him four children. Mr. G. performed a variety of odds-and-ends jobs in his father's tailoring shop. His mother saw to it, however, that he did no "hard or dirty work," just helping about and "overlooking" the other employees. As a consequence, Mr. G. learned none of the skills of the tailoring trade.

Shortly before the outbreak of World War II, Mr. G. came to visit two of his sisters who previously had emigrated to the United States; when hostilities erupted in Europe he was unable to return home. All members of his family, with the exception of a young son, perished in the war.

During the ensuing years, he obtained employment at a garment factory owned by his brothers-in-law. Again he served as a helper, not as a skilled workman. Although he bore the brunt of essentially good-humored teasing by his co-workers throughout these years, he maintained a friendly and helpful attitude, pleasing them by getting sandwiches, coffee and cigarettes at their beck and call.

He married again to a hard-working, motherly type woman who provided the greater portion of the family income. Shortly thereafter, the son of his first wife emigrated to this country. Although the son was only 19 at the time, he soon found himself guiding his father's affairs, rather than the other way around.

Mr. G. was never troubled by his "failure" to mature and seemed content to have others take care of him, even though this meant occasional ridicule and humiliation. His present difficulty arose when the factory closed. Lacking the wherewithal of a skilled trade and the initiative to obtain a new position, he "decided" to stay at home, quite content to remain dependent on others.

(From T. Millon, *Modern Psychopathology: A Biosocial Approach to Maladaptive Learning.* Philadelphia: Saunders, 1969. Used with permission of the author.)

The case of Harry G. represents one variation of the dependent personality disorder. The case of Harry may be summed up in one word, inadequate.

CLINICAL PICTURE

Docility, a clinging helplessness and a search for support and reassurance characterize dependent personalities. They are self-deprecating, they feel a sense of inferiority and are willing to abdicate self-responsibility and self-control to others. That is, these individuals subordinate their desires to others; they will even submit to intimidation and abuse in hopes of avoiding loneliness and abandonment. When left alone, they feel impotent to affect a constructive lifestyle. These persons appear to be in search of guidance for making even the most simple decisions.

The dependent personality disorder may be thought of as a pathological syndromal elaboration of the normal cooperative personality described in Chapter 2. According to the American Psychiatric Association (1980), the dependent disorder is diagnosed far more frequently among women than men.

The dependent personality may be thought of as stretching across a continuum, thereby possessing mild variations as well as more severe variations of the disorder. As the degree of pathology increases, so does a sense of selflessness, an inability to function autonomously, and a complete abdication of rights and desires to others. Let us take a closer look at the dependent personality disorder through the use of our standardized clinical criteria. A multidimensional summary of the dependent personality is provided in Table 6.1.

Behavioral Appearance

Dependent personalities may project many images; in general, however, their behavioral appearance ranges from appearing incompetent in milder variations to appearing pitifully helpless in more severe variations of this disorder.

The absence of self-confidence is apparent in the posture, voice, and overall mannerisms of these individuals. Friends often view dependent personalities as generous and thoughtful, but they may note that they seem to be unduly apologetic and obsequious. Neighbors and coworkers are often impressed by the humility, cordiality, and gentility of their behavior. Beneath the surface of this warm and gentle exterior, however, lies a solemn and somewhat apprehensive individual who is in search of acceptance, approval, nurturance, and support.

Table 6.1 A Multidimensional Appraisal of the Dependent Personality Disorder

1. Behavioral appearance: incompetent to helpless.
2. Interpersonal conduct: submissive to clinging.
3. Cognitive style: naive to gullible.
4. Affective expression: pacific to timid.
5. Self-perception: inept to inadequate.
6. Primary defense mechanism: introjection.
7. Differential personality diagnosis:
   a. histrionic personality disorder
   b. avoidant personality disorder

In many instances, dependent individuals project an image of in-competence, that is, the inability to interact effectively with their en-vironment. They appear to lack many of the functional skills that most people simply take for granted. As a result, they lack self-assertion and seem passive as they withdraw from mature responsibilities.

The case of Harry G. represents one variation of the dependent disorder whose behavioral appearance can be summarized as being inadequate. All through his life Harry G. allowed others to care for him. As a result, he was never given the opportunity to mature and to ac-quire basic adult competencies. His role of helper was obvious to all, including himself. But Harry seemed content to allow that image to prevail.

In extremely severe manifestations of this disorder, there is a con-stant apprehension of being left alone. This fear drives these indi-viduals to totally submerge themselves in the whims and desires of others. In effect, they become totally selfless individuals. Also charac-teristic of extreme variations of this disorder may be the presence of a chronic state of fatigue. Any form of exertion brings on the need to rest and recuperate. Many wake up exhausted, ready for another night's sleep. Concerted effort or work out of the ordinary routine tend to exhaust these individuals. They hesitate to engage in new tasks for fear of becoming too tired. They frequently lack sexual interest and may experience sexual impotency. The mere thought of extending themselves beyond their normal work load results in weakness, anx-iety, and a sense of being weighted down.

Interpersonal Conduct

Passive-dependent individuals often seek out benefactors. These are single, all-powerful helpers. They are partners in whom the dependent individuals may place their trust, depend on for creature comforts, and look to for protection against the responsibilities of an adult world. So, we see the interpersonal conduct of the dependent personality may range from submissive to clinging.

When supplied with a nurturant and dependable partner, they may function with ease. They are interpersonally sociable, they can display, warmth, affection, and generosity to others. At times, these individuals may be overly cooperative and acquiescent. They generally prefer to yield and placate rather than assert themselves. Harry G. demonstrated these submissive characteristics from an early age. He allowed his mother, sisters, and later his wife and son to run his life for him. "Being small and unassertive by nature, he accepted the comforts of his role in a quiet and unassuming manner." Even though he often bore the brunt of teasing he consistently maintained a friendly attitude, content to be dependent on others.

At times, when dependent individuals are deprived of the affection and protection they need, they will tend to withdraw, become tense and apprehensive, even depressed and despondent.

In sum, then, the interpersonal conduct of these dependent personalities is characterized by interpersonal submissiveness, conciliation, abdication of personal rights and responsibilities, and, at times, a tendency to cling to others for support and protection. Large groups and noisy affairs are often significant sources of stress for dependent individuals. They will often go to great pains to avoid such circumstances.

Cognitive Style

Cognitively dependent individuals limit their awareness of self and others. They often adopt a Pollyanna attitude toward the world. They minimize difficulties that may arise. They are basically naive, with a tendency to be easily persuaded and taken advantage of. Their cognitive style appears to range from naive to gullible.

Dependents constrict their world, they become unperceptive and uncritical. They generally only see the "good" in people and circumstances. Despite this Pollyanna veneer, these individuals still lack the joy of living. If they truly let go, they report emerging feelings of pessimism, discouragement, and gloom. They appear, then, to suffer alone in silence. So, to experience intrapersonal harmony, these individuals must rationalize their inadequacies.

Harry G. was obviously content to be trusting, weak and dependent. But clearly, he similarly demonstrated these traits to a naive degree. By claiming weakness and incompetence, individuals like Harry G. absolve themselves of the tasks and responsibilities they know they should assume, but would rather not. Likewise, self-deprecation evokes sympathy, attention, and care from others for which dependents are likely to experience guilt. Dependents will sometimes cover up their fundamental need to be dependent by attributing them to physical illness, bad luck, etc. The social affability that these individuals often express not only serves to prevent social condemnation, but also protects them from being harsh with their own shortcomings. So, not only are dependents interpersonally naive and gullible to others, but they are naive and gullible with themselves as well.

Intrapsychically, dependent individuals like Harry G. possess relatively underdeveloped and undifferentiated cognitive processes. There appears to be both a deficit and a lack of diversity in intrapsychic regulatory abilities.

Affective Expression

Affectively, dependent personalities range from being pacific to timid. In addition, an anxious and somber quality of their mood suggests an intrinsic melancholic temperament. In effect, dependent individuals may possess an affective status characterized by fear and sadness. The pacific aspects of their felt emotion are characterized by warm, docile, and noncompetitive behavior. The timid aspects of their affect express themselves as interpersonal timidity, avoidance, and withdrawal. Harry G. is seen to behave more pacifically as opposed to timidly. He expressed a docility and noncompetitive lifelong status as helper, despite the fact that he was sometimes ridiculed for that status.

In sum, the thrust of affective expression for dependents will be a manifest pacific, somber, and timid affect founded on what may be an intrinsically melancholic temperament.

Self-Perception

The apparent self-image of dependent individuals is that of considerate, thoughtful, and cooperative persons. Closer examination will reveal that these individuals see themselves as ranging from inept to grossly inadequate. These dependent individuals are basically insecure and magnify their failures and inadequacies. They minimize what successes or attributes they may have. Dependents commonly assume personal blame for the problems and difficulties of others, despite the fact that objectively they would be considered blameless. Clinically, these self-depreciating tendencies may be viewed as a strategy by which these individuals may extract from others assurances that they are not worthless persons.

The self-perception of inadequacy can not only serve the dependent as a tool for avoiding responsibilities, but it may also serve to prohibit these individuals from seeking to become competent. In effect, this self-perception can become a self-fulfilling prophecy of ineptness and fundamental inadequacy. Harry G. saw himself as basically inadequate. This he believed and was content to allow others to run his life for him.

Primary Defense Mechanism

We have described the passive-dependent personality as one in which the individuals who possess it are docile, clinging, timid, and usually inadequate. These persons, as their labeling denotes, are dependent on others for approval, attention, and support. The defense mechanism they most commonly employ is *introjection.*

Introjection may be thought of as the tendency of dependent individuals to develop an extreme devotion to their significant others. Introjection is not just identification with, or dependence on, others. Rather, it is the internalization of others with the hopes of creating an inseparable interpersonal bond. These dependent individuals appear content to lose their own identity and autonomy if it strengthens the relationship between themselves and those on whom they depend. Introjection is a defense mechanism that is used preventively to preclude threats and conflicts in relationships.

The opening case described Harry G., a dependent 57-year-old man. Harry G. not only depended on his family for support, but he went beyond that, integrating himself first with his mother, then with his brothers-in-law, and later with his second wife and his son. Harry G.'s use of introjection could be seen as his autonomy and independence that were voluntarily abdicated into the will of those on whom he depended. It also helps to explain why Harry G. was more distressed at displeasing his wife than he was at losing his job of 15 years. Thus, dissociation was a defense mechanism for Harry G. because it allowed him to minimize the chances of conflict between himself and those on whom he depended. In other words, introjection reduced the chances that Harry G. would lose his supportive, significant others.

Differential Personality Diagnosis

Diagnostic discriminations involving the dependent personality disorder are most commonly complicated by the similarities between the dependent personality and the histrionic and avoidant personalities.

These two patterns are those with which the dependent disorder most frequently combines or overlaps. Thus, diagnosis is further complicated.

If one had to sum up the key feature differentiating the dependent disorder from the histrionic disorder in one word, it would be the *passivity* demonstrated on the part of the dependent personality. Dependents are submissive, docile, and self-effacing. Histrionics, on the other hand, are far more active. They are overtly gregarious, manipulative, seductive, and even charming.

The key feature differentiating the dependent from the avoidant disorder revolves around the issue of trust. Both dependents and avoidants have strong needs for affiliation, affection, and nurturance. Yet, the avoidant cannot seem to trust others in the same manner as the dependent does. The avoidant questions the motives of others, anticipates rejection and humiliation, and, therefore, withdraws from others. The dependent, on the other hand, puts his/her trust in others and anticipates that he/she will be cared for, supported, and nurtured.

ETIOLOGY AND DEVELOPMENT

We have described passive-dependents as passive, submissive, incompetent, and possessing an inadequate self-image. These are generally thought to be undesirable characteristics by most. What forces come to bear to create such a personality?

Biogenic Factors

It seems no less plausible to suggest that biogenic factors play a role in the development of the dependent personality disorder as any other personality disorder. Research on this topic is lacking however. Therefore, the following comments are offered purely as speculation.

Temperamentally, the dependent infant might, at birth, present tendencies to be fearful, withdrawing, and even sad. Such behavior is likely to elicit an increased amount of protective behavior on the part of the parents. Such parental behavior reinforces the preceding biological phenomena and the infant perceives no need to alter his/her basic biogenic temperament.

It has been noted that dependent personalities may be accounted for from physical exertion. Biogenically, this phenomenon may be accounted for by way of a hypometabolic condition mediated through a chronic thyroid insufficiency, yet within "normal" limits. Similarly, it has been noted (Millon, 1969) that dependent personalities tend to have endomorphic (heavy and cumbersome) or ectomorphic (thin and frail) body builds. Either extreme condition could contribute to low energy thresholds and a seeming lack of vigor that often typifies the dependent personality disorder.

Despite the biogenic potentials for the determination of the dependent personality, it is unreasonable to believe that biogenic factors act alone without being shaped by environmental factors.

Environmental Factors

Assuming for the moment that biogenic factors are, indeed, at work in the determination of the dependent personality disorder, their manifestation will clearly be shaped by environmental factors. On the other hand, if biogenic factors play no role at all in the development of this disorder, then even greater deterministic emphasis must be placed on environmental factors. In either case, we have listed below some of the most prevalent environmental influences that may shape the dependent personality disorder.

Parental Overprotection. Although all infants are helpless and dependent on parents for protection in the early stages of life, it may be possible to be overly protective. Should the infant's parents be too protective, that is, shelter the infant from all adversity long beyond the infantile stage, then the child fails to develop any autonomous coping behavior. In effect, the child becomes "attached" and dependent on parental protection for physical and psychological shelter. This point is clearly brought out in the case of Harry G., who was pampered and overprotected. His mother failed to allow him to exert himself. As a result, he failed to develop any significant physical or mental competencies.

Competitive Deficits. A major nonparental environmental factor that may shape the development of the dependent personality disorder is repeated competitive deficits. Feelings of unattractiveness or competitive inadequacy, especially during adolescence, can have a devastating impact on the individual. Such conditions may result in social humiliation and self-deprecation and doubt. Should these events or relationships continue, the child soon learns that it is better to be submissive rather than competitive.

Adherence to Social Roles. Briefly note that more women than men develop the dependent personality disorder. It may be suggested that this trend is due to an inherent submissive disposition on the part of females. Of course, such a suggestion is likely to arouse angry accusations of sexist bias. Furthermore, there is little evidence to support such a claim. More plausible is the thesis that the cultural roles that are sanctioned in most societies reinforce the learning of passive-dependent behaviors among women. So, in effect, the fact that more women develop the dependent personality disorder compared to men may be a function of the cultural programming that girls and women receive.

It is also important to note that social-role expectations may be at work in the case of the endomorphically and ectomorphically built males as well. The cultural roles for the heavy and cumbersome as well as the thin and frail are often roles of submission and dependence.

In summary, from an environmental perspective, we see parental overprotection, competitive deficits, and adherence to social expectations as potential determinants of the dependent personality disorder.

Neuropsychological Development

The neuropsychological stages of development, a forum where biological and environmental factors become integrated, play a particularly important role in the development of the dependent personality. Let us follow the course of neuropsychological development and see how the major environmental determinant of the dependent personality, that is, parental overprotection, acts to shape these all important developmental stages:

1. The first stage of neuropsychological development, the sensory-attachment stage, serves as the foundation for future growth. If the child is supplied with adequate amounts of beneficial stimulation, both interpersonal sensitivity and trust will develop.

    It seems plausible that children who receive adequate stimulation, but almost exclusively from one source (usually the mother), will be disposed to develop a passive and dependent personality. Although these children are neither impoverished for stimulation nor are they overstimulated, they do suffer from stimulation initiated from an unusually narrow sphere of origin. As a result of this lack of variety in sources of stimulation, the child tends to form a singular attachment, or fixation, to one source of stimulation, to the exclusion of others. In the case of Harry G., he was protected as a family heirloom from the day he was born and his mother served to overprotect him as long as she lived.

2. An infant who retains an exclusive attachment to the mother during the sensory-attachment stage is likely to have that attachment continued in the next neuropsychological stage—the sensorimotor-autonomy stage. In the process, dependence behavior is strengthened and perpetuated. On the other hand, dependence behavior need not always originate in the sensory-attachment stage. There are many youngsters who were not especially attached to their mothers in the first stage who develop such attachment subsequently.

In the normal progression of this second stage, children will assert their growing capacities and strive to be more autonomous. This normal progression can be interfered with by physical trauma or disease, parental anxieties, or other disruptive forces. For example, some overly protective mothers may discourage their child's independence for fear of "losing their baby." They create innumerable barriers and distractions to keep the child from gaining greater autonomy. Almost always, however, such behavior is believed to be in the best interest of the child. In the case of Harry G., his mother never really allowed him to grow personally because of excessive sheltering. He was never really allowed to exert himself. Rather than let him stumble and perhaps even fail on his own, Harry's mother shaped his destiny from the day he was born, through the army, up until her death.

3. Parental pampering and overprotection, if continued into the third neuropsychological stage of development, can have devastating effects on the child's self-image.

First, overprotection on the part of the child's parent, or other caregiver, may result in an inability on the part of the child to develop a self-concept independent from the parent. Overprotection has deprived the child the opportunity to do things for himself/herself. As a result, the child may fail to develop a sense of what he/she is good at and ultimately who he/she is. Second, it is implicit in parental overprotection that the child cannot take care of himself/herself. The protected child is likely to develop a self-concept as one who requires special attention because he/she is unable to care adequately for himself/herself. Third, because parental overprotection has restricted the child from developing any real skills (as in the case of Harry G. who never learned to do much of anything professionally), any ventures into the "real" world are likely to be met with frustration and failure. Thus, the notion of incompetence and the resultant poor self-image is reinforced. So, the dependent has no real option but to turn to others for strength and support as he/she has done all his/her life. This is exactly the scenario we see unfold in the case of Harry G. who depended on his mother, sisters, and finally his wife for strength and support.

SELF-PERPETUATION OF THE DEPENDENT PERSONALITY DISORDER

We have described the dependent personality disorder as one characterized by submissiveness, passivity, and an inferior self-image. How can such a disorder be self-perpetuated? Let us turn to a discussion of how the dependent personality perpetuates itself. We will discuss three major factors: reinforcement of dependent behavior, avoidance of growth-promoting activities, and self-deprecation.

Reinforcement of Dependent Behavior

Being dependent can be reinforcing for two reasons. Dependence behavior can be positively reinforcing and it can be negatively reinforcing.

Dependence behavior can be positively reinforcing because it allows the individual to accrue that which he/she seeks—the strength and support of others. In the case of Harry G., he "was never troubled by his 'failure' to mature and seemed content to have others take care of him, even though this meant occasional ridicule and humiliation." Thus, by being dependent on others, Harry's need seemed to be taken care of. Even when the factory closed and he lost his job, he was content to allow his wife to support him.

Dependence behavior can not only be positively reinforcing, it can be negatively reinforcing as well. Dependence behavior can be negatively reinforcing because it can result in the elimination of that which is deemed undesirable (the definition of negative reinforcement). In the case of Harry G., his dependency on his mother and sisters contributed to their ultimately spiriting him away from the army into which he had been drafted. Thus, by allowing others to dictate the major aspects of his life, Harry was removed from serving in the army, a condition that he found anguishing. For dependent individuals, in general, passive-dependent behavior may be negatively reinforcing because it helps them avoid their greatest fear—that of being abandoned and left alone to provide for themselves. Thus, we see in the case of

Harry G. as well as other dependent personality disorders, dependence is not necessarily undesirable. In fact, it can be quite reinforcing; so, it goes on.

Avoidance of Growth-Promoting Activities

Because of the excessive parental protection received by dependent children, they miss many chances to develop competencies. This lack of competency soon becomes obvious to the dependent individual and to those around the child. This condition then breeds a sense of inadequacy and fear of failure on the part of the dependent individual.

The dependent individual, having now developed deeply rooted fears of inadequacy, hesitancies, and a general fear of failure, avoids activities that might be challenging, threatening, or anxiety producing. Unfortunately, this often precludes most activities that are growth promoting as well. In the case of Harry G., he shied away from any such "threats," fearing that he would fail. He preferred to remain inept. Thus, this self-imposed restriction on trying to do anything that might be challenging or growth promoting, leads to a perpetuation of the person's current condition of dependency.

Self-Deprecation

Not only do the dependent personalities observe real deficits in their competencies, but they deprecate whatever talents or virtues they do possess. Through such deprecation, they are able to prevent others from expecting them to assume any responsibilities they would rather avoid. So, we see another example of dependency leading to negative reinforcement.

Indeed, each time dependent persons publically declare their dependency, they convince not only others, but also themselves that they are defective, dependent, or basically inferior. Self-deprecation can become a trap in which, through their own persuasiveness, dependent individuals develop an increasing sense of the futility of independence. Thus, they try less and less to be independent and overcome their inadequacies. Thus, the disorder is perpetuated.

In summary, we see that because dependence is both positively and negatively reinforcing, because dependent personalities avoid challenging, growth-promoting activities, and because they engage in significant self-deprecation, the dependent personality disorder is self-perpetuating.

ASSOCIATED DISORDERS

We have seen the dependent personality as one that seeks nurturance and support through dependence on others. Let us now examine the disorders that are associated with the dependent personality.

Mixed Personality Disorders

When we examine the dependent personality disorder as a basis for other personality disorders with which it blends, or mixes, we find the avoidant and histrionic patterns most frequently interacting with the dependent pattern.

Dependent-Avoidant Mixed Personality Disorder. Perhaps the most common personality disorder found combining with the dependent disorder is the avoidant pattern—the combination creating the dependent-avoidant mixed personality disorder. This mixed disorder is often encountered wherever institutional or environmental contingencies reinforce such behavior. Case 6.2 describes a 57-year-old unmarried World War II veteran. He has remained in outpatient treatment at a mental hygience clinic since the early 1950s. He has continued to receive a 75% psychiatric disability since that time.

CASE 6.2

The Dependent-Avoidant Mixed Personality Disorder

57-Year-Old Man, Unmarried, Unemployed World War II Veteran

The patient's behavior may be characterized as submissively dependent, self-effacing, and noncompetitive. Others are leaned upon for guidance and security, and a passive role is assumed in relationships. There is a striking lack of initiative and a general avoidance of autonomy. The patient is exceedingly dependent, not only in needing attention and support from others to maintain equanimity but in being especially vulnerable to separation from those who provide support. However, intense resentment is felt toward those upon whom there is dependence since he has been subjected to frequent rebuff and disapproval. Outbursts of anger have been directed toward others for having failed to appreciate the patient's needs for affection and nurturance. The very security that he needs is threatened, however, when such resentments are expressed.

The patient has become apprehensive and has acquired a pattern of withdrawing from social encounters. Further, he has built a tight armor to damp-down and deaden excessive sensitivity to rejection. Loneliness and isolation are commonly experienced. Although efforts are made to be pleasant and agreeable, there is an underlying tension and emotional dysphoria, expressed in disturbing mixtures of anxious, sad, and guilt-ridden feelings. Insecurity and fears of abandonment underlie what may appear on the surface to be a quiet, submissive, and benign attitude toward difficulties. Despite past rebuff and fears of isolation, he continues to evidence a clinging helplessness and a persistent search for support and reassurance.

Complaints of weakness and easy fatiguability may reflect an underlying mood of depression. Having experienced continuing rebuff from others, the patient may succumb to physical exhaustion and illness. Under these circumstances, simple responsibilities demand more energy than the patient can muster. He expresses the feeling that life is empty but heavy, experiencing a pervasive sense of fatigue and apathy.

(From T. Millon, *Disorders of Personality: DSM-III, Axis I.* New York: Wiley, 1981. Used with permission of the author.)

The key features of the case provided are the patient's obvious dependency combined with his avoidant, socially withdrawing behavior and the manner in which environmental contingencies maintain the disorder.

Dependent-Histrionic Mixed Personality Disorder. Another frequent combination of personality disorders is found in the mixture of dependent and histrionic disorders. Cluster analyses (Millon, 1982) have indicated that this combination is particularly prevalent among women as they approach midlife. Case 6.3 exemplifies such a pathological mix and clearly portrays the dependent and histrionic characteristics blended into one presenting personality disorder.

CASE 6.3

The Dependent-Histrionic Mixed Personality Disorder

37-Year-Old Woman, 3 Children, Divorce Pending

The patient's behavior is best characterized by a submissive dependency and a leaning upon others for affection, nurturance, and security. The fear of being abandoned leads the patient to be overly compliant and obliging. At times, she handles this fear by being socially gregarious and superficially charming, often evident in the seeking of attention and in self-dramatizing behaviors. The patient typically reveals a naive attitude toward interpersonal problems. Critical thinking rarely is evident and most cognitive knowledge appears to be unreflected and scattered. In an effort to maintain an air of buoyancy, she tends to deny all disturbing emotions, covering inner disharmonies by short-lived enthusiasms. In part, this may stem from a tendency to be genuinely docile, soft-hearted, and sensitive to the desires of others. The patient is more than merely accommodating and docile in efforts to secure dependency needs. She is admiring and loving, giving all to those upon whom there is dependence. The patient has also learned to play the inferior role well, providing partners with the rewards of feeling useful, sympathetic, stronger, and more competent. There is often an active solicitousness of praise, a marketing of appeal, and a tendency to be seductive and entertaining.

The patient persistently seeks harmony with others, if necessary at the expense of internal values and beliefs, and is likely to actively avoid all situations that may involve personal conflict. To minimize distressing relationships, she avoids self-assertion and abdicates autonomous responsibilities, preferring to leave matters in the hands of others. The preoccupation with external rewards and approval has left her bereft of an identity apart from others. The patient values herself not in terms of intrinsic traits but in terms of relationships. By submerging or allying herself with the competencies and virtues of others, the patient not only is bolstered by the illusion of shared competence but finds solace in the belief that bonds so constructed are firm and inseparable.

The patient feels helpless when faced with responsibilities that demand autonomy or initiative. The loss of a significant source of support or identification often prompts severe dejection. Under such conditions of potential rejection or loss, she will openly solicit signs of reassurance and approval. Guilt, illness, anxiety, and depression are frankly displayed since these tend to deflect criticism and transform threats of disapproval into those of support and sympathy. When dependency security is genuinely threatened, the patient will manifest an anxious depressiveness covarying with other, more extreme reactions such as brief manic periods of either euphoria or disorganized hostility.

(From T. Millon, *Disorders of Personality: DSM-III, Axis I.* New York: Wiley, 1981. Used with permission of the author.)

Associated Axis I Disorders

Our discussion now turns to the Axis I disorders that are highly correlated with, and may indeed emerge from, the dependent disorder. We find numerous Axis I possibilities.

Anxiety Disorders. Dependent personalities are extremely vulnerable to anxiety disorders. Of particular relevance is *separation anxiety.* As Millon (1981) notes, "Having placed their welfare entirely in the hands of others, they expose themselves to conditions that are ripe for generalized anxieties. There may be an ever present worry of being abandoned by their sole benefactor and left alone to struggle with their meager competencies" (p. 117).

It should noted, having just presented the preceding analysis, that anxiety is also likely to evoke nurturance and sympathy from others. Therefore, anxiety may also be used as a tool by the dependent to elicit the support and nurturance he/she so desperately needs.

Phobic Disorders. Dependent personalities appear to develop *phobic disorders* (specific and irrational fears) when their security is threatened or when they are placed in situations that exceed their perceived abilities to perform or meet demands. Social phobias are rather common among dependent personalities. Intense feelings of anxiety may arise when these individuals are placed in new or socially competitive situations. The social-learning histories of these individuals have left them ill prepared to meet the challenges of many social situations. Thus, usually lacking social skills, their perceived ability to perform adequately in social situations is minimal; hence, their aversion to most social situations. Once again, it should be noted that phobic reactions are likely to gain the attention and support of others. Thus, these reactions may be useful to these personalities for securing their dependent needs.

Somatoform Disorders. *Conversion reactions* and *somatization disorders* are commonly seen among dependent personalities. It will be recalled that the major clinical features of these disorders is the existence of physical symptoms, yet there are no demonstrable pathophysiological mechanisms of organic nature for them.

It may be argued that these symptoms promote the avoidance of undesirable responsibilities. In addition, these symptoms as noted earlier, tend to elicit the sympathy and nurturance the dependent personalities need. According to Millon (1981), "It is notable that their symptoms often are located in their limbs, a way perhaps of demonstrating to others that they are disabled and, therefore, incapable of performing even routine chores" (p. 118).

In addition to conversion and somatization disorders, *hypochondriacal symptoms* are likely to arise among dependent personalities. The principle goals of such symptoms, once again, may be to elicit attention, support, and nurture from others.

Factitious Disorders. As a result of their social-learning histories, dependent personalities have been well trained in the role of "patient." This is a role that is characterized by weakness and inadequacy. As a result these individuals are especially prone to have *factitious disorders*.

Factitious disorders are physical or psychological symptoms that are unreal. According to DSM-III, they are "physical or psychological symptoms that are produced by the individual and are under voluntary control," yet these symptoms are unreal, not genuine, or unnatural (American Psychiatric Association, 1980, p. 285). Factitious disorder should be distinguished from malingering. Malingering refers to unreal or unnatural symptoms that the patient controls for a goal that is obviously recognizable. In the case of factitious disorders, the symptoms are again unreal or unnatural and under voluntary control, yet there is no recognizable goal involved other than that of simply playing the role of patient.

Etiologically, overdependency and excessive parental solicitousness may have taught these individuals as children that the role of "patient" will elicit protection and nurturance.

Affective Disorders. Dependent personalities, like the histrionics described in Chapter 5, are especially susceptible to separation anxiety and feelings of helplessness and abandonment. The actual loss of a supportive person or relationship may promote *dysthymic reactions, major depressive episodes,* or even *bipolar disorders.*

Summary

In this chapter, we have described the nature and development of the dependent personality disorder. Let us review our main points:

1. The clinical picture of the passive-dependent, dependent personality disorder may be summarized as follows:

   a. Behaviorally, dependents appear to others as ranging from incompetent to helpless. These individuals are unwilling and unable to assume autonomous roles.

   b. Interpersonally, dependent individuals range from being submissive to clinging. They tend to subordinate their desires and needs to others from whom they derive support.

   c. Cognitively, these individuals range from being naive to gullible. They are easily persuaded.

   d. Affectively, dependents range from being pacific to being timid. They are timid, yet warm and accepting.

   e. Dependents generally see themselves as ranging from inept to inadequate. They perceive themselves as weak and fragile and as self-doubting.

   f. The primary defense mechanism used by dependents is introjection.

   g. Differential diagnoses should include the histrionic personality disorder and the avoidant personality disorder.

2. Parental overprotection, competitive deficits, and social-role programming contribute to the development of the dependent personality disorder. There is also some evidence that biogenic factors play a role in the development of this personality disorder.

3. The dependent personality disorder is self-perpetuated through a process that involves the positive and negative reinforcement of dependent behaviors, the avoidance of growth-promoting activities, and self-deprecation. The apparent motive for this pattern is a need for interpersonal affection and support.

4. The most common mixed personality disorders that are anchored to the dependent personality are the dependent-avoidant mixed personality disorder and the dependent-histrionic mixed personality disorder.

5. Common DSM-III, Axis I disorders that appear related to the dependent personality are anxiety disorders, phobic disorders, somatoform disorders, factitious disorders, and numerous affective disorders.

PART Four

THE AMBIVALENT PERSONALITY DISORDERS

In this section we examine the passive-aggressive personality disorder and the compulsive personality disorder. Within the context of the present theory, these personality disorders are examples of the basic *ambivalent* pattern.

Conflict is an inevitable part of living. The repetitive manner in which individuals attempt to resolve conflicts often reveals a major aspect of their fundamental personality. We have seen that independent personalities turn to themselves for the resolution of conflicts and for reinforcement in general. Dependent individuals, on the other hand, have learned to depend on others for the resolution of their conflicts and for reinforcement in general. Ambivalent individuals, however, are trapped in continuous conflict because of their inability to know how or where to turn to resolve conflict and seek reinforcement. Two types of ambivalent personalities exist: the *passive-ambivalent* personality and the *active-ambivalent* personality.

Passive-aggressive individuals may be considered active-ambivalents. These individuals are trapped in a web of instability and indecision. These unstable and erratic personalities experience significant tension as they vacillate between dependency and conformity, on the one hand, and negativism and autonomy, on the other.

Individuals who possess the compulsive personality disorder may be considered passive-ambivalents. On the surface, these individuals appear to have turned completely to others for approval and reinforcement, yet they are actually struggling to restrain impulses toward autonomy and self-assertion. To control these impulses, passive-ambivalents resort to extreme rigidity and conformity. Therefore, in both the active- and passive-ambivalents, we see contradictory desires and feelings towards themselves and others.

CHAPTER 7

The Passive-Aggressive Personality Disorder

In Chapter 2, the reader was introduced to the ambivalent personality disorders. In this chapter, we will address the first of two ambivalent patterns—the active-ambivalent or passive-aggressive personality disorder. As you read the case of Ann W., make note of any major examples of these descriptive criteria:

1. Behavioral appearance.
2. Interpersonal conduct.
3. Cognitive style.
4. Affective expression.
5. Self-perception.
6. Primary defense mechanism.

CASE 7.1

The Passive-Aggressive Personality

Ann W., Age 27, Married, Three Children

For many years Ann had periodic "spells" of fatigue, backaches and a variety of discomforting gastrointestinal ailments. These recurred recently and, as in the past, no physical basis for her complaints could be established. In his interviews with her,

Ann's physician concluded that there was sufficient evidence in her background to justify recommending psychiatric evaluation.

In his report, her physician commented that Ann had withdrawn from her husband sexually, implored him to seek a new job in another community despite the fact that he was content and successful in his present position, disliked the neighborhood in which they lived and had become increasingly alienated from their friends in past months. He noted the fact that a similar sequence of events had occurred twice previously, resulting in her husband's decision to find new employment as a means of placating his wife. This time Ann's husband was "getting fed up" with her complaints, her crying, her sexual rebuffs, her anger and her inability to remain on friendly terms with people. He simply did not want to "pick up and move again, just to have the whole damn thing start all over."

When Ann first was seen by her therapist she appeared contrite and self-condemning; she knew the physical problems she had been experiencing were psychosomatic, that she caused difficulties for her husband and that she precipitated complications with their friends. This self-depreciation did not last long. Almost immediately after placing the burden of responsibility on her own shoulders, she reversed her course, and began to complain about her husband, her children, her parents, her friends, her neighborhood and so on. Once she spilled out her hostility toward everyone and everything, she recanted, became conscience-smitten and self-accusing again.

The first item to which Ann referred when discussing her past was the fact that she was an unwanted child, that her parents had to marry to make her birth "legitimate." Her parents remained married, though it was a "living hell much of my life." A second girl was born two years after Ann, and a third child, this time a boy, five years thereafter. In the first two years of life, Ann was "clung to" by her mother, receiving a superabundance of [her] mother's love and attention. "It seems as if my mother and I must have stuck together to protect ourselves from my father." Apparently, parental bickering characterized home life from the first day of their marriage. Ann's father remained antagonistic to her from the very beginning, since Ann represented for him the "cause" of his misery.

The protection and affection that Ann received from her mother in her first two years was substantially reduced with the advent of her sister's birth. Mother's attention turned to the new infant and Ann felt abandoned and vulnerable. She recalled the next several years as ones in which she tried desperately to please her mother, to distract her from her sister and recapture her affection and protection. This "worked at times." But as often as not, Ann's mother was annoyed with her for demanding more than she was able to provide.

By the time the third child appeared on the scene, parental conflicts were especially acute, and Ann was all the more demanding of support and attention as a means of assuaging her increased anxieties. It was not long thereafter that she began to hear the same comment from her mother that she had heard all too often from her father: "you're the cause of this miserable marriage." Mother would feel pangs of guilt following these outbursts, and would bend over backwards for brief periods to be kind and affectionate. But these moments of affection and love were infrequent. More common were long periods of rejection or indifference.

Ann never was sure what her mother's attitude would be toward her, nor what she could do to elicit her love and attention. Thus, at times when she attempted to be helpful, she gained her mother's appreciation and affection; at other times, when [her] mother felt tired, distraught or preoccupied with her own problems, the same behavior would evoke hostile criticism.

Ann hated her sister "with a vengeance," but feared to express this hostility most of the time. Every now and then, as she put it, she would "let go," tease her unmercifully or physically attack her. Rather interestingly, following these assaults, Ann would "feel terrible" and be contrite, becoming nurturant and protective of her sister. She quickly recognized in therapy that her behavior with her sister paralleled that of her mother's. And, in time, Ann observed that this vacillating and ambivalent pattern served as the prototype for her relationships with most people.

Until college, Ann's peer relationships were not unusual, although she reported never having been a member of the "in group." She had her share of friends nevertheless. Ann attended an all-girls college where she frequently experienced problems in social relationships. She had a sequence of ill-fated friendships. For example, during her first two years, she had four different roommates. Typically, Ann would become "very close" to her roommate. After a short period, usually less than a semester, she would become disillusioned with her friend, noting faults and finding her disloyal. Eventually, Ann would become "blue," then "nasty" and hostile.

When Ann met her future husband, during the first semester of her junior year, she decided to move into a single room in her dormitory. Though not a total isolate, she rarely mingled socially with the other girls. The courtship period with her boyfriend had its trying moments. Ann was inordinately jealous of his friends, and feared that he would leave her. Quite often, she would threaten to break off the romance so as not to be hurt should it progress further. This threat served to "bring him back" to her.

Ann's marriage has mirrored many of the elements she experienced and observed in her childhood. She is submissive and affectionate, then sickly, demanding and intimidating of her husband, a pattern not unlike the one she saw her mother use to control her father. Ann's husband spent much of his energies trying to placate her, but "Ann is never content." During the six years of their marriage, she seemed satisfied only when they first moved to a new location. But these "bright periods" dimmed quickly, and the same old difficulties emerged again. This time, however, her husband would have "none of this," and refused to budge. Ann again began to experience her physical symptoms, to withdraw affection, vent anger and vacillate in her moods.

(From T. Millon, *Modern Psychopatholgy: A Biosocial Approach to Maladaptive Learning and Functioning.* Philadelphia: Saunders, 1969, Used with permission of the author.)

The case of Ann W. represents one variation of the active-ambivalent, passive-aggressive personality disorder. As such, it is an example of one of the most frequently encountered mild personality disorders.

Table 7.1   A Multidimensional Appraisal of the Passive-Aggressive Personality Disorder

1. Behavioral appearance: stubborn to contrary.
2. Interpersonal conduct: ambivalent to uncooperative.
3. Cognitive style: inconsistent to disorienting.
4. Affective expression: irritable to agitated.
5. Self-perception: discontented to mistreated.
6. Primary defense mechanism: displacement.
7. Differential personality diagnosis:
   a. antisocial personality disorder
   b. avoidant personality disorder

CLINICAL PICTURE

The passive-aggressive personality is an active-ambivalent personality disorder. It may be thought of as a pathological syndromal extension of the normal "sensitive" personality pattern described in Chapter 2, as such it is far broader in its nature than the current DSM-III formulations. The passive-aggressive disorder is best conceptualized as stretching across a continuum from mildly pathological to more severely pathological. As the degree of pathology increases, so does the negativity and basic ambivalence that characterizes this pattern.

Millon (1969) has referred to this disorder as a negativistic personality. This label is based on the tendency for individuals who possess this disorder to be contrary, unaccommodating, sulky, pessimistic, and chronically complaining. Passive-aggressives tend to dampen everyone's spirits. They tend to be sullen malcontents, sour pusses and demoralizing. Their actions often serve to obstruct the efforts and pleasure of those around them. "The name of this disorder is based on the assumption that such individuals are passively expressing covert aggression" (American Psychiatric Association, 1980, p. 328). Let us take a closer look at this personality disorder using the 7-point standardized clinical criteria used in other chapters. These points are summarized in Table 7.1.

Behavioral Appearance

Passive-aggressive individuals appear negativistic to others. They are resistant and erratic. Behaviorally, they range from being stubborn in mild variations of the disorder to being generally contrary in more severe forms of the disorder. The stubborn and contrary tendencies of passive-aggressive individuals may manifest themselves in unpredict-ability, procrastination, impatience, intentional inefficiency, im-pulsivity, and generally erratic behavior. Their behavior is even more erratic than what we would expect from individuals who were deprived of consistent parental models during childhood. In more severe forms of the disorder, their contrary nature is disclosed by their tendencies to be generally pessimistic, highly irritable, resentful of others, inten-tionally forgetful and their tendency to derive gratification from demor-alizing others or actually undermining the pleasures and aspirations of others.

The case of Ann W. is an example of a woman whose behavior is seen as erratic and fundamentally negativistic. She cleverly uses her illnesses to manipulate her husband and at the same time engages in self-deprecation in what appears to be a half-hearted attempt at atone-ment for her manipulative actions. Finally, her manipulative, com-plaining, and oppositional behavior took its toll on her husband who got fed up with her complaints, crying, and sexual rebuffs.

Interpersonal Conduct

The unpredictable, impulsive, and negativistic reactions of passive-aggressive individuals make it difficult for others to feel comfortable around them. Although there are periods of pleasant sociability, most acquaintances of these individuals feel on edge waiting for them to display a sullen look or to become obstinate or nasty. Thus, their inter-personal conduct may range from being ambivalent to resistant and uncooperative.

The history of Ann W. reveals an individual who had significant interpersonal problems. In college she had four roomates in 2 years. Once losing interest in her roomates, Ann would have a tendency to follow a pattern of becoming "blue" then "nasty" and finally "hostile." Eventually, she moved into a single room of her own. Ann was inor-dinately jealous and played numerous games to ensure the affection of her boyfriend.

In sum, passive-aggressive individuals typically behave in an am-bivalent interpersonal fashion and often act blatantly uncooperative. Their interpersonal ambivalence may express itself as vacillation be-tween conflicting social roles and relationships, especially between de-pendent acquiescence and aggressive independence. A powerful tool in the hands of many passive-aggressives is that of guilt. They can use guilt to manipulate those around them and to achieve their desired ends. Their uncooperative nature inhibits not only themselves, but also those with whom they live and work. Indecisiveness, procrastination, pessimism, impatience, complaining, and irritability are each, different ways of being uncooperative.

Cognitive Style

Cognitive ambivalence characterizes the thinking of passive-aggressive individuals. No sooner do they see the merits of solving their problems one way than they find themselves finding reasons not to follow through. Thus, the cognitive style of passive-aggressives ranges from being cognitively inconsistent to disorienting.

Passive-aggressive individuals are fearful of committing themselves and unsure of their own competencies and the loyalities of others. They generally find their thoughts shifting from one solution to another. Because of intense ambivalencies, they often end up acting precipitously, on the spur of the moment.

A distinguishing clinical characteristic of passive-aggressives is their lack of cognitive controls. Cognitive dissonance is a ubiquitous companion. They find themselves thinking and repeatedly expressing attitudes that are contrary to their inner feelings. Fundamentally, passive-aggressives harbor conflicting thoughts towards self and others. Ann W. is a good case in point. She appeared contrite and self-condemning when she first saw her therapist. She admitted that the physical symptoms she was experiencing were tools she used to manipulate her husband and others. She admitted causing difficulties for her husband and becoming antagonistic towards her friends. Yet, "almost immediately after placing the burden of responsibility on her own shoulders, she reversed her course, and began to complain about her husband, her children, her parents, her friends, her neighborhood and so on." Then, she reversed her behavior again. Thus, intrapsychically, we would be likely to deduce that there exists a discordant intrapsychic organization. Incompatible impulses seem to be interwoven in such a manner as to facilitate the cognitive dissonance that characterizes this disorder.

Affective Expression

The affective expression of passive-aggressive individuals ranges from irritable to agitated and is characterized by lability and vacillation.

Passive-aggressive individuals display a rapid succession of moods and seem restless, unstable, and erratic in their feelings. These persons are easily offended. There is a low tolerance for frustration. Passive-aggressives may seem chronically impatient, fidgety, and irritable. They may vacillate from being distraught and despondent, at one instance, to being petty, spiteful, stubborn, and contrary, at another instance. Sometimes these individuals actually seem enthusiastic and cheerful, but this mood is short-lived. The emotions of passive-aggressives are worn on their sleeve. Ann, for example, clearly felt no need to hide her emotions. It was always clear how she was feeling. The impulsive, unpredictable, and often explosive reactions of passive-aggressive individuals make it difficult for others to relax in their presence.

Self-Perception

The self-perception of passive-aggressive individuals appears to range from discontented to mistreated. Self-reports alternate between preoccupations with their own personal inadequacies, bodily ailments, and guilt feelings, on the one hand, to resentments, frustrations and disillusionments, on the other hand.

Passive-aggressives characteristically voice their dismay about the sorry state of their life, their worries, their sadness, their disappointments, their nervousness, and so on. They express a desire to be rid of distress and difficulty, but they seem unwilling to do so. Thus, they see themselves as misunderstood and unappreciated. They feel they are constantly demeaned by others and generally mistreated.

In extreme cases, the passive-aggressive reports being trapped by fate—nothing ever works out favorably. These persons express envy and resentment over the easy life of others. They will then be critical and cynical with regard to what others have achieved, yet they will covet those achievements themselves.

In sum, these passive-aggressive individuals feel discontented, cheated, and unappreciated. They have been misunderstood, taken advantage of, and they are disillusioned. These descriptors summarize Ann's self-perception and help explain many of her interpersonally contrary behaviors.

Primary Defense Mechanism

The passive-aggressive personality has been described as an active-ambivalent personality disorder in which the individual's behavior may be observed to be unpredictable, indecisive, erratic, negativistic, impatient, irritable, and resentful. The basic ambivalence that is the foundation of this personality results in a host of frustrations and emotions that churn on the brink of consciousness, ready to explode into one of the brief, but dramatic, negativistic tirades that characterizes this disorder. It should come as no surprise to find the most commonly employed defense mechanism is *displacement.*

Displacement refers to the shifting, or transfer, or negative or hostile emotions from the people, places, or things that aroused them to other settings—usually other people in the case of the passive-aggressive—of lesser importance or power. Frequently, these hostile emotions are expressed in passive ways, such as acting in what appears to be perplexed, incompetent, altruistic, or self-sacrificing ways. The mechanisms of displacement serve to minimize the risk of rejection or retaliation from the original or true source of the passive-aggressive individual's hostile feelings.

In the case of Ann W., displacement can be found early in her developmental history. Ann stated that she hated her sister "with a vengeance," yet it is more reasonable to assume that this hatred for her sister was really displaced resentment for the rejection she felt from her mother after the third child was born. In effect, the hatred for her sister was really her way of getting even with her mother.

In her later life, Ann can be seen to employ displacement again. Ann constantly found fault with her neighbors and, therefore, often wanted to move to new neighborhoods. The hostility she felt towards her neighbors was often displaced on to her husband in rather indirect ways. For example, as her relationship with her neighbors deteriorated, she would develop chronic fatigue, backaches, and gastrointestinal ailments. All of these symptoms obviously inhibited her sexual desire and performance. The result was sexual rebuffs to her husband. Thus, through the mechanism of displacement, Ann W. can be observed to not only ventilate her frustrations and hostilities, but also to exert some control over her environment.

Differential Personality Diagnosis

The traits that comprise the passive-aggressive disorder actually share innumerable features with personality and symptom disorders listed in the DSM-III. For example, the moodiness of the passive-aggressive disorder is a central feature in most DSM-III affective disorders. The quick-tempered irritability and contrary disposition of the passive-aggressive are also found in the aggressive antisocial personality. The self-discontent and interpersonal ambivalence of the passive-aggressive are common among avoidant personalities as well. In general, the *heterogeneity* and distinct *variability* of presenting characteristics represents the essence of this disorder (i.e., the passive-aggressive has a propensity to vacillate between widely divergent symptoms and mood states, whereas antisocial and avoidant personalities show more homogeneity and far less variability in the symptoms and mood states they present). Its heterogeneity is what distinguishes it from other disorders that, ostensibly, seem very similar.

ETIOLOGY AND DEVELOPMENT

The clinical picture of the passive-aggressive personality disorder is that of an active-ambivalent reinforcement pattern. These individuals are clearly resistant, immature, moody, and discontented.

Biogenic Factors

The passive-aggressive pattern can be observed among family members. Whether this phenomenon is a function of genetic factors or environmental factors is unclear. It is, however, reasonable to speculate that certain aspects of the passive-aggressive personality disorder may rest upon biological substrates.

According to Weil (1974), the structure and function of the limbic system may play a significant role in the manifestation of human emotions (see also Gellhorn, 1957). Weil speculates that low stimulation thresholds in structures within the limbic circuitry may give rise to what we will refer to as affective irritability, as observed in the passive-aggressive disorder.

From a different perspective, it seems reasonable to speculate that children who undergo an uneven maturational process may be prone to another one of the components of the passive-aggressive disorder. Such uneven maturation fosters feelings of frustration and discontent as well as features that are associated with this passive-aggressive personality (Millon, 1969).

Finally, Millon (1969) has observed the passive-aggressive disorder to occur in greater frequency among women than men. Conceivably, many passive-aggressive women may be subject to "extreme hormonal changes during their menstrual cycles, thereby precipitating marked, short-lived and variable moods. Such rapid mood changes may set into motion sequences of erratic behavior and associated interpersonal reactions conducive to the acquisition of perpetuation of this pattern" (Millon, 1969, p. 292). This hypothesis is, of course, highly speculative, though not inconsistent with recent work on what is called the Premenstrual Syndrome (PMS).

Environmental Factors

Biogenic factors notwithstanding, it seems likely that environmental factors shape the major aspects of what we know as the passive-aggressive personality disorder.

Parental Inconsistency. Although all children are exposed to parental inconsistencies as they are raised, passive-aggressive children are likely to be exposed to more than their fair share. Their parents are likely to have swayed from affection to rejection and from love to hostility. This erratic pattern was probably frequent, prolonged, and pronounced.

As a result of this pattern of erratic parental behavior, these children are likely to develop a variety of pervasive and deeply ingrained conflicts, such as trust versus mistrust, competence versus doubt, and initiative versus guilt and fear. Their self-concept is then likely to be composed of contradictory appraisals. Every judgment is likely to be matched against an opposing one. Every course of behavior will have its positive and negative side. Thus, these children are caught in a bind: they have no way of knowing which course of action is appropriate. As a result, these children vacillate, feeling hostility, guilt, compliance, assertion, and so on. They shift erratically and impulsively from one action to another. Unable to predict what kinds of reaction their behavior will elicit, these children remain constantly on edge, in a steady state of tension and alertness. This chronic state of tension is likely to lead to a potentially explosive emotional status. At the slightest provocation, these individuals are likely to explosively react.

The case of Ann W. demonstrates the notion of parental inconsistency. First, one parent showed affection; the other did not. Later, with the birth of Ann's sister, her mother, who had originally been affectionate, now vacillated between affection, on the one hand, and frustration and resentment, on the other hand.

We may usefully summarize the effects of parental inconsistency. First, the child learns to imitate the erratic behavior of his/her parents. Second, the child never clearly learns what is appropriate behavior. Third, the child internalizes the series of conflicting messages and attitudes. The result is a general sense of frustration and ambiguity. Fourth, because the child is unable to predict the consequences of his/her behavior, the frustration and ambiguity result in a chronic state of affective tension, which may ignite into an explosion of impulsive and emotional behavior.

Family Schisms. Inconsistent and contradictory parental behavior can often be found in schismatic families, that is, families in which the parents are frequently in conflict with one another. This was the case in Ann's family where parental bickering created a condition where Ann felt she was in a "living hell much of my life".

Children raised in a schismatic family not only suffer from the constant threat of family dissolution, but are also forced to contend with the chronic tension that characterizes the family. Oftentimes, these children try to play moderator. This very role, one of switching from one point of view to another, may begin to develop into an habitual pattern. The result is that these children have conflicting parental models—both of which the child has learned to imitate. Thus, we see that the schismatic family literally breeds ambivalence.

Sibling Rivalry. The case of Ann W. portrays many features common to the developmental history of the passive-aggressive personality. It is not uncommon to find sibling rivalries in the development of passive-aggressive personalities.

Many such individuals report feeling replaced by a younger sibling. In such instances, parental attention and affection may be redirected to the newborn child. Of course, it should be noted that such events are not unique to the families of passive-aggressive individuals. Exactly what *is* unique about such families that foster the development of such a personality disorder may be the unique combination of biogenic and environmental factors that contribute to the development of this disorder. In passive-aggressive children, the shock of being replaced may be so great that deeply rooted feelings of resentment and jealousy emerge. Although these feelings are, indeed, genuine, these children quickly learn that it is inappropriate to display such feelings towards their younger siblings. As a result, they learn to be sneaky and perhaps even physically abusive towards their siblings when the parents are absent. This was the case in Ann W.'s family as she learned to hate her sister "with a vengeance."

Learned Vacillation. We know behavior that is perpetuated is, in some way, reinforcing. This is true of the vacillating passive-aggressive as well. Switching back and forth among the roles of the martyr, the affronted, the aggrieved, the misunderstood, the guilt-ridden, the sickly, the overworked, and so on, is a clever tactic of interpersonal behavior that gains passive-aggressive individuals several things. They are able to accrue attention, reassurance, and dependency; at the same time, they are able subtly to vent their anger and resentments. Vacillation is positively reinforcing because it allows one to derive the rewards from both sides of the fence: the dependent side and the autonomous side. Thus, by playing opposing, vacillating roles, the passive-aggressive can have his/her emotional needs met under the guise of social responsibility. Ann used this maneuver quite effectively in her married life to motivate her husband to move, change jobs, and to comply with her other wishes.

Neuropsychological Development

The primary factor affecting the neuropsychological development of the active-ambivalent individual is parental inconsistency.

Parental inconsistency begins to affect developmental processes during the sensory-attachment stage. The inconsistent messages received by the child inhibit the natural process of psychological attachment. On the one hand, the child may receive messages of affection, on the other hand, the same parental figure may be rejecting and punitive.

The child moves into the second stage, the sensorimotor-autonomy stage without a clearly developed sense of security. During this stage, vacillating role behavior begins to emerge. Similarly, the child's sense of an autonomous self has been greatly retarded without a sense of parental support and without a clear sense of role identity.

SELF-PERPETUATION OF THE PASSIVE-AGGRESSIVE PERSONALITY DISORDER

The passive-aggressive personality disorder, unlike most other disorders we will discuss, lacks stability. These individuals seem to be constantly in a state of discontent and turmoil. In addition, their misery provokes them to behave unpredictably, to appear restless, sullen, and obstructive much of the time. Therefore, not only do they suffer an ever-present sense of inner turmoil, but they also act out their discontent for all to see and to share with them. Let us examine the major processes that serve to perpetuate and intensify the miseries of the passive-aggressive individual.

Emotional Undercontrol

Passive-aggressive individuals are noted for their general lack of emotional controls. Deprived of necessary environmental guidance and support for acquiring self-controls, these individuals are usually forced to model themselves after what may be erratic and undisciplined parents. As a result, these individuals seldom learn to conceal their emotions. Whatever emotions they experience, they quickly rise to the surface to be expressed.

The passive-aggressive personalities experience an undercurrent of inner turmoil and anxiety that is rooted in deep personal ambivalencies. They are extremely unstable. In short, passive-aggressive personalities generally suffer from a wide range of intense and conflicting emotions that characteristically surge to the surface, as they did in the case of Ann, because of weak emotional controls and a lack of self-discipline.

This erratic and sometimes intense display of emotions is distressing to those around the passive-aggressive individual. At first, they try to be understanding and, in many instances, they are deceived by the vacillating moods. Yet, over time, those around the passive-aggressive individuals seem to simply burn out. They express frustration and disgust. This reaction then serves to reinforce the confusion, discontent, and turmoil experienced by the passive-aggressive individual. Thus, the disorder perpetuates itself.

Anticipation and Creation of Disappointment

Not only does the passive-aggressive personality prompt real difficulties by the very nature of the disorder, but he/she often anticipates and perceives difficulties where none, in fact, exist.

Passive-aggressive personalities, raised in erratic environments, have learned that good things do not last. Ann W. learned this based on the erratic and confusing manner in which her mother treated her. She also learned it throughout her adult life as she moved from one location to another. She was continually able to find fault and disappointment with all of her "friends" no matter who they were or where they lived.

Rather than be disappointed, again and again, passive-aggressive individuals anticipate being betrayed, let down, or generally disappointed. After a series of disappointments, these individuals become extremely hesitant to allow anyone to become close enough to them to disappoint them. This in itself frustrates and embitters them even further. Thus, their own anticipation of being frustrated prompts these individuals to create a self-fulfilling prophecy of disillusionments and frustration.

Operant Conditioning

A final consideration in the self-perpetuation of the passive-aggressive personality disorder is the reinforcement of the behavior itself. The characteristic vacillation of the ambivalent passive-aggressive disorder appears to be a source of positive reinforcement. Through alternating, vacillating behavior, individuals can play the middle of the road. That is, they can accrue the benefits of being passive and dependent and at the same time accrue the benefits of expressing their urges for independence and autonomy. It is this dilemma that appears to render these persons indecisive, that is, they are ambivalent about just what position to take, yet they can derive reinforcement to some degree from both postures by vacillating between the two. Thus, the disorder goes on.

In summary, then, we find that the lack of emotional control and the self-fulfilling anticipation of disappointment lead the passive-aggressive individual to distrust others and freely display his/her frustration and discontent. These patterns become circular, and the end result is that the passive-aggressive personality disorder perpetuates itself. Finally, we find that the vacillating ambivalent behavior is capable of providing positive reinforcement itself. So the disorder is perpetuated.

ASSOCIATED DISORDERS

We have seen the passive-aggressive personality as a plethora of ambivalent manifestations. Let us examine disorders that appear related to this pathological personality.

Mixed Personality Disorders

Cluster analyses and clinicial observation (Millon, 1982) suggest that the passive-aggressive personality disorder has the propensity to blend with two other personality disorders: the histrionic and the borderline.

Passive-Aggressive-Histrionic Mixed Personality Disorder. The passive-aggressive-histrionic mixed personality disorder is most commonly observed among women patient populations in family counseling agencies and in private practice settings. When it occurs in men patient populations, it is usually found in drug abuse rehabilitation programs.

Case 7.2 describes a 36-year-old married woman with two young children. The case demonstrates how the passive-agressive and histrionic disorders are likely to coexist.

CASE 7.2

The Passive-Aggressive-Histrionic Mixed Personality Disorder

36-year-old Woman, Married, Two Children

The patient's behavior is typified by a high degree of emotional lability and short periods of impulsive acting out, alternating with depressive complaints, moodiness, and sulking. Notable also are hypersensitivity to criticism, a low frustration tolerance, immature behaviors, short-sighted hedonism, and a seeking of excitement and stimulation. Emotions surge readily to the surface, untransformed and unmoderated, evident in a distractible, flightly, and erratic style of behavior. Whatever inner feelings she may sense, be they guilt, anger, or desire spill quickly to the surface in pure and direct form.

Moods tend to be brittle and variable with periods of high excitement and affability alternating with a leaden paralysis, fatigue, oversleeping, overeating, and an overuse of alcohol. She displays short lived, dramatic, and superficial affects, reporting a tendency to be easily excited and then quickly bored. Mood levels are highly reactive to external stimulation. Feelings of desperation or euphoria are expressed histrionically and more intensely than justified by the situation. The patient behaves by fits and starts, shifting capriciously down a path that appears to lead nowhere, often precipitating wrangles with others and disappointments for self.

Cut off from needed external attentions, the patient may engage either in a frantic search for approval, become easily nettled and contentious, or become dejected and forlorn. There may be extreme cyclical swings, alternating periods of simulated euphoria and illusory excitements, intermingled with moments of hopelessness and self-condemnation. There are frequent depressive complaints, usually to the effect that others misunderstand her and that life has been full of disappointments. She may become disgruntled, critical, and envious of others, grudging their good fortunes with a jealous, quarrelsome, and irritable reaction to minor slights. There may be an unusual preoccupation with bodily functions and health, an overreaction to illness, and unreasonable complaints about minor ailments. Symptoms may be displayed exhibitionistically to gain attention and support.

(From T. Millon *Disorders of Personality: DSM-III, Axis II.* New York: Wiley, 1981, Used with permission of the author.)

Passive-Aggressive-Borderline Mixed Personality. The second most frequent passive-aggressive profile is seen in the passive-aggressive-borderline mixed personality disorder. In this pathological mix, the more severe features of the borderline disorder seem to accentuate the emotional lability and unpredictability that are characteristic of the passive-aggressive disorder. The end result is a more severe variation of the passive-aggressive disorder as it approaches the borderline on a continuum of syndromal continuity. Case 7.3 summarizes the passive-aggressive and borderline disorder when they combine. This pathological combination is commonly encountered in VA clinics, alcoholism treatment centers, and halfway houses for women psychiatric patients.

CASE 7.3

The Passive-Aggressive-Borderline Mixed Personality Disorder

28-Year-Old Man, Divorced, Vietnam Veteran

The patient's behavior is typified by highly variable and unpredictable moods, an embittered and resentful irritability, and an untrusting and pessimistic outlook, notably the feelings of having been cheated, misunderstood, and unappreciated. An intense conflict between dependency and self-assertion contributes to an impulsive and quixotic emotionality. He exhibits deficient regulatory controls with fleeting thoughts and emotions impulsively expressed in unmodulated form and external stimuli evoking capricious and vacillating reactions. There is a pattern of negativism, sullen pouting, fault finding, and stubborness that is punctuated periodically by short-lived enthusiasms, belligerent, and querulous outbursts and expressions of guilt and contrition.

The patient anticipates being disillusioned in relationships with others and often precipitates disappointments through obstructive behaviors. Though desperately seeking closeness and intimacy, he is deeply untrusting and fearful of domination, resists external influence, and is suspiciously alert to efforts that might undermine self-determination and autonomy. Personal relationships are fraught with wrangles and antagonisms, provoked often by his bitter complaining, passive-aggressive behaviors, touchiness, and characteristic irascible demeanor. The struggle between feelings of resentment and guilt, and the conflict over dependency and self-assertion permeate all aspects of his life.

The patient displays an unpredictable and rapid succession of moods, is invariably dysphoric in affect, seems restless, and is capricious and erratic in the expression of feelings. There is a tendency to be easily nettled, offended by trifles, and readily provoked into being fretful, contrary, and hostile. There is a low tolerance for frustration and he is impatient and fractious unless things go as desired. He will vacillate between being distraught and despondent, at one time; and being irrationally negativistic, petty, spiteful, and contentious, another. His disputatious and abrasive irritability precipitates exasperation in others, leading them to stereotype him as a person who dampens everyone's spirits, a perennial malcontent whose very presence demoralizes and obstructs the pleasures of others. There is a struggle between acting out and curtailing resentments. The sulking and unpredictable "blowing hot and cold" behaviors prompt others into reacting in a parallel capricious and inconsistent manner, causing them to weary quickly of him. As a result, he reports feeling misunderstood and unappreciated, at one time, and turning inward, expressing self-condemnation, the next.

The patient is overly sensitive to the attitudes of others, exhibiting an agitated defensiveness and brooding suspiciousness. Others are often seen as devious and hostile, and he repeatedly distorts their incidental remarks so as to appear deprecating and vilifying. He hesitates displaying weakness lest these be fatal concessions that will be misused by the malice anticipated from others. There is an alert vigilance against the possibility of attack or derogation, a defensive stance from which he can react at the slightest hint of threat. Feelings of retribution for past mistreatment underlie his hostility, envy and, suspiciousness. Unfortunately, these behaviors often set into motion a self-fulfilling prophesy, driving away potential well-wishers and creating unnecessary frictions, which are then seen by him as proof and justification for suspicion and hostility.

(From T. Millon, *Disorders of Personality: DSM-III, Axis II.* New York: Wiley, 1981, Used with permission of the author.)

Associated Axis I Disorders

Before continuing, it may be valuable to recall for the reader some of the factors that interrelate Axis I and Axis II disorders.

First, Axis I clinical syndromes usually take the form of dramatic signs that are easily contrasted to the patient's ubiquitous pattern of behaving, that is, the patient's personality. Second, we believe that to understand Axis I disorders, it is necessary to understand the patient's personality. The personality pattern serves as the basis for the emergence of the Axis I disorders. Similarly, Axis I disorders may be seen as extensions of the basic personality.

Finally, specific Axis I clinical symptoms are less a function of present precipitants (e.g., psychosocial stressors) than they are of the synthesis of biogenic and environmental factors that have shaped the patient's development.

Having reviewed these points, let us now turn to a discussion of the DSM-III, Axis I clinical syndromes most frequently associated with the passive aggressive personality disorder.

Anxiety Disorders. It may be observed that passive-aggressive personalities experience prolonged and generalized anxiety disorders. These individuals openly display their discomfort as a means of upsetting others or soliciting the attention and support of others. According to Millon (1981) "Typically passive-aggressives color their apprehensions with depressive complaints, usually to the effect that others misunderstand them and that life has been full of disappointments. These complaints not only crystallize and vent their tensions but are also subtle forms of expressing anger and resentment" (p. 258).

The anxiety felt by these passive-aggressive personalities is most likely to be ventilated in brief but frequent doses, thereby decreasing the likelihood of a significant build-up of tension.

Psychosomatic Disorders. According to the DSM-III, psychosomatic disorders are classified under the heading of "psychological factors affecting physical conditions." In the previous edition of the DSM, the DSM-II, these disorders were termed "psychophysiological disorders" and defined as being physical disorders of presumably psychological origin.

These disorders frequently arise in patients who repeatedly find themselves in unresolvable conflicts. And these are the types of situations in which passive-aggressive personalities often find themselves. It is quite common to find passive-aggressives as well as compulsives trapped between a need to discharge anxiety and to act independently and assertively, on one hand, and to acquiece to others, on the other hand. This seemingly constant psychic struggle appears capable of activating neuroendocrine and endocrine mechanisms in sufficient intensity and chronicity so as to result in numerous psychosomatic manifestations (Everly & Rosenfeld, 1981).

Somatoform Disorders. It is not uncommon to see passive-aggressive individuals display *hypochondriacal* and *somatization* symptoms along with their psychosomatic disorders. Discontented and irritable, these individuals often use physical complaints as a disguise for hostile impulses of anger and resentment. Oftentimes, such physical complaints may be used as an attempt to manipulate others, creating in them feelings of guilt, grief, and frustration, even to the point of incurring financial losses. Some diagnosticians may argue that many passive-aggressive individuals are consciously aware of their manipulative behaviors and, as such, this warrants the diagnosis of *factitious disorders* when imaginary physical symptoms arise.

Affective Disorders. Affective disorders are quite common among passive-aggressive personalities. *Dysthymic reactions* (defined earlier) and *cyclothymic disorders* (defined as mood disturbances of at least 2 years' duration with periods of depression and hypomania, yet not severe enough to warrant full depressive or manic diagnoses) seem rather prevalent among these individuals.

Passive-aggressive individuals characteristically vacillate between anxious futility, despair and self-deprecation, on the one hand, to bitter discontent and demanding irritability on the other hand. A generalized pessimism often engulfs them and those around these individuals. As these feelings persist, a host of affective disorders may be seen to arise.

Summary

We have examined the passive-aggressive personality disorder, let us now review the main points:
1. The clinical picture of the active-ambivalent, passive-aggressive personality disorder may be summarized as follows:
    a. Behaviorally, passive-aggressive individuals range from appearing stubborn to contrary. They typically procrastinate, perform inefficiently, and take advantage of opportunities to demoralize others
    b. Interpersonally, they conduct themselves in a manner that ranges from ambivalent to uncooperative. They vacillate between dependency and independent behavior
    c. Cognitively, these individuals range from being inconsistent to disorienting. They typically experience contradictory thoughts and desires
    d. Affectively, passive-aggressives range from being irritable to agitated. They are touchy, impatient, fretful, and generally negative
    e. The self-perception of passive-aggressives apparently ranges from seeing themselves as discontented in some cases to being mistreated in more severe cases. They are pessimistic.
    f. Their primary defense mechanism is displacement
    g. Potential differential personality diagnoses would include the antisocial personality and the avoidant personality disorder
2. Environmental factors such as parental inconsistency, family schisms, sibling rivalry, and learned vacillation are all factors that contribute to the etiology and development of the passive-aggressive disorder.
3. The passive-aggressive personality disorder is self-perpetuated through the absence of emotional controls, the anticipation and creation of disappointment, and the positive reinforcement of passive-aggressive behavior.
4. The most common mixed personality disorders that are based in the passive-aggressive personality disorder are the passive-aggressive-histrionic mixed personality disorder and the passive-aggressive-borderline mixed personality disorder.
5. Finally, common DSM-III, Axis I disorders that appear to be associated with the passive-aggressive personality disorder include anxiety disorders, psychosomatic disorders, somatoform disorders, and affective disorders.

CHAPTER 8

The Compulsive Personality Disorder

In chapter 7, we examined the active-ambivalent, passive-aggressive personality disorder. We will now turn our attention to the passive-ambivalent variation—the compulsive personality disorder. As you read the case of Wayne B., make a note of any major examples of these descriptive criteria:

1. Behavioral appearance.
2. Interpersonal conduct.
3. Cognitive style.
4. Affective expression.
5. Self-perception.
6. Primary defense mechanism.

CASE 8.1

The Compulsive Personality Disorder

Wayne B., Age 40, College Dean, Married, No Children

Wayne was advised to seek assistance from a therapist following several months of relatively sleepless nights and a growing immobility and indecisiveness at his job. When first seen, he reported feelings of extreme self-doubt and guilt and prolonged periods of tension and diffuse anxiety. It was established early in therapy that he always had experienced these symptoms. They were now merely more pronounced than before.

The precipitant for this sudden increase in discomfort was a forthcoming change in his academic post. New administrative officers had assumed authority at the college, and he was asked to resign his deanship to return to regular departmental instruction. In the early sessions, Wayne spoke largely of his fear of facing classroom students again, wondered if he could organize his material well, and doubted that he could keep classes disciplined and interested in his lectures. It was his preoccupation with these matters that he believed was preventing him from concentrating and completing his present responsibilities.

At no time did Wayne express anger toward the new college officials for the "demotion" he was asked to accept. He repeatedly voiced his "complete confidence" in the "rationality of their decision." Yet, when face-to-face with them, he observed that he stuttered and was extremely tremulous.

Wayne was the second of two sons, younger than his brother by three years. His father was a successful engineer, and his mother a high school teacher. Both were "efficient, orderly and strict" parents. Life at home was "extremely well planned," with "daily and weekly schedules of responsibility posted" and "vacations arranged a year or two in advance." Nothing apparently was left to chance. Both boys were provided with the basic comforts of life, enjoyed the rewards of a well-run household, but knew exactly what was expected of them, and knew that their parents would be punitive and unyielding if they failed to adhere to these expectations.

Wayne perceived his brother as the more preferred and dominant child in the family. He felt that his brother "got away with things," was a "show-off" and knew how to "get around his mother." Begrudgingly, Wayne admitted that his brother may have been a brighter and more attractive child. Nevertheless, he asserted that there was "not much of a difference" between them, and that he had been "cheated and overlooked by the fraud." This latter comment spilled forth from Wayne's lips much to his surprise. Obviously, he harbored intense resentments toward his brother which he desperately tried to deny throughout his life. He feared expressing hostility in childhood since "mother and father would have nothing to do with emotions and feelings at home, especially angry feelings toward one another." The only way in which Wayne could express his resentment toward his brother was by "tattling"; he would experience great pleasure when able to inform his parents about things his brother had done of which they would disapprove. Not until therapy, however, did Wayne come to recognize that these self-righteous acts were less a matter of "sticking to the rules" than of trying to "get back at him."

Wayne adopted the "good boy" image. Unable to challenge his brother either physically, intellectually or socially, he became a "paragon of virtue." By being punctilious, scrupulous, methodical and orderly, he could avoid antagonizing his perfectionistic parents, and would, at times, obtain preferred treatment from them. He obeyed their advice, took their guidance as gospel and hesitated making any decision before gaining their approval. Although he recalled "fighting" with his brother before he was six or seven, he "restrained his anger from that time on and never upset his parents again."

Peer experiences were satisfactory throughout schooling, although he was known as a rather serious and overconscientious student. With the exception of being thought of as "a sort of greasy grind," his relationships during adolescence were adequate, if not especially rewarding.

At 27, Wayne completed his doctorate in political economics, married a rather plain but "serious-minded" girl and obtained his first regular academic appointment at a small college. Two years later he moved to his present institution. His "fine work" in advising freshmen students led to his appointment as Dean of Freshmen, and eventually to that of Dean of Students, a position he has held for seven years.

Although Wayne demonstrated a talent for "keeping the rules" and for assuming his responsibilities with utmost conscientiousness, he had been accused by both students and faculty as being a "stuffed shirt," a "moralist" with no real sympathy or understanding for the young. His lack of warmth and frequent, harshly punitive decisions with students were out of keeping with the new administration's policies and led to the request that he step down.

(From T. Millon, *Modern Psychopathology: A Biosocial Approach to Maladaptive Learning and Functioning.* Philadelphia: Saunders, 1969, Used with permission of the author.)

The reader may be struck by the grim, cheerless character of the compulsive personality. Wayne B. represents but one variation of this passive-ambivalent personality disorder.

CLINICAL PICTURE

The compulsive personality disorder may be considered a pathological extension of the "respectful" personality described in Chapter 2. It represents a passive variation of the basic ambivalent pattern. It will be recalled, ambivalence is a conflict, an opposition between contrary tendencies. The compulsive personality represents an unresolved mixture of thoughts and feelings that on the one hand represent a desire to be assertive and to act autonomously, yet, on the other hand, represent a need to derive the support and comfort that can be obtained through conformity. Although this conflict is quite similar to that experienced by the active-ambivalent, passive-aggressive personality, the two ambivalent disorders differ, in that passive-aggressives outwardly display their felt ambivalency through vacillating and erratic behavior, whereas the compulsives submerge their ambivalency in a pool of overconforming, oversubmissive, and overly rigid behavior.

Certainly, morals and ethics are requisites to civilized life, but compulsives are so inflexible in their pursuit of them that they become trapped in a quagmire of indecision and conformity, afraid of making the slightest mistake—afraid of the slightest derivation from the

Table 8.1   A Multidimensional Appraisal of the Compulsive Personality Disorder

---

1. Behavioral appearance: disciplined to perfectionistic.
2. Interpersonal conduct: respectful to ingratiating.
3. Cognitive style: constricted to blocked.
4. Affective expression: solemn to grave.
5. Self-perception: conscientious to righteous.
6. Primary defense mechanism: reaction formation.
7. Differential personality diagnosis:
    a. dependent personality disorder
    b. paranoid personality disorder

"norm." In a word, the compulsive personality may be summed up as "conforming." Certainly, the compulsive personality is best conceived of as occurring in varying degrees spread along a continuum ranging from mildly pathological to more severely pathological.

In its mildest forms, the compulsive disorder may fit with little dysfunction within settings that demand a rigid adherence to rules, principles, and guidelines, for example, military and quasi-military organizations, research settings for the basic sciences, or even in fields such as accounting, finance, and computer sciences.

In its more severe forms, however, the rigid adherence to conforming standards becomes self-destructive. According to the American Psychiatric Association (1980), the basic features of more severe manifestations of this disorder are a "restricted ability to express warm and tender emotions; perfectionism that interferes with the ability to grasp the 'big picture'; insistence that others submit to his or her way of doing things; excessive devotion to work and productivity to the exclusion of pleasure; and indecisiveness" (p. 326).

Having presented this overview of the compulsive personality disorder, let us now take a closer look at this pattern. To do so, we will employ our standardized descriptive format, which is summarized in Table 8.1.

Behavioral Appearance

Socially, compulsive individuals appear to others as ranging from disciplined to perfectionistic. They are viewed as being industrious and efficient, though lacking in flexibility and spontaneity. At times, they may appear stubborn, stingy, possessive, uncreative, and unimaginative. They tend to procrastinate and they seem indecisive. Unfamiliar conditions, unexpected occurrences, and deviations from generally accepted guidelines can promote anxiety and even panic attacks in these individuals.

Compulsive individuals seem most content to put their nose to the grindstone and work diligently, patiently, and meticulously on projects that require these characteristics. Some people will view this as a sign that these individuals are orderly and methodical, others view this same behavior as being petty and picayune. Compulsives are generally concerned with matters of detail and organization. At times, these individuals will be rigid and unbending about rules and procedures. This was the case with Wayne B. He appeared to be cold and aloof to others, concerned only with details and operating procedures. His overly rigid enforcement of the student code of conduct contributed to the accusations that he was a "stuffed shirt" and a "moralist" with no real sympathy for others. Ultimately it became apparent that Wayne B.'s inflexibility and "harshly punitive decisions" towards students were the major factors that lead to his dismissal as Dean of Students, a position he had held for 7 years.

Interpersonal Conduct

The interpersonal behavior of compulsive individuals may be characterized as ranging from respectful to ingratiating. Clearly these individuals behave in a polite and rather formalized way. However, they relate to others in terms of their rank and status, that is, compulsives tend to be more authoritarian rather than equalitarian. This assumption is based on the very different way in which they act around their superiors as opposed to their subordinates. In extreme moments, they become deferential, ingratiating, even obsequious with their superiors. They go out of their way to impress these individuals with their efficiency and no-nonsense attitudes. They constantly seek approval and reassurance from their superiors. Compulsives are likely to experience chronic anxiety and tension should such approval not be forthcoming on a regular basis. This behavior is markedly different than that displayed around their subordinates. Under these conditions, compulsive individuals are often quite aggressive, autocratic, and condemnatory. They may act confident, self-assured, even pompous and self-righteous. Yet these attitudes are usually cloaked in adherence to rules and regulations, so it is difficult to see the aggressive interpersonal aspects of their behavior.

Wayne B. shows both sides of the compulsive's interpersonal profile. He experienced considerable tension when around his superiors. He always tried to present his best qualities in their presence. Even when he was demoted he remained respectful and conforming. Yet with his students, Wayne was aggressive, overly rigid and punitive. He presented the classical picture of the authoritarian Dean of Students, an image that simply was not consistent with the new administration's policies. As a result, Wayne B. was demoted.

Cognitive Style

Cognitively, compulsive individuals generally range from being constricted to being blocked and extremely dogmatic. Cognitive constriction refers to the tendency of these individuals to construct a world in terms of rules, regulations, schedules, and hierarchies. Cognitive constriction inhibits imagination and leaves these individuals vulnerable to distress from novel, unexpected, or unpredictable situations. In extreme cases, these individuals become cognitively blocked. That is to say, they become so narrow-minded and dogmatic that their minds become resistant to any new ideas or new ways of doing things.

Although they appear on the surface to be deliberate and well poised, these compulsives sit atop cognitive/affective powder kegs. Their consciousness is beset by intense ambivalent conflicts and inner turmoil. Their adherence to rules and regulations, their dogmatic cognitive disposition is simply a way of avoiding the intrusion of explosive contrary thoughts and feelings. Compulsives, then, must avoid events that might unleash these forces. We see then that *self-control* becomes the paramount issue for compulsive individuals.

This point is clear in Wayne B.'s developmental history. He was constantly fearful of displeasing his parents. So, despite contrary feelings, he would work hard to control counterproductive impulses. He adopted a pattern of strict adherence to rules and parental expectations. By doing so, he increased his chances of receiving parental approval and at the same time controlling any contrary impulses.

Intrapsychically, it may be argued that compulsives have created a highly organized system for segregating cognition, affect, motivation, and so on. Need gratification is highly regulated. Forbidden impulses are rigidly bound, conflicts are defensively denied and kept from awareness. Wayne B., for example, most likely experienced some degree of disappointment on being demoted, yet he denied those feelings the same way he denied his contempt for his brother for years, until in therapy, that contempt was allowed to surface.

Affective Expression

One is often struck by the affective expression of most compulsives that seems to range from solemn to grave. Thus, their typical affective demeanor is grim, cheerless, and overly serious.

The compulsive personality disorder often presents itself in individuals as a contempt for people who behave frivolously and impulsively. Compulsives usually consider emotional behavior, even the expression of positive emotions, as immature and irresponsible. Rather, affect-void objectivity is what these individuals respect and cling to. They evaluate others on the basis of the time-proven rules and regulations of an organized society. Conventional values are the rules these individuals live by.

Emotional displays are threatening to compulsive individuals. They seldom understand such displays and are too inhibited to allow themselves the experience. Wayne B. was observed to be a serious-minded individual who married a woman of like affective disposition.

In sum, compulsive individuals are affectively restrained, solemn, and even grave. They distrust their own affect for fear that they will experience a tirade of uncontrollable explosive, and contrary emotions.

Self-Perception

Compulsive individuals see themselves as being somewhere between conscientious and righteous. They are usually careful about avoiding the contradictions between unconscious impulses and overt behavior. Thus, their conscientious, even righteous, self-perceptions are but smoke screens: their effort to avoid meaningful introspection. Compulsives see themselves as industrious, reliable, dependable, meticulous, and efficient. They are fearful of misjudgment and errors; as a result, they become overly attuned to their conscientious behavior and oblivious to their ambivalence.

As a protective device, compulsives disdain introspection as signs of immaturity and self-indulgence. So, despite his intelligence, Wayne B. had no conscious awareness of his overly rigid behavior and accused modern-day students of being immature, self-indulgent, and undisciplined.

Often dominating the self-perception of compulsive individuals is a strong sense of loyalty to others. They feel they have unalterable obligations to those who trust or depend on them. Wayne showed this tendency by expressing his confidence that his superiors were right in their decision to demote him.

Primary Defense Mechanism

So far we have described the compulsive personality as a conforming, overcontrolled, rigid, methodical, and highly disciplined individual. Compulsive individuals favor the use of *reaction formation* as their primary defense mechanism. Reaction formation represents a process in which individuals repress their undesirable impulses and form a diametrically opposite conscious attitude. For example, a hostile patient may display a facade of extreme friendliness or a rebellious adolescent may become very polite and gracious. Reaction formations serve not only to maintain conformity and social acceptability, but also they serve to maintain control over socially unacceptable impulses that threaten to disrupt psychological homeostasis.

The case of Wayne B. is an example of the compulsive personality disorder. As such, we would expect to see reaction formation appear at points in his development. During therapy Wayne B. admitted, much to his own surprise, a great degree of resentment and hostility towards his brother. Yet, overtly displaying such resentment would have been intolerable to his parents. As a result, he adopted the mechanism of reaction formation. He adopted a "'good boy' image" (something far more pleasing to his parents) and "became a 'paragon of virtue.'"

Even in later life, Wayne can be seen to continue to employ the mechanism of reaction formation. It will be recalled that at no time had Wayne overtly expressed anger or even disappointment at his demotion from the position of Dean of Students. In fact, consistent with the mechanism of reaction formation, Wayne expressed "his 'complete confidence'" in the new administration's decision to demote him. Yet, it is interesting to note that when Wayne was forced to interact with the new college officials, he consistently displayed signs of distress before, during, and after the interaction.

In sum, reaction formation is a tool that allows its users to display an image of reasonableness, maturity, and social acceptability when faced with circumstances that would normally evoke anger, dismay, or embarrassment. The case of Wayne provides subtle examples of how reaction formation may be used by compulsive individuals.

Differential Personality Diagnosis

According to Millon (1981), "Few problems of differential diagnosis are likely to arise with the compulsive personality" (p. 236). Perhaps the major difficulty that will be encountered diagnostically will come in identifying the mixed personality disorders within which the compulsive occurs. These will be discussed later in this chapter.

ETIOLOGY AND DEVELOPMENT

We have found the compulsive personality disorder to be one in which individuals seem perfectionistic, conscientious, and well organized, but rigid and superficial in their interpersonal relationships and often indecisive. We will now attempt to trace the roots of this passive-ambivalent disorder.

Biogenic Factors

There is little evidence to suggest that biogenic influences contribute in any distinctive manner to the development of the compulsive personality disorder. On examination, we find a wide variety of overt physical traits and infantile reaction patterns among compulsives. No biological features appear to discriminate or be highly correlated with this personality disorder.

Environmental Factors

Having found no credible biogenic determinants of the compulsive personality disorder, we must, once again, turn our focus to environmental factors and assume that they play a major role in the etiology of this disorder.

Parental Overcontrol. The notion of parental overcontrol as a childrearing practice may best be understood by comparing it to other child-rearing practices.

Overcontrol differs from overprotection, as we saw in the dependent personality disorder, in that overcontrol stems from an attitude of parental firmness and repressiveness. Overprotection, on the other hand, usually reflects a loving and gentle disposition on the part of the parents. Although overcontrolling parents may well be caring parents, they seem to be concerned with keeping the child in line and preventing the child from causing trouble for himself/herself and others. In the case of Wayne B., we see a fairly typical example of overcontrolling parents who were "punitive and unyielding" when the children would misbehave.

Overcontrol is similar, in some respects, to the practice of parental hostility that we saw in the development of the antisocial personality, in that there are rigidly punitive aspects to both. But there is an important difference as well. The hostile parent is punitive regardless of the child's behavior, whereas the overprotective parent is punitive only if

THE COMPULSIVE PERSONALITY DISORDER

the child misbehaves or fails to live up to expectations. Recall the case of John W. (Case 3.1) in which his father was a tough, rigid man who dominated the family and even physically abused his family near the end of his life. On the other hand, Wayne B.'s parents (Case 8.1) expected him to live up to certain expectations and condemned him only if he failed to achieve the standards they imposed.

Learned Compulsive Behavior. The notion that aspects of the compulsive disorder are learned directly and indirectly from the family situation seems extremely viable. Let us note what may be some of the major processes at work.

First, the child instrumentally learns to avoid punishment by agreeing to parental demands and by meeting parental expectations. The child is, in effect, shaped by fear and intimidation to be obedient and conforming to the expectations and standards set down by the parents. This was very much the case in Wayne B.'s childhood. The children knew what was expected of them and knew they would be punished if they did not conform to parental expectations of obedience.

Second, the child vicariously learns to accrue aspects of the compulsive personality through a process of modeled compulsive behavior on the part of the parents. In effect, he/she learns to imitate the models set forth by the parents (both Wayne B.'s parents "were 'orderly and strict . . . . well-planned'"). In doing so, the child develops a positive self-image as being an obedient, conforming offspring. Wayne described himself as adopting "the 'good boy' image." However, in using parents as role models, the child also adopts their strictness and punitive disposition.

Third, as the child is being shaped by parental expectation and is similarly using parental models around which to develop his/her own personality, the child has failed to learn to behave autonomously. The form of learning experienced by these children is inadequate to facilitate autonomous behavior. Without the ability to generate alternatives and explore options of their own, these children are left no other course than to adhere rigidly to the models that have been provided them.

Responsibility Training. Another feature found commonly in the developmental history of the compulsive disorder is the exposure to conditions that teach a deep sense of responsibility to others. Similarly, these children are taught to feel guilty when these responsibilities are not met. Oftentimes, these children are taught that it is shameful and irresponsible to engage in frivolous play and to act on impulse; rather, they should behave constructively and responsibly. Their actions should be well planned and well organized.

Perhaps the major driving force behind the behavior of the compulsive personality is an intense fear of disapproval and a concern for avoiding punishment. This fear can be well understood given a history of perfectionistic and punitive parents.

This passive-ambivalent personality is extraordinarily careful to pay proper respect to authorities. Such individuals are polite and orderly. They take great pains to display loyalty. Their conduct is usually beyond reproach. They are punctual and often meticulous in fulfilling the duties and obligations expected of them. Wayne B. epitomized these characteristics. He was well organized, "a 'paragon of virtue,'" and he even expressed "his 'complete confidence'" in his superiors when they decided to demote him.

Despite all that has been described, the compulsive personality often experiences intense urges towards self-assertion and rebellion. It is the presence of these internal contrary impulses that cause these individuals concern. "It is the everpresent threat that these impulses will break into the open that serves as the basis for his fear of disapproval" (Millon & Millon, 1974, p. 264).

So, in summary, we see that through the environmental factors of parental overcontrol, various learning paradigms, and training in accepting authority, the compulsive personality is shaped.

Neuropsychological Stages

Let us now turn to a discussion of how parental overcontrol may act to affect the neuropsychological development of the child. It should be kept in mind that parental overcontrol is a restrictive childrearing practice in which punitive measures are used to set distinct limits on the child's behavior.

1. In the first stage of neuropsychological development, the child's environment was likely to be quite organized and rigid. The child's behavior was likely to be very scheduled. But such behavior is not unique to the compulsive personality. Therefore, we will move to the second stage of neuropsychological development.

2. In this second stage, the sensorimotor-autonomy stage, the child begins the struggle to achieve a sense of self-competence. During this developmental period, most children begin to be assertive and resistant. But, overcontrolling parents will

respond to these efforts with firm and harsh discipline. They will withdraw their love and support and will physically curtail the child. As a result, children are unable fully to develop any assertive behavior—they are generally forced to submit to parental perogatives.

This behavioral pattern has certain consequences attached to it. The child's ultimate degree of autonomy is restricted. The child will fail to develop a normal sense of self-competence. As a result, the child will be fearful of deviating from the straight and narrow and other well-planned courses of action. The child will hesitate to act impulsively and will avoid venturesome behavior. In effect, we see this child in a similar dependent position as the passive-dependent personality. Yet, the difference is that the passive-dependent child has accepted the dependent role as this role grew out of parental *love* and *protection*. The compulsive child has accepted a rather dependent role out of *fear* of the consequences for not doing so.

3. The third neuropsychological stage, under normal conditions, is characterized by the assumption of initiative behaviors, the expression of autonomy, and the formation of an independent self-image. In the case of a parentally overcontrolled child, however, these processes are stifled.

Parental overcontrol at this stage of development has taken away the child's opportunities to find his/her own identity. As a result, the child has few options but to imitate the parental models. Such imitation occurs at relatively young ages, younger than one might expect for such behavior. For example, in the case of Wayne B., he was able to recall with some pride that he was often referred to as a little gentleman ever since he was very young. Similarly, he was made to wear a coat and tie to class in high school and college.

The end result of parental overcontrol in this third stage of development is that the child lacks initiative and is overly cautious in virtually every aspect of life. The child grows into an adult who is fearful of new interpersonal and, in the case of Wayne B., employment situations. These individuals are plagued with indecisiveness that can be not only anxiety producing, but immobilizing as well. They seem to need a guarantee that everything will turn out favorably concerned with the fear of making a wrong decision. To add security to their world, these individuals often resort to organizing and planning their entire environment compulsively. They are most comfortable in familiar surroundings in which there is a clear set of rules and regulations. Such conditions reduce, or virtually eliminate, the need to act spontaneously or unconventionally.

Wayne B. exemplifies the compulsive personality, from his overprotected childhood to his current psychiatric complaint.

SELF-PERPETUATION OF THE COMPULSIVE PERSONALITY DISORDER

Given the restrictive and anxiety-producing aspects of the compulsive personality disorder, it seems reasonable to ask the question, why these individuals fail to explore alternative coping measures.

Germane to all personality disorders are the facts that change, itself, is anxiety-producing; similarly, personality disorders are deeply ingrained habits. In short, the numerous personality disorders we are examining are all self-perpetuating traps; they are self-made prisons that continually act to strengthen pathological restraints. Let us take a look at four self-perpetuating processes that characterize the compulsive personality.

Cognitive and Behavioral Rigidity

It must be remembered that individuals possessing the passive-ambivalant personality hate to make mistakes. They fear taking risks for just this reason. Therefore, as a defensive maneuver they restrict themselves to those thoughts, aspirations, and behaviors that tend to be conservative or with which they are familiar. These individuals tend to see things in extremes: right or wrong, good or bad, black or white, and so on. They have little ability to consider the gray areas. As a result, there is a lot of familiar repetition in the lives of these individuals. They tend to be highly predictable. Some may consider them boring. Their cognitive and behavior styles may be considered deliberate, even mechanical. Such inflexibility characterized Wayne B.—He had been criticized for being too rigid on numerous occasions.

Adherence to Rules and Regulations

Most people recognize the need for rules and regulations in a civilized society, but most people seek to minimize such constraints. The compulsive personality is an exception to this observation.

Individuals who possess the compulsive personality have learned not only to live by such rules, but also to prefer situations in which appropriate behavior is clearly spelled out by a system of rules and regulations. By rigidly adhering to such codes of behavior, the ambiguities of life are drastically reduced. These individuals receive a sense of security through the adherence to rules and regulations. Not only do such rules make life less ambiguous, but they also are effective controls for the impulses and urges that may be dwelling inside these individuals. By adhering to rules, mores, and social convention, these individuals do not have to worry as much about controlling their impulses—the rules do it for them. Finally, when in doubt, these individuals search for further rules and guidelines that will dictate their behavior.

Rigid adherence to such rules, regulations, mores, and so on, is important because compulsive individuals perceive flexibility as a weakness. It is virtually impossible for these individuals to make any exceptions to the rules by which they live. To do so would be like opening Pandora's infamous box. No longer would they have a strict code to live by, and no longer could they be sure that their impulses could be held under control. To show any flexibility, to make any exceptions destroys the entire system—no longer would it provide any security. Therefore, rigid adherence is the only way of maintaining interpersonal and intrapersonal security. The case of Wayne B. points this out in as much as the major reason for his demotion was his insistence on inflexible adherence to the rules governing the college life of students. Despite his demotion, Wayne B. voiced his "'complete confidence' in the 'rationality of their decision'" to demote him.

A classic personification of rigid adherence to regulations and unquestioning loyalty to authority can be found in the tenacious Detective Javert; the antagonist in the French novel *Les Miserables.* Javert's total being was consumed by an adherence to the letter of the law. Yet, his inflexible rigidity left him without the ability to function autonomously—a trait that would contribute to his self-destruction.

Self-Criticism

A third major factor that serves to perpetuate the compulsive disorder is the tendency for compulsive individuals to engage in self-criticism and to possess a tendency to blame themselves for adversity. In the case of Wayne B., one reason he first sought counseling was because he complained of extreme feelings of self-doubt, anxiety, and especially guilt about his inability to perform his assigned tasks at work.

By the time the compulsive child reaches adolescence, he/she has usually developed an almost merciless conscience that serves to help regulate behavior. This conscience is a relentless gauge to which the compulsive person must measure up. It dictates "proper" behavior in all circumstances and renders powerful and swift punishment in the form of guilt should the individual deviate from the rules, regulations, mores, or general social conventions. Thus, these powerful inner controls serve to hinder any spontaneous or adventuresome behavior— and the pattern is perpetuated.

Operant Conditioning

A final consideration in the self-perpetuation of the compulsive personality disorder must be the issue of the reinforcing aspects of the compulsive behavior itself. What is it about the compulsive pattern that could be reinforcing? Close examination reveals that rigid, controlled behavior is negatively reinforcing.

The compulsive individual lives in constant fear of being wrong, of eliciting disapproval from others, especially significant others. In sum, compulsives are chronically fearful of making social, interpersonal, and professional mistakes. The rigid, conforming ritualistic, ultraconservative behavior that characterizes the compulsive pattern is a most effective preventive strategy against making errors. In effect, compulsive behavior is negatively reinforcing because it decreases the probability of performing unacceptable acts—so, the disorder is self-perpetuated.

In summary, despite its restrictive and often colorless nature, the compulsive personality disorder is maintained through an interaction of cognitive and behavioral rigidity; a strict adherence to numerous rules, regulations, mores, and general social conventions; a strong tendency to be highly critical of self; and the operant conditioning of the compulsive behavior itself. The cognitive rigidity serves to make decisions easier. Issues are either good or bad, right or wrong, and so on. Such inflexibility serves to reduce any anxiety associated with flexibility and ambivalence. Strict adherence to rules and regulations serve to structure the life of the compulsive individual and to reduce the chance that undesirable impulses will arise. Self-criticism serves to keep the compulsive individual in line. It restricts adventuresome behavior and restrains impulsiveness. Finally, the negatively reinforcing characteristics of the compulsive behavior pattern ensures the avoidance of social, interpersonal, and professional unacceptability. Thus, the disorder goes on.

ASSOCIATED DISORDERS

Mixed Personality Disorders

With perhaps one or two exceptions, compulsives can be found to blend with almost every other personality disorder. Research (Millon, 1982) has narrowed the most frequent combinations to two: one characterized by strong dependent traits of moderate severity, the other by significant paranoid features with more severe psychopathology.

Compulsive-Dependent Mixed Personality Disorder. Research has shown (Millon, 1982) that the compulsive personality disorder frequently combines with the dependent disorder to create a compulsive-dependent mixed personality disorder. This pathological mixture commonly emerges within the context of psychosomatic treatment centers and appears in about a 2:1 ratio of women to men.

Case 8.2 provides a description of just what the compulsive-dependent mixed disorder looks like. The woman described was referred for psychological evaluation following on extended history of psychosomatic complaints.

CASE 8.2

The Compulsive-Dependent Mixed Personality Disorder

42-Year-Old Woman, Extended History of Psychosomatic Complaints

This patient's behavior is typified by a submissive dependency, a compliance to rules and authority, and a willing submission to the wishes and values of others. There is a tendency to be self-effacing and noncompetitive, a fear of independent self-assertion, and a surface compliance to the expectations and demands of others. She voices a strong sense of duty to others, feeling that they must not have their expectations unmet. Her self-image, on the surface, is that of a considerate, thoughtful, and cooperative person, prone to be unambitious and modest. There are marked feelings of personal inadequacy as she tends to minimize attainments, underplay attributes, and downgrade abilities. The patient is overly respectful, even ingratiating with those in authority. The fear of provoking condemnation creates considerable tension for her, as well as occasional expressions of guilt. Her submissive behavior with those in authority may be traced in part to a reversal of hidden rebellious feelings.

Lurking behind her front of propriety and restraint are intense contrary feelings that occasionally break through her controls. Rarely daring to expose these feelings, she binds them so tightly that life becomes overorganized in an anxiously tense and disciplined self-restraint. She lacks spontaneity and flexibility, is often indecisive, tends to procrastinate, and is easily upset by deviations from routine. There is a marked denial of discordant emotions and a tendency to neutralize feelings normally aroused by distressful events.

The patient dreads making mistakes and fears taking risks lest these provoke disapproval and punishment. To avoid transgressions and obviate the unknown and potentially dangerous, she conveys a front of equanimity and social agreeableness. She is minimally introspective and displays a rigorous internal conscience, an inner gauge that serves to counter oppositional urges and thoughts. As a consequence of constraining feelings and denying emotional conflicts, she is inclined to develop numerous and persistent psychophysiological symptoms.

(From T. Millon, *Disorders of Personality: DSM-III, Axis II*. New York: Wiley, 1981, Used with permission of the author.)

Compulsive-Paranoid Mixed Personality Disorder. Perhaps the second most significant disorder combination based on the compulsive pattern is the compulsive-paranoid mixed personality disorder. This mixed pathological pattern is more severe than the compulsive-dependent disorder. The paranoid components seem to accentuate the basic compulsive disorder. In doing so, we may consider this disorder as a syndromal extension of the milder compulsive pattern, yet not as severe as the full-blown paranoid disorder.

Case 8.3 depicts one manifestation of this mixed disorder. It is the case of a 55-year-old field engineer who was referred for evaluation following repeated difficulties with his subordinates. This individual was known as a tough but competent manager. Recently, he had begun to encounter difficulty with his subordinates as well as with the division's vice president. The engineer claims he was not receiving adequate recognition for his work.

CASE 8.3

The Compulsive-Paranoid Mixed Personality Disorder

55 year-old male; Field engineer

The patient's behavior is typified by a highly controlled but conflictful conformity to the conventions of propriety and authority. Also evident are periodic displays of suspiciousness, irritability, obsessional ideation, and moodiness. There is a tendency to compulsivity and denial, with a notable defensiveness about admitting psychological problems. However, there are occasional reports of feeling tense and high-strung. He anticipates derogation and humiliation from others, and there has been an inclination to self-blame and self-punishment that may have recently given way to outbursts of anger and persecutory accusations. There is a fear of expressing emotions, admitting shortcomings, and losing control.

Efforts are made to maintain a disciplined self-restraint, and the patient rarely relaxes or lets down a guarded defensiveness. He typically appears grim and cheerless, exhibiting an anxiously tense serious-mindedness or perfectionism. Beneath a cooperative and controlled facade are marked feelings of personal insecurity, and he is vigilantly alert to avoid social transgressions that may provoke humiliation and embarassment. The patient's major defense has been to be excessively conforming, inhibiting behaviors that might evoke ridicule and contempt. There is a pattern of avoiding situations that may result either in personal censure or derision, and there is a dread of making mistakes or taking risks, lest these provoke disapproval. As a defensive maneuver, he restricts activities, operates within narrow boundaries, and confines himself to a rigid and, at times, self-righteous conformity to rules and regulations. By adhering vigorously to propriety and convention, by following the straight and narrow path, he seeks to minimize criticism and punitive reactions, particularly from persons in authority.

The patient's defensive style has been undermined repeatedly, and there has been a growing tendency to be argumentative, resentful, and critical of others. His marked self-doubts and deflated sense of self-esteem resulted in an earlier style of attachment to supportive institutional or bureaucratic organizations. In this way, the patient sought to associate his actions by identifying them with those in authority. Efforts are made to maintain a behavioral pattern that is consistent and unvarying, one in which independent actions are restrained and the strictures of authoritarian rules are rigidly complied with. Tendencies to perfectionism and concern with minor irrelevancies have distracted his attention from deeper sources of anxiety, inadequacy, and anticipated derogation.

To display weakness or abrogate the rules of social conventions was felt as a threat that might expose the patient to disapproval. Given his past experiences, the patient knows that others cannot be trusted to provide support. With each acquiescent submission to others, he has built an ever-larger residue of resentment. Thus, lurking behind his facade of propriety is a growing bitterness and disillusionment. These animosities churn within him. They will either break through to the surface in angry upsurges or be countered in ritualistic precautions or obsessive ruminations. Guilt and self-condemnation may be periodically exhibited, as when he turns his feelings inward and imposes severe punitive judgments and actions upon himself. Despite the tension it generates, such self-reproval is likely to serve as a release for his hostile and forbidden feelings. However, ambivalence is constantly present. On the one hand, there are strong desires to discharge hostility and, on the other, a constant fear that such expressions will prompt derision and rejection. As a residual of this ambivalence, he may have a history of persistent tensions, possibly evident in psychosomatic symptoms.

(From T. Millon, *Disorders of Personality:DSM-III, Axis II.* New York: Wiley, 1981, Used with permission of the author.)

Associated Axis I Disorders

We will now examine the major Axis I clinical syndromes that are highly related to, and that appear to emerge from, the compulsive personality disorder.

Obsessive Compulsive Disorders. It is generally believed that compulsive personalities do indeed suffer more *obsessive* or *compulsive disorders* when compared to noncompulsive personalities. It will be recalled that obsessions are recurrent, persistent thoughts, ideas, or images, whereas compulsions are "repetitive and seemingly purposeful behaviors that are performed according to certain rules or in a sterotyped fashion" (American Psychiatric Association, 1980, p. 235).

Preoccupation with thoughts, especially doubts, and ritualistic, repetitive behaviors accomplishes two goals. First, it allows these individuals to distract themselves from hostile, bizarre, erotic or other socially unacceptable thoughts. Second, it decreases the chances that these individuals will act in socially unacceptable ways. Thus, it may be argued that obsessive compulsive disorders emerge as a defense mechanism (albeit maladaptive) in response to a decompensation, or failure, in the basic compulsive personality coping pattern.

Phobic Disorders. Phobic disorders are persistent irrational fears of people, places, or things that result in anxiety and avoidance behavior (American Psychiatric Association, 1980). These disorders are prevalent among compulsive individuals primarily owing to their aversion to failure, being humiliated, being wrong, or engaging in socially unacceptable behavior.

Compulsives develop simple phobias primarily as a function of three anxiety precipitants:

1. Decision—making situations in which they could be faulted or criticized.
2. Real failures they wish to avoid.
3. Surging impulses to think or perform in a socially unacceptable manner.

The compulsives, then, tend to displace their anxieties onto the phobic stimuli, thereby allowing them to reify the fears onto tangible objects that can be controlled or avoided.

Anxiety Disorders. Compulsives are among the most frequent candidates for generalized anxiety disorders. The presence of anxious tension is a part of their everyday life. They live in constant fear of social disapproval and humiliation. The characteristic diligence and consci-entiousness of compulsives reflect, in a large measure, their need to control themselves. Should their ability to control themselves and their environment be lost or even become questionable, *acute anxiety attacks* or *panic disorders* will emerge.

Somatoform Disorders. *Somatization* and *hypochondriacal* disorders are sometimes employed by compulsives as a way of rationalizing failures and inadequacies. To cover up these shortcomings, com-pulsives are inclined to use physical illness as a "legitimate" excuse for some failure or social inadequacy. Not only do symptoms of physical illness suffice as reasons for failure and error, but they also are actually likely to elicit praise for having accomplished that which has indeed been achieved considering the physical handicap.

Compulsives do frequently suffer real fatigue and physical symp-toms as a consequence of their obsessive compulsive behavior pattern and their constant struggle to control themselves and their environ-ment.

Psychosomatic Disorders. Compulsive individuals are prime candidates for *psychosomatic disorders.* Their use of suppression and repression, and the undischarged, chronic state of tension and arousal sets the stage for the exhaustion of some physiological target organ (Everly & Rosenfeld, 1981). Psychophysiological symptomatology is likely to emerge within gastrointestinal and cardiovascular systems, although any physiological system can certainly be a candidate for a psychoso-matic complaint. It is interesting to note that the so-called Type *A* personality is partially characterized by obsessive and compulsive characteristics. The Type *A* personality is recognized by the National Heart Lung and Blood Institute as a behavioral risk factor for coronary heart disease (Cooper et al., 1981).

Brief Reactive Psychoses and Schizophreniform Disorders. When com-pulsive individuals lose control, when their highly structured environ-ment breaks down, we are likely to see a gross decompensation occur. Beyond simple panic attacks, we are likely to observe *brief reactive psychoses* and *schizophreniform disorders.*

Brief reactive psychoses refer to psychotic symptoms that follow a psychosocial stressor and last less than 2 weeks. A schizophreniform disorder refers to a psychopathological condition in which the symp-toms are identical to those of schizophrenia, but with a duration of more than 2 weeks but less than 6 months.

These dramatic and severe reactions can be understood in light of the fact that the compulsives' world is held together and derives meaning from the highly structured cognitive and behavioral patterns they use to maintain control. When these individuals perceive a loss of control, it may literally mean that the order and meaning that once characterized their entire existence is now gone.

Affective Disorders. More typical than the psychotic episodes described are the compulsive's tendency to experience affective disorders. *Dysthymic disorder* is a common affective reaction to the realization that these persons lead empty, excessively conforming lives. According to Millon (1981), "More commonly, compulsives will exhibit classic forms of agitated depression, noted primarily by diffuse apprehension, marked feelings of guilt, and a tendency to complain about personal sin and unworthiness . . . compulsives are likely to turn the angry and resentful components of their ambivalence inward and against themselves, claiming that they truly deserve punishment and the misery they now suffer" (p. 234).

Summary

This chapter has described the nature and development of the compulsive personality disorder. Let us review some of the major points we have addressed:

1. The clinical picture of the compulsive personality disorder may be summarized as follows:
   a. Behaviorally, compulsives appear to others as ranging from disciplined to perfectionistic. They live a highly structured, repetitive lifestyle intertwined with a rigid adherence to rules and regulations.
   b. Interpersonally, compulsives behave in a manner that ranges from respectful to ingratiating. They are polite, but formal, and usually loyal.
   c. The cognitive style of compulsives ranges from constricted to dogmatically blocked. They are typically unimaginative and wary of new ideas. Problems without clear-cut answers are highly frustrating for these individuals.
   d. Affectively, these individuals range from solemn to grave. They are tense, unrelaxed, and they keep their emotions under tight control.
   e. Their self-perceptions appear to range from conscientious to righteous. They see themselves as loyal, reliable, and efficient.
   f. Compulsives most commonly employ the defense mechanism of reaction formation.
   g. Differential personality diagnosis might include the dependent personality disorder as well as the paranoid personality disorder.
2. Because there are no major biogenic foundations for the compulsive disorder, we must consider the prepotency of environmental factors in the etiolo-

gy and development of this personality disorder. Parental overcontrol, learned compulsive behavior, and training in responsibility to others are environmental factors proposed to contribute to the compulsive pattern.

3. The compulsive disorder is self-perpetuated through cognitive and behavioral rigidity, the dogmatic adherence to rules and regulations, tendencies to be self-critical, and the operant conditioning of the compulsive behavior itself. These individuals appear to have a need to be "proper" and avoid errors.

4. The most commonly encountered mixed personality disorders that use the compulsive pattern as a basis are the compulsive-dependent mixed personality disorder and the compulsive-paranoid mixed personality disorder.

5. Commonly DSM-III, Axis I disorders associated with the compulsive disorder are obsessive-compulsive disorders, phobic disorders, anxiety disorders, somatoform disorders, psychosomatic disorders, brief reactive psychoses, schizopheniform disorders and affective disorders.

Five

THE DETACHED PERSONALITY DISORDERS

We will describe here the avoidant personality disorder and the schizoid personality disorder. These disorders represent the basic *detached* personality patterns.

Detached individuals are typically introverted, aloof, and seclusive. They have difficulty establishing interpersonal relationships. They tend to avoid social activities and are usually quite uncomfortable in such activities when they are forced to participate. The detached disorders may be divided into two broad subcategories: the *active-detached* (avoidant) and the *passive-detached* (schizoid).

Active-detached avoidant individuals experience significant degrees of interpersonal anxiety. They fear being rejected or humiliated so that they possess little interpersonal trust. Yet, these avoidant individuals desire interpersonal affiliation.

Passive-detached individuals, on the other hand, exhibit emotional and cognitive deficits

beyond those of the avoidants. These deficits
interfere with their ability to relate
interpersonally. So, although the avoidants
actively seek social isolation as a defense against
rejection and humiliation, schizoids simply find
it difficult to relate interpersonally owing to
significant cognitive and affective deficits.

9

The Avoidant Personality Disorder

Having provided a general introduction to the basic detached personality disorders, we will now turn our focus to the first of 2 such detached patterns—the active-detached, avoidant personality disorder. As you read the case of James M. be sure to make note of any major examples of these descriptors:

1. Behavioral appearance.
2. Interpersonal conduct.
3. Cognitive style.
4. Affective expression.
5. Self-perception.
6. Primary defense mechanism.

CASE 9.1

The Avoidant Personality Disorder

James M., Age 27, Unmarried

James was a bookkeeper for nine years, having obtained this position upon graduation from high school. He spoke of himself as a shy, fearful and quiet boy ever since early childhood. He currently was living with his mother, a socially insecure, periodically alcoholic and anxious woman who kept her distance from others. His father, also described as an alcoholic, was "mean to his mother" and deprecating to his children. He died when James was 14. A sister, four years older than James, lives in another city, had recently been divorced and was referred to by James as "being just like my father," dominating and rejecting.

James was characterized by his supervisor as a loner, a peculiar young man who did his work quietly and efficiently. They noted that he ate alone in the company cafeteria and never joined in coffee breaks or in the "horsing around" at the office. Some years back he signed up for a company-sponsored bowling league, but withdrew after the first session.

As far as his social life was concerned, James had neither dated nor gone to a party in five years. He dated a girl "seriously" while in high school, but she "ditched" him for another fellow. After a lapse of about three years, he dated a number of different girls rather sporadically, but then stopped "because I didn't know what to say to them, and I thought they must have liked someone else." He now spent most of his free time reading, watching TV, daydreaming and fixing things around the house.

James experienced great distress when new employees were assigned to his office section. Some 40 people worked regularly in this office and job turnover resulted in replacement of four or five people a year. He feared constantly that he was going to be "fired," despite the fact that his work was competent and that the firm almost never dismissed its employees.

In recent months, a clique formed in his office. Although James very much wanted to be a member of this "in-group," he feared attempting to join them because "he had nothing to offer them" and thought he would be rejected. In a short period of time, he, along with two or three others, became the object of jokes and taunting by the leaders of the clique. After a few weeks of "being kidded," he began to miss work, failed to complete his accounts on time, found himself unsure of what he was doing and made a disproportionate number of errors. When his supervisor discussed with him his increasingly poor performance, James displayed extreme anxiety and complained of being "nervous, confused, tired and unhappy much of the time." Although he did not connect his present discomfort to the events in his office, he asked if he could be reassigned to another job where he might work alone.

The counselor to which he was directed found him to be of average intelligence and extremely conscientious, but lacking in confidence and fearful of competition. It became clear in further discussions that many of his traits could be traced to the humiliation and deprecation he suffered at the hands of his father, the rejection he experienced with his peers and in dating and his life-long [sic] identification with, and exposure to, his mother's fearful attitudes which he imitated unconsciously.

(From T. Millon, *Modern Psychopathology: A Biosocial Approach to Maladaptive Learning and Functioning.* Philadelphia: Saunders, 1969, Used with permission of the author.)

The case of James M. represents one variation of a personality disorder that is characterized by a hypersensitivity to interpersonal rejection or humiliation.

Table 9.1   A Multidimensional Appraisal of the Avoidant Personality Disorder

1. Behavioral appearance: guarded to alarmed.
2. Interpersonal conduct: aversive to withdrawn.
3. Cognitive style: distracted to perplexed.
4. Affective expression: anguished to overwrought.
5. Self-perception: alienated to rejected.
6. Primary defense mechanism: fantasy.
7. Differential personality diagnoses:
   a. schizoid personality disorder
   b. schizotypal personality disorder
   c. borderline personality disorder

CLINICAL PICTURE

The avoidant personality disorder represents an active-detached personality disorder. According to the biosocial learning theory described in Chapter 2, these are individuals who actively strive to be aloof and seclusive. They derive reinforcement from neither self nor others.

The avoidant personality disorder may be thought of as a pathological syndromal extension of the normal inhibited personality described in Chapter 2. The avoidant pattern is best conceived of as a personality disorder that ranges in varying degrees along a symptomatological continuum, from mild forms to extremely severe forms. In its milder forms, this disorder is characterized by feelings of isolation and loneliness combined with fears of interpersonal humiliation and rejection. In its more severe forms, this disorder is characterized by a hypersensitivity not only to humiliation and rejection, but also to shame. These individuals are unwilling to enter interpersonal relationships. They have very poor self-esteem and withdraw interpersonally whenever given the opportunity. In both the milder and more severe variations, individuals characteristically possess a desire for interpersonal affiliation, yet withdraw owing to their fear of being rejected. Let us take a closer look at the clinical picture of this disorder using our standardized descriptive format. Table 9.1 summarizes the avoidant personality disorder from that perspective.

Behavioral Appearance

A shy and apprehensive quality characterizes these individuals, though their appearance may range from being guarded in mild variations to alarmed in more severe variations of this disorder. They not only appear awkward and uncomfortable in social situations but seem actively to shrink from the reciprocal give-and-take of interpersonal relations.

To most observers who have peripheral contact with them, avoidant individuals appear to be timid, withdrawn, or perhaps cold and strange. Those who relate to these individuals more closely, however, recognize their sensitivity, evasiveness, and mistrustful qualities.

Their speech is generally slow and constrained. There are frequent hesitations, fragmented sequences of thought, and an occasional confused or irrelevant digression.

The physical behavior of avoidant individuals is usually controlled and underactive, although it may be marked with bursts of fidgety or rapid staccato movements.

James M. was seen by his supervisor as a "peculiar young man who did his work quietly and efficiently." Although James desired to be a member of the in-group at work, he was perceived to be seclusive and aloof.

In general, then, we see the avoidant individual as an individual who warily scans the environment for potential threats, overreacts to innocuous events, and is constantly anticipating ridicule or rejection. In effect, they are constantly on guard.

Interpersonal Conduct

Interpersonal activity, for the avoidant personality, may be summarized as ranging from being aversive to withdrawn. In face-to-face contact, avoidants often impose a strain on others. Their aversive view of others, that is, their discomfort and mistrust, take the form of subtle testing operations, that is, a set of carefully guarded maneuvers by which they check whether others are sincere in their friendly overtures or are deceptive and represent potential threats to their security. Thus, if a new office employee would be friendly to him on a one-on-one basis, James M. would make it a practice to talk to him when others were around, checking to see if the new employee would continue the conversation with him or would turn his attention to others.

Avoidant individuals fear placing their welfare and feelings in the hands of others. They are hesitant to trust or confide in others. Thus, their social detachment and social withdrawal does not stem from deficit drives and sensibilities but from an active and self-protective restraint. Although chronically lonely, avoidant individuals choose not to expose themselves to the potential rejection and humiliation that others can put on them. This pattern is typified in the social life of

James M.: "He ate alone in the company cafeteria and never joined in coffee breaks or in 'horsing around' at the office." James did sign up for a company bowling league but quit after one session. Even in his adolescence, James anticipated social rejection, and perhaps saw such rejection when it was not even there.

In extreme cases of the avoidant disorder, individuals become hypersensitive to insult and rejection and may withdraw to the point of being seclusive. James was approaching this point when he entered counseling.

Cognitive Style

The cognitive processes of avoidant individuals range from being distracted to perplexed. They are not only interfered with by their hypersensitivity and the resultant flooding of irrelevant environmental details, but they are complicated further by emotional disharmony. In general, digressive thoughts appear to disrupt not only coherent cognitive processes, but seem to disrupt social communication as well. Cognitive interference is one of the cardinal characteristics of the avoidant personality. It is especially pronounced in social settings where the perceptual vigilance of these individuals is most acute.

The intrapsychic organization of avoidant individuals appears to be highly fragile, subject to the slightest disruption. Once disrupted, one may observe a regressive decompensation emerge.

In the case of James M., we see an individual who is cognitively distracted in social situations and who became perplexed as he became the center of jokes and other forms of ridicule. James began making mistakes and losing confidence in himself. It was clear that at that point he was losing what reins he held over his cognitive capabilities.

Affective Expression

The dysphoric affect of avoidant individuals may present itself as ranging from anguished to overwrought. Expressions conveying disharmonious emotions and feelings of emptiness and depersonalization are especially common. Because the affect of avoidant individuals cannot be overtly expressed, they accumulate and are often vented in an inner world of rich fantasy and imagination. Their need for affect and interpersonal affiliation may ultimately be expressed in the forms of music, poetry, or diaries that no one will ever read.

In many instances, the chronically tense and anguished state that avoidants find themselves "pulls" ridicule and depreciation from others. This was clearly the case in James M.'s bearing the brunt of jokes and depreciation from his coworkers who saw him as aloof, seclusive, and tense. It is not uncommon to see affective states of tension, anxiety, sadness, and anger vacillating within the same individual.

Self-Perception

Avoidant individuals generally describe themselves as chronically tense and fatigued, yet descriptions are generally based on the assumption that they have been alienated or rejected by their peers and significant others. Feelings of loneliness and of being unwanted and isolated are quite common, as are a general fear and distrust of others.

Avoidant individuals tend to be extremely introspective and self-conscious. They often perceive themselves as different from others, and they tend to be unsure of their identity and self-worth. They tend to lack overall self-esteem. They will characteristically devalue their own achievements, seeing themselves as isolated, discontent, and empty, and experiencing feelings of depersonalization.

James M. saw himself as basically an unworthy individual. He was convinced that girls found him unattractive and were dating him until someone better came along. Similarly, he wanted to join the in-group at work, but felt he was unworthy and had nothing to contribute.

Primary Defense Mechanism

The active-detached, avoidant personality disorder is one in which the individuals who possess it appear apprehensive, mistrustful, tense, and shy, yet desirous of interpersonal affiliation. The primary defense mechanism utilized by these individuals is *fantasy.*

Fantasy is a semiconscious process of imagination that serves to gratify the needs and wishes that cannot be fulfilled in reality. Fantasies are a tool to provide its user a "safe" medium in which to discharge affection, aggression, or other impulses that would otherwise be inappropriate, uncomfortable, or impossible to achieve in reality. Owing to the fact that most interpersonal exchanges are threatening to avoidants, the possibility of withdrawing into fantasy is a welcomed opportunity.

James M. frequently employed fantasy as a means of avoiding interpersonal humiliation or rejection, at the same time discharging impulses that were difficult for him to express socially. He spent a considerable amount of time daydreaming and watching TV—both forms of fantasy. Thus, fantasy is a defense mechanism because it provided

James M. with a "safe" opportunity to discharge impulses he might otherwise be ridiculed or rejected for displaying.

Differential Personality Diagnosis

In differentiating between the avoidant personality disorder and other personality disorders, some confusion may occur in separating the avoidant from the schizoid, schizotypal, and borderline disorders.

A major point of distinction between the avoidant and the schizoid lies in the fact that the avoidant individual desires social acceptance and regrets the social isolation in which he/she lives. The schizoid, on the other hand, is genuinely indifferent to social interaction.

Schizotypal personalities differ from the avoidants in their obviously bizarre behavior. For example, they tend to engage in odd speech, fantasy, and generally odd behavior patterns. The avoidants do not demonstrate such bizarre behavior patterns, but rather display low self-esteem and the expectation of rejection and humiliation.

Finally, although avoidants and borderlines share many socially inhibited features, avoidants exist in social isolation, yet at the same time desire to be accepted by others. Borderlines, on the other hand, are impulsive and more emotionally labile than are avoidant personalities.

If placed on a continuum, both the schizotypal and the borderline disorders may be considered more severe personality disorders when compared to the avoidant disorder.

ETIOLOGY AND DEVELOPMENT

We see, then, that the avoidant personality represents an actively detached personality disorder. These individuals long for companionship but fear rejection and the humiliation that they feel accompanies it.

Biogenic Factors

Venables (1968) hypothesized that the vigilance that characterizes the avoidant personality may be indicative of a low autonomic arousal threshold. Millon and Millon (1974) have concurred with this conclusion in stating "the aversive feature of the active-detached pattern centers on a possible functional dominance of the sympathetic nervous system" (p. 229). The predicted effects of such a condition on brain function have been hypothesized by Millon (1969), "uninhibited neural transmission may generate many pathological consequences; it can make normally discriminable stimuli functionally equivalent, allow irrelevant impulses to intrude upon logical associations, diminish the control and direction of thought and permit the emergence of inappropriate memory traces—in short, it can result in marked interference with normal cognitive processes" (p. 235).

Should these speculated biological substrates exist within the avoidant personality, they do nothing more than to act as a biological foundation for the emergence of the disorder itself. The actual shaping of the disorder occurs from the influence of environmental factors.

Environmental Factors

Evidence for the existence of major biogenic influences in the etiology and development of the avoidant personality disorder is highly speculative and generally weak. Rather, it seems more plausible that environmental factors shape the course of this disorder. We will now examine two of the more commonly encountered factors that may contribute to the development of the avoidant personality disorder.

Parental Rejection. Even normal, attractive, and healthy infants may encounter varying degrees of parental rejection. This appears to be a prevalent factor in the development of the avoidant personality. In the case of this personality disorder, however, the amount of parental rejection seems to be particularly intense and/or frequent. The result of such rejection is easy to predict. The children will have their natural optimism and energy crushed, and acquire, instead, attitudes of self-depreciation and feelings of social alienation.

Conditions of parental rejection appear to be particularly devastating because they are interpreted as exceptions to the edict of unconditional parental acceptance and love towards their offspring. After all, as the common notion is held, if your parents cannot accept you, who will? Yet, these children learn that their parents do not accept them.

In the case of James M., his father actively rejected him through his deprecating behavior and his mother passively rejected him through her alcoholism. Furthermore, his sister appeared to assume the rejecting role of his father after his death. We see, then, in the case of James M. that he was rejected not only by his father but by mother and sister as well. This rejection came from those closest to him, those who knew him best. It is easy to see why James M. began to develop self-deprecating attitudes—he had been rejected completely by those who were closest to him.

Peer-Group Rejection. Familial rejection, as experienced by James M., need not result in self-deprecating attitudes. In many instances, children leave the hostile family situation and encounter positive, reinforcing experiences from others outside of the home. However, should the child encounter prolonged familial rejection and then experience rejection by a peer group, the prognosis points even more decisively in the direction of the avoidant disorder. Furthermore, even in instances where the child has received familial support, peer-group rejection can be especially devastating.

As children venture into conditions that require greater social interaction with peers, for example, at school, on the playground and athletic field, or at dances, they are exposed to repetitive social challenges. Should these interactions lead to rejection over a sustained period of time, they will act to wear down any sense of self-competence and self-esteem. Many such children are shattered by daily reminders of their scholastic ineptitude, athletic incompetence, or social awkwardness. As a result, they may be humiliated and experience cruel derogation at the hands of their peers. Unable to prove themselves in any of the avenues open to children, they may not only be ridiculed and isolated by their peers, but they may also begin to become sharply critical of themselves. Their feelings of loneliness and rejection are now compounded further by severe self-judgments of personal inferiority and unattractiveness. In the case of those children who were rejected by parents and family as well, they see peer rejection as validation of the family's judgments. These children are now unable to turn to family or peers for gratification and many are not even able to turn to themselves.

Given the significance of familial and peer rejection in childhood, such patterns are likely to continue into adolescence and adulthood, fostered by the highly correlated feelings of self-doubt and self-deprecation.

In the case of James M., not only did his family reject him, but his dates "rejected" him as well. Finally, the incident that seemed to be at the root of his work performance and anxiety problems also involved rejection, this time by his coworkers.

Thus, the avoidant personality emerges as an anxiety-ridden and deeply mistrusting individual. Similarly, these persons will have significantly deflated notions of self-esteem. They have learned that the world is unfriendly, punishing, and cruel and that they have little or no attributes to affect the dismal condition in which they find themselves. As a result, they withdraw from others and from themselves.

Neuropsychological Development

The consequences of rejection, especially parental rejection, are numerous and diverse.

1.   Parents who handle their children in a cold and callous manner during the sensory-attachment stage of neuropsychological development generally promote feelings of tension and insecurity in these children. These infants are likely to acquire a sense that the world is harsh, unwelcoming, and discomforting. They are likely to learn, in their primitive way, to avoid attaching themselves to others. They will acquire a sense of mistrust. As a result, these children are likely to feel isolated, abandoned, and helpless.

2.   Parents who scorn, ridicule, and reject their children during the sensorimotor-autonomy stage will diminish feelings of self-competence and inhibit the growth of self-confidence. Although normal language and motor development is likely to occur, the children will probably be hesitant to seek any challenge or extension of these skills.

     These children are likely to view the parental rejection they have experienced as valid and, thereby, engage in a process of self-deprecation. Harsh, self-critical attitudes are likely to have devastating consequences. By employing self-doubt and self-criticism, these children are unable to turn to themselves for comfort when family and peers are rejecting. These children are caught in a web of social deprecation *and* self-deprecation—not only does society punish these children, but they punish themselves as well. In the case of James M., when dates would stop seeing him, he would naturally assume they dropped him for another, more desirable person.

3.   The roots of self-deprecation that were begun in the sensorimotor-autonomy stage take a firmer hold in the intracortical-initiative stage. The image of being weak, unlovable, and unworthy forms a strong cognitive basis. Children who have been consistently rejected often perceive themselves as being unattractive, incompetent, and the major reason things go wrong around them. These individuals, by the time they reach adulthood, often feel that they deserve to be ridiculed. Having accepted the role of an incompetent and unattractive person, there is seldom any effort to improve themselves at this late stage of development.

SELF-PERPETUATION OF THE AVOIDANT PERSONALITY DISORDER

We have seen that the avoidant personalities expect to be rejected and have even learned to reject themselves. They are hyperalert and hypersensitive to criticism and rejection. Their lifestyle is one designed to avoid the pain of rejection. They convince themselves that they need to depend on no one. Furthermore, they learn to turn away from themselves to avoid the conclusion that they are unattractive or incompetent. Why does such a self-punishing pattern of behavior persist? What are the mechanisms by which the avoidant personality disorder perpetuates itself?

Restricted Social Experience

Persons with the avoidant personality pattern assume that the atypical treatment they received in early life will continue throughout their lifetime. In defense of such a painful recurrence, they begin to narrow or restrict the range of activities in which they engage. By reducing their exposure to others, they reduce the chances of being rejected.

This notion of avoiding others in order to avoid rejection was clearly demonstrated in the case of James M. James quit dating, had not been to a party in several years, and had even dropped out of a bowling league after attending only once. He ate lunch by himself and liked working alone.

Avoidant, withdrawing behavior tends to remove one from others; when observed by others, such behavior is likely to evoke reciprocal actions. In other words, when people see that the avoidant individual actively seeks to withdraw from social contact with them, they usually respond with antagonism directed towards the avoidant individual. They tend to ridicule him/her, and, in effect, reject that person. Furthermore, signs of interpersonal weakness tend to attract those individuals who enjoy belittling others. In the case of James M., his obvious sensitivity to criticism and rejection and his nonassertive manner evoked ridicule from his coworkers. This ridiculing, rejecting behavior on the part of James M.'s coworkers, then, only served to further reinforce his desire to withdraw. So, the avoidant behavior is perpetuated.

Hypersensitivity

Avoidant personalities are painfully alert to signs of rejection, ridicule, and deception. They detect the most minute traces of annoyance in others. They tend to make mountains out of molehills. In effect, they seize every opportunity to catastrophize about any minor disturbance or problem. James M., for example, dated sporadically but always felt that the women he dated were simply dating him until they found someone better.

Although the hypersensitivity of the avoidant personalities serves as a method for self-protection, it also serves to foster a perpetuation of the problem. As a result of their overalertness and hypersensitivity, the avoidant personalities actually increase the chances that they will encounter specifically those aversive conditions they are trying to avoid. Their hypersensitivity picks up reactions that most people would overlook. In effect, the hypervigilance and the hypersensitivity strategies backfire. Although they are designed to protect these individuals from rejection, they serve to uncover rejection in its most minute forms—hypervigilance and hypersensitivity may actually serve to find rejection where it does not really exist. Thus, the pattern goes on—the world becomes as rejecting as the avoidant personality had feared it would be—so, their avoidance is perpetuated. The avoidant personality seems to live in a world of self-fulfilling prophecy.

Excessive Introspection

Withdrawing from social conditions brings little relief. Having actively detached themselves from others, avoidant personalities are left to become preoccupied with themselves. Limited to themselves as their major source of stimulation, they can only ponder and reflect on their misery. Unlike the passively detached, schizoid personality, who does not desire to be with others, the avoidant personality actually desires companionship and social interaction. The history of James M. clearly showed various attempts at such social interaction. Yet, avoidant individuals, usually because of their hypersensitivity to rejection, will end up withdrawing from social exchange. Thus, they are forced to retreat into themselves where they, again, are left to ponder their pitiful situation. The tendency cognitively to withdraw and examine the undesirable life that is being led often serves to foster the conclusion that the avoidant individual simply does not deserve to be accepted by others. The result is a painful reduction of self-esteem. The conclusion that the avoidant individual does not deserve to be accepted by others, then, serves to foster even more avoidance and subsequent alienation. The pattern is continued.

Operant Conditioning

A final factor to be considered when addressing factors that serve to sustain or perpetuate the avoidant personality disorder is the operant conditioning of the avoidant behavior pattern itself. It has been stated throughout this chapter that the avoidant individual desires social affiliation, yet is fearful of interpersonal rejection and humiliation. The avoidant behavior pattern itself, that is, the seclusive, aloof, withdrawing, and hypersensitive pattern of behavior, is negatively reinforcing to these individuals considering this fear. The rationale for this conclusion lies in the fact that through such avoidant behaviors, these individuals can actually reduce the chances that they will be rejected or humiliated. Thus, the behavior is negatively reinforced—and the disorder goes on.

In summary, we see that avoidant individuals restrict their social experiences, are hypersensitive to rejection, and are excessively introspective. These three factors serve as mechanisms for the self-perpetuation of the avoidant personality disorder. By restricting their social milieu, they fail to increase their social competence and often evoke the ridicule of others for their asocial behavior. By being hypersensitive and hypervigilant to rejection, they interpret even minute rebuffs as major signs of rejection and sometimes see rejection where there is none. And by being excessively introspective, they are forced to examine the sorrowful condition they have created for themselves. The likely conclusion to be reached on the basis of the conditions enumerated is that they do not deserve to be accepted by others. Finally, we must add the self-perpetuating factor of the operant conditioning of the avoidant behavior itself. These four sustaining factors then, do much to ensure the perpetuation of the avoidant personality disorder.

ASSOCIATED DISORDERS

Mixed Personality Disorders

Aspects of the avoidant personality disorder develop in virtually all of the other personality disorders as their severity increases and social withdrawal becomes a common response to increased adversity. Research utilizing the Millon Clinical Multiaxial Inventory (MCMI) (Millon, 1982) has indicated that mixed personalities utilizing the avoidant pattern are most frequently found in the following combinations:

avoidant-dependent (discussed in Chapter 6), avoidant-passive-aggressive and avoidant-borderline.

Avoidant-Passive-aggressive Mixed Personality Disorder. The avoidant-passive-aggressive mixed personality disorder is found to be prevalent in chronic, yet ambulatory, outpatient treatment centers, such as halfway houses (Millon, 1982).

The avoidant-passive-aggressive disorder is described in Case 9.2. This man was attending an outpatient medication group at the time of his evaluation. He had recently engaged in several aborted suicide attempts.

CASE 9.2

The Avoidant-Passive-Aggressive Mixed Personality Disorder

46-Year-Old Man, Korean War Veteran

This patient's behavior is typified by a conflict between desiring detachment from others and fearing to be independent. He would like to be close and show affection but anticipates pain and disillusionment. Complicating the concern about venturing into close relationships is his markedly deflated self-esteem. Thus, any effort to make a go at independence is constrained by the fear that it will fail and result in humiliation. Although he has no alternative but to depend upon supporting persons and institutions, this behavior overlies deep resentments. Others have either turned against him or disapproved his efforts to achieve autonomy. He is often petulant and passively aggressive, and on occasion will attack others for failing to recognize his need for affection and nurturance. The dependency security he seeks is seriously jeopardized under these circumstances. To bind anger, and thereby protect against humiliation and loss, he has become anxious and withdrawn, feeling a pervasive dysphoric mood.

The patient's discontent, outbursts, and moodiness frequently evoke humiliating reactions from others, and these rebuffs only serve to reinforce his self-protective withdrawal. Every avenue of gratification seems trapped in conflict. He cannot act alone because of marked self-doubts. On the other hand, he cannot depend on others because of a deep social mistrust. Disposed to anticipate disappointments, he often precipitates disillusionment through obstructive and negative behaviors. He reports feeling misunderstood, unappreciated, and demeaned by others; voices a sense of futility about life; has a deflated self-image; and frequently refers to self with contempt and deprecation. A depressive tone and anxious wariness are ever-present, evident in erratic displays of moodiness.

Unable to muster the wherewithal to overcome deficits, and unable to achieve the support desired from others, he is disposed to turn against himself, expressing feelings of unworthiness and uselessness. Expecting to be slighted or demeaned, he has learned to be watchful and on guard against the ridicule and contempt anticipated from others. He is therefore ever-alert and sensitive to minute signs of censure and derision. Looking inward offers him no solace since he sees none of the attributes admired in others in himself. This awareness intrudes upon his thoughts and interferes with effective behavior, upsetting his cognitive processes and diminishing his capacity to cope effectively with ordinary life tasks. During periods when stresses are minimal, he may deny past resentments and attempt to portray an image of general well-being and contentment. These efforts, however, give way readily under the slightest of pressures.

(From T. Millon, *Disorders of Personality: DSM-III, Axis II.* New York: Wiley, 1981, Used with permission of the author.)

Avoidant-Borderline Mixed Personality Disorder. The second prevalent mix involving the avoidant personality disorder is composed of the avoidant and the borderline disorders. This pathological combination is to be considered more severe than the avoidant-passive-aggressive disorder. It is commonly found among patients who have experienced repeated psychotic episodes. The automated MCMI printout is presented in case 9.3 and is based on the responses given by a divorced woman whose two preadolescent children were placed in a foster home several years earlier. This individual's psychiatric record shows more than 10 brief psychiatric hospitalizations.

CASE 9.3

The Avoidant-Borderline Mixed Personality Disorder

40-Year-old Woman, Divorced, Two Preadolescent Children

This patient's behavior is characterized by a pervasive apprehensiveness and intense and variable moods that are noted by prolonged periods of dejection and self-deprecation, interspersed with normal spans, as well as episodes of withdrawn isolation or unpredictable and erratic anger. The expectancy that people will be rejecting and disparaging precipitates profound gloom, at one time, and irrational negativism or excitement, another. At times, despite a longing to relate and be accepted, she constrains these needs, protectively withdraws from threats to her fragile emotional balance, and maintains a safe distance from any psychological involvements. Retreating defensively, she may become remote from others and from needed sources of support. A surface apathy may be exhibited in these efforts to damp down or deaden excess sensitivities. Nevertheless, intense contrary feelings occasionally break through in manipulative and immature outbursts.

Deep resentments are difficult to bind toward those whom she has felt have been unsupportive, critical, and disapproving. The little security that she possesses, however, is threatened when these resentments are discharged. To protect against further loss, she makes repeated efforts to resist expressing anger, albeit unsuccessfully. When not withdrawn and drifting aimlessly in peripheral social roles, she is unpredictable, irritably edgy, and negativistic, engaging in innumerable wrangles and disappointments with others, vacillitating between moments of being agreeable, sullenly passive, and explosively angry. These difficulties are frequently complicated by genuine expressions of guilt and contrition that are mixed with feelings of being misunderstood, unappreciated, and demeaned by others.

Deprived of a sense of self-worth, she suffers constantly from painful thoughts about the pitiful and futile state of being oneself. This is compounded by her tendency to be extremely introspective. Thus, the alienation that she feels from others is paralleled by a feeling of alienation from self. There is a constant and confusing undercurrent of tension, sadness, and anger. Vacillation is exhibited between desires for affection, fear, and a general numbness of feeling. She has learned to be watchful, on guard against ridicule, and ever-alert to signs of censure and derision. She detects the most minute traces of annoyance expressed by others and makes the mole hill of a minor and passing slight into a mountain of personal ridicule and condemnation. She has learned that good things don't last, that affection will capriciously end, followed by disappointment and rejection. Anticipating rejection and deprecation, she frequently jumps the gun with impulsive hostility. What is seen is a cyclical variation of constraint followed by angry acting out, followed in turn by remorse and regret. These erratic emotions not only are intrinsically distressing, but they upset her capacity to cope effectively with everyday tasks. Unable to orient emotions and thoughts logically, she may at times become lost in personal irrelevancies and autistic asides. This inability to order ideas and feelings in a consistent and relevant manner only further alienates her from others.

(From T. Millon, *Disorders of Personality: DSM-III, Axis II.* New York: Wiley, 1981, Used with permission of the author.)

Associated Axis I Disorders

Avoidant personality types are among the most vulnerable of the personality disorders to further psychopathology. Not only do they tend to exhibit more disorders, but they also experience these difficulties more frequently and more intensely than all other personality types, with perhaps the exception of the borderline disorder.

Anxiety Disorders. Avoidant individuals seem characteristically "on edge, unable to relax, easily startled, tense, worrisome, irritable, preoccupied with calamities, and prone to nightmares; and they have poor appetites and suffer fatigue and intangible physical ailments" (Millon, 1981, p. 308). The most common of the avoidant's symptoms is *generalized anxiety disorder*. It seems to evolve out of these individuals' inability to handle the prolonged strain of social interaction and interpersonal competition. Not only have these individuals acquired a marked distrust of others, but they lack the self-esteem to cope with social inadequacy, insult, or humiliation. The fear that social interaction will lead to such humiliation hangs heavy over their heads during even the most minimal of social contact. As a result, feelings of frustration and general tension build into prolonged anxiety, which, very likely, may erupt into an acute *panic attack.*

Somatoform Disorders. *Hypochondriacal symptoms* and *conversion* disorders may be commonly exhibited by avoidant personalities. Hypochondriacal symptoms may serve these avoidant individuals as means of coping with feelings of depersonalization as well as a reason for not interacting socially. It may be argued that such symptoms also serve as a form of self-punishment for an inability to interact socially.

Conversion disorders, ranging from minor tics to motor paralyses, may occur in avoidant individuals. The more severe conversion disorders are unlikely, however, owing to the desire of these individuals to attract attention. Nevertheless, when these individuals are unable to avoid social pressure or deprecation, their fear and feelings of inadequacy may become manifest in conversion symptoms. Some conversion patients exhibit *la belle indifférence,* that is, a lack of concern about their bodily symptoms. One explanation for such a disorder would be the patient's need to justify social inadequacies, yet the desire to avoid attracting attention.

Dissociative Disorders. Avoidant personalities are especially prone to experience varied forms of *dissociative disorders.* Feelings of estrangement may arise as a protective maneuver to diminish the impact of excessive stimulation or the pain of social humiliation. Similar symptoms may also reflect the patient's devalued self-concept. Self-estrangement may also be traced to avoidant individuals' tendency to engage in cognitive interference.

Affective Disorders. According to the biosocial learning theory, the avoidant personality represents a "detached" personality. This refers to the observation that these individuals appear to seek reinforcement from neither themselves nor others. Thus, it would seem unlikely that these individuals would suffer affective disorders. Yet, affective disorders do, indeed, occur among this group of individuals. The answer as to why lies in the fact that these individuals do desire constructive social interaction, yet their fears keep them from pursuing such interaction. As a result, we may observe sadness, emptiness, and loneliness in these individuals. Many of these individuals express a yearning for the approval and affection they have been denied. In some cases, we are likely to see a self-contempt and self-deprecation for their perceived unlovability. These processes further promote and potentiate a wide range of affective disorders.

Schizophrenic Disorders. The severe psychopathological disorders of *disorganized schizophrenia, catatonic schizophrenia,* and *paranoid schizophrenia* may emerge from the avoidant personality disorder.

Disorganized schizophrenia is marked by "incoherence and flat, uncongruous, or silly affect. There are no systematized delusions although fragmentary delusions . . . are common" (American Psychiatric Association, 1980, p. 190). This decompensated disorder represents a complete breakdown of all coping strategies. Avoidant individuals are prone to this disorder because of their tendency to become easily overwhelmed and their tendencies to engage in cognitive interference.

Catatonic schizophrenia is defined as a "marked psychomotor disturbance, which may involve stupor, negativism, rigidity, excitement, or posturing. Sometimes there is rapid alternation between the extremes of excitement and stupor" (American Psychiatric Association, 1980, p. 190). When avoidant individuals decompensate into this disorder, it may be seen as a protective withdrawal, a retreat into indifference and a voluntary, purposeful dissociation with most aspects of life, presumably owing to its disappointing and aversive aspects.

Finally, paranoid schizophrenia may be described as a constellation of suspicious, persecutory, or grandiose delusions and hallucinations (American Psychiatric Association, 1980). These symptoms are likely to occur in avoidants because symptoms such as these (and distortions in reality in general) are a common consequence of prolonged isolation and distainful views of others.

Summary

In this discussion, we have examined the avoidant personality disorder. Let us review the main points addressed:
1. The clinical picture of the active-detached, avoidant personality disorder may be summarized as follows:
   a. Behaviorally, avoidants appear to others in a range from guarded to alarmed. They are highly vigilant for potential interpersonal threats.
   b. Interpersonal situations are viewed as being aversive and are coped with through withdrawal. Although these individuals desire affiliation they maintain a social distance.
   c. The cognitive style of avoidant individual ranges from being distracted to perplexed, often preoccupied with vigilant appraisal.

    d. Affectively, these avoidants seem to range from being anguished to overwrought.

    e. The self-perception of avoidants ranges from being alienated to rejected. They often see themselves as being isolated.

    f. Their primary defense mechanism is fantasy.

    g. Differential personality diagnoses would include the schizoid personality disorder, the schizotypal personality disorder, and the borderline personality disorder.

2. The etiology and development of the avoidant personality represents an intertwined constellation of biogenic and environmental factors:

    a. Biogenically, low arousal thresholds for the autonomic nervous system have been hypothesized as an etiological factor.

    b. Parental rejection, peer-group rejection, and self-rejection serve as powerful environmental factors that contribute to the etiology and development of the avoidant disorder.

3. Four major factors contribute to the self-perpetuation of the avoidant personality disorder:

    a. Restricted social experience.

    b. Hypersensitivity.

    c. Excessive introspection.

    d. Operant conditioning of the avoidant behavior itself. The avoidant's motivation appears linked to a fear of social rejection and humiliation.

4. The major mixed personality disorders that are anchored to the avoidant disorder are the avoidant-passive-aggressive mixed personality disorder and the avoidant-borderline mixed personality disorder.

5. Common DSM-III, Axis I disorders that are related to the avoidant personality disorder include anxiety disorders, somatoform disorders, dissociative disorders, affective disorders, and schizophrenic disorders.

10

The Schizoid Personality Disorder

In Chapter 9, we discussed the active-detached, avoidant personality disorder. In this chapter, we will turn our attention to the passive-detached, schizoid personality disorder. As you read the case of Roy L., make note of any of these clinically relevant aspects:

1. Behavioral appearance.
2. Interpersonal conduct.
3. Cognitive style.
4. Affective expression.
5. Self-perception.
6. Primary defense mechanism.

CASE 10.1

The Schizoid Personality Disorder

Roy L., Age 36, Married, Two Children

Roy was a successful sanitation engineer involved in the planning and maintenance of water resources for a large city; his job called for considerable foresight and independent judgment but little supervisory responsibility. In general, he was appraised as an undistinguished but competent and reliable employee. There were few demands of an interpersonal nature made of him, and he was viewed by most of his colleagues as reticent and shy and by others as cold and aloof.

Difficulties centered about his relationship with his wife. At her urging they sought marital counseling for, as she put it, "he is unwilling to join in family activities, he fails to take an interest in the children, he lacks affection and is disinterested in sex."

The pattern of social indifference, flatness of affect and personal isolation which characterized much of Roy's behavior was of little consequence to those with whom a deeper or more intimate relationship was not called for; with his immediate family, however, these traits took their toll.

In the early years of marriage, his wife maneuvered Roy into situations which might interest him, getting him involved in bridge clubs, church activities, sports and so on. These not only proved of no avail in activating Roy, but they seemed to make him grumpy and antagonistic.

Eventually, it was she who became discontent and irritable, and in time, she began to cajole, hound and intimidate Roy. Finally, sensing the grave changes that were beginning to take place within herself, she beseeched him to seek help, not so much "because of his behavior, but because I felt I was turning into a frustrated and irritable shrew." It soon became apparent that her difficulties stemmed from Roy's impassivity and self-absorption.

(From T. Millon, *Modern Psychopathology: A Biosocial Approach to Maladaptive Learning and Functioning*. Philadelphia: Saunders, 1969, Used with permission of the author.)

Case 10.1, the case of Roy L., is but one variation of the schizoid personality disorder. Yet, a generic theme of interpersonal, cognitive, and affective deficits seems blatantly apparent. For example, the dysfunctional nature of Roy L.'s interpersonal behavior might never have come to the attention of a clinician were it not for his wife's discontent. As for himself, Roy L. was generally unclear as to the purpose of counseling and simply regarded himself as a quiet and rather serious individual.

CLINICAL PICTURE

The passive-detached, schizoid personality disorder may be viewed as a dysfunctional syndromal extension of the normal introversive personality discussed in Chapter 2. Yet, the schizoid pattern itself as formulated in this text, appears in various graduated symptomatological forms and intensities, ranging from mildly dysfunctional to more severely dysfunctional. As a result, the schizoid disorder presented here will be somewhat broader in scope than the schizoid disorder as presented in the DSM-III.

In mild variations, schizoid personalities remain in the background of social life. They work quietly at their jobs and rarely do they attract any attention from those who have contact with them. They tend to fade into the scenery and would prefer to live their lives undisturbed were it not for others who place certain social expectations on them. Because they experience few rewards from social interaction, schizoid personalities often turn their attention and talents to interests that do not demand interpersonal contact. It is not uncommon to find these individuals seemingly preoccupied with hobbies (e.g., stamp or rock collecting), raising animals, academic pursuits (e.g., math or science), and mechanical or electronic gadgetry. In general, a key theme in the schizoid disorder may be summed up in the term asocial. A similarly important feature in this disorder is the steady and even state of hyporesponsiveness to virtually all sources of stimulation. Events that might provoke anger, elicit joy, or evoke sadness in other individuals seem to have minimal if any effects on schizoids.

In their more extreme variations, schizoids appear emotionally cold, indifferent to interpersonal interaction, and have few if any close friends (American Psychiatric Association, 1980). Excessive daydreaming and elaborate fantasies may also be part of the more severe schizoid variant. Let us take another look at the schizoid personality disorder through case 10.2.

CASE 10.2

Another Variation of the Schizoid Personality Disorder

Margaret L., Age 20, College Junior, Unmarried

Margaret was an extremely pretty, petite brunette, who personified the young college coed in appearance. She sought counseling on the urging of her dormitory roommate because both felt she might have latent homosexual tendencies. This concern proved unjustified, but there were other characteristics of a pathological nature that clearly were evident.

Margaret rarely enjoyed herself on dates; not that she found herself "disgusted" or "repelled" with necking and petting, but she simply "didn't experience any pleasure" in these activities. She went out of her way to avoid invitations to parties, preferring to stay in her room, either watching TV or working at her studies. She was an excellent student, majoring in geology and hoping for a field career in forestry, petroleum research or archeology.

Margaret was viewed as rather distant and aloof by her classmates. She rarely engaged in social activities, turned down an opportunity to join a sorority and had no close friends, in fact, few friends at all, except for her roommate and one girl back home. Despite her good looks, she was asked to date infrequently; when she did date, it usually was a one or two date affair in which either the boy failed to ask again or she refused to accept the invitation. The little reputation she had on campus was

Table 10.1   A Multidimensional Appraisal of the Schizoid Personality Disorder

1. Behavioral appearance: lethargic to sluggish.
2. Interpersonal conduct: aloof to remote.
3. Cognitive style: impoverished to barren.
4. Affective expression: flat to bleak.
5. Self-perception: complacent to lifeless.
6. Primary defense mechanism: intellectualization.
7. Differential personality diagnosis:
   a. avoidant personality disorder
   b. schizotypal personality disorder

that she was a "cold fish" and "a brain," someone who would rather talk about her courses and career plans than dance, drink and be merry.

One relationship with a boy lasted several months. He seemed to be a quiet and introversive young man who joined her in taking hikes, in demeaning the "childish" behaviors of their classmates and in discussing their mutual interest in nature, trees and rock formations. Their relationship faltered after 10 to 12 outdoor hiking dates; they seemed to have nothing more to say to each other. Margaret would have liked to continue this friendship, but she experienced no dismay over its termination.

Further explorations showed that Margaret rarely experienced either joy, dismay or anger. She seemed content to "let matters ride along," sitting on the sidelines while others became perturbed, ecstatic or hostile about "silly little things between them." This viewpoint, however, reflected less a well-reasoned philosophy of life than an inability to grasp "what it is that got people so excited."

In describing her few relationships, past and present, she seemed to be vague, superficial and naive, unable to organize her thoughts and tending to wander into irrelevancies such as the shoes certain people preferred or the physical characteristics of their parents.

(From T. Millon, *Modern Psychopathology: A Biosocial Approach to Maladaptive Learning and Functioning.* Philadelphia: Saunders, 1969, Used with permission of the author.)

With both the case of Roy L. (Case 10.1) and the case of Margaret L. (Case 10.2) in mind, let us now examine the schizoid personality disorder from the perspective of our standardized format. This perspective is summarized in Table 10.1.

Behavioral Appearance

As suggested earlier, schizoids appear to others as being hypoactive. They generally range in their behavioral appearance from seeming lethargic in mild forms of the disorder, to appearing sluggish in more severe forms of the disorder.

Throughout the spectrum of this disorder, one is struck by the lack of vitality, the low energy, and the general deficits that appear to be present with regards to spontaneity and expressiveness. These individuals seem to experience chronic fatigue and hypoactive motoric displays. For example, their habits of speech are typically slow and monotonous. Their overall communicative behavior may be characterized by obscurities that point to their inattentiveness or inability to grasp subtle emotional aspects of interpersonal communication. Overt musculoskeletal behaviors appear to be lethargic and void of any rhythmic or expressive nature. Without much effort, readers may be able to identify acquaintances who seem slow and chronically lethargic, who never seem to perk up, and who seem continually preoccupied.

Both Roy L. and Margaret L. could be summarized as lacking zest or vigor. In the case of Margaret L., she was seen by her peers as being "a 'cold fish' and a 'brain' who was more interested in books and rocks than people.

In sum, schizoids appear to others as being chronically underresponsive to all sources of stimulation. They seem to display a lack of spontaneity, ressonance, and color. They may also appear clumsy and boring in interpersonal relationships.

Interpersonal Conduct

Interpersonally, schizoid individuals range from being aloof to remote. That is, they are rarely responsive to the actions or feelings of others. They possess minimal "human" interests and possess few friends or close relationships. Schizoids appear interpersonally bland and passive. This passivity may be interpreted by others as a sign of hostility or rejection; in reality, it merely represents a fundamental incapacity to sense the moods and needs of others.

The blatant inability of schizoid individuals to engage in the give-and-take of interpersonal relationships is obvious to virtually everyone who has contact with these individuals. They tend to maintain a rather vague and peripheral interest in group discussions. Roy's wife, for example, complained of his inability to involve himself in even the most fundamental of familial activities. When social interaction is necessary, at school or at work, schizoids participate on the most superficial of levels and with a considerable degree of resistance even then. Margaret L. avoided parties at school and found no pleasure at the thought of interpersonal displays of affection, such as petting or kissing. Most of her dates, seldom as they occurred, were with different individuals because she seemed unable or uninterested in starting any kind of ongoing relationship. Margaret's basic interpersonal indifference showed itself clearly on one occasion, when a young man she had been dating terminated their relationship. Even though she would have desired to continue with the relationship, she showed no remorse or feelings of any kind.

In the case of Roy L., his wife noted that any efforts on her part to get him involved in social activities outside the family were usually met with resistance, even irritability and hostility.

In sum, the schizoid personality disorder is perhaps best thought of as an asocial personality pattern.

Cognitive Style

Cognitively, schizoid individuals are minimally introspective because the rewards of self-evaluation are relatively few for those incapable of experiencing existential thought or emotion. Schizoids suffer from an apparent cognitive deficit. They may range from being cognitively impoverished to being virtually barren of higher, meaningful cognitive abilities. Their thought processes tend to be obscure. Their patterns of thought and communication are easily derailed through internal or external distraction.

The case of Margaret L. demonstrates a form of deficit in cognitive processing, sometimes referred to as cognitive slippage. In her clinical interview, "she seemed vague, superficial and naive, unable to organize her thoughts and tending to wander into irrelevancies such as the shoes certain people preferred or the physical characteristics of their parents."

The DSM-III notes that in some cases, "Individuals with this disorder are often unable to express aggressiveness or hostility. They may seem vague about their goals, indecisive in their actions, self-absorbed, absentminded, and detached from their environment ('not with it' or 'in a fog'). Excessive daydreaming is often present" (American Psychiatric Association, 1980, p. 310).

The key feature in the cognitive style of the schizoid individual is an apparent cognitive deficit. Such a deficit will also appear in the discussion that follows.

Affective Expression

Schizoid personalities manifest a steady state of underresponsiveness to all sources of external stimulation. Events that might provoke anger or elicit joy or sadness in others brings no such response in schizoid individuals. There appears, therefore, to be a pervasive deficit in the domain of affective expression. There are few emotions felt; neither joy, anger, fear, nor anxiety appear to be experienced by these individuals to any significant degree. For this reason, it can be argued that schizoid individuals affective expression generally ranges from flat to bleak. In other words, these individuals appear unable to experience happiness, sadness, or even anger in any depth. They are emotionally cold and present a lack of warmth for others.

Both Roy L. and Margaret L. seemed unable to give or receive affection. Margaret L., especially, seemed to be disdainful of pursuits in which her peers outwardly displayed joy or happiness. She felt such activities were immature. But, Margaret L. also seemed to be unmoved by having been rejected by her last boyfriend. Thus, her felt emotions seemed blunted no matter what their nature, positive or negative. Therefore, to combine with the cognitive deficits discussed earlier, we would now add affective deficits as well to the key features of the schizoid personality.

Self-Perception

Schizoid personalities characterize themselves as ranging from complacent in mild variations to lifeless in extreme cases. In general, schizoids tend to view themselves as bland and introverted. They seem satisfied with their lives and are content to remain aloof. They segregate themselves from the social aspirations and competitiveness they see in others. As noted earlier, schizoids are minimally introspective. As obvious as Margaret L.'s social and emotional deficits were to others, she was unable to see them herself. Only the concern of "latent homosexual tendencies" motivated her to seek counseling. As for Roy L., he was content living his seclusive lifestyle, only the urgings of his wife motivated him to enter therapy.

Primary Defense Mechanism

The passive-detached, schizoid personality is one that appears colorless, asocial, insensitive, and uncommunicative. Their defense mechanism of choice appears to be *intellectualization.*

Intellectualization refers to the tendency of some individuals to think of, and describe, their affective and interpersonal experiences in matter-of-fact terms. They approach even the most emotional of issues or events from an impersonal, almost mechanical perspective. Individuals who employ intellectualization pay primary attention to formal and objective aspects of social and emotional events. They will tend to view displays of emotion as childish and immature. The defense mechanism of intellectualization provides schizoid individuals with a tool for remaining aloof as well as remaining socially and affectively uninvolved with their environment.

The case of Margaret L. provides us with examples of how the mechanism of intellectualization may present itself. Margaret L. rarely showed any emotion at all. She seemed to "'let matters ride along.'" Even when her friendship with a male college student was terminated, contrary to her preference, she showed no emotion and viewed the whole matter objectively. Margaret L. had no close friends apparently because of her cold, aloof attitude towards others. She seemed content to pursue abstract, impersonal interests.

Differential Personality Diagnosis

When we consider the personality disorders most likely to be confused with the schizoid disorder, we must consider the schizotypal disorder and the avoidant disorder.

When compared to schizoid individuals, we find that the schizotypal individual displays more dramatically eccentric behavior. Schizoids tend to be more affectively flat, colorless, and dull, whereas schizotypals manifest a more severe disorder, exhibiting several classic signs of schizophrenia (with the exception of hallucinations and delusions). Examples are magical thinking, (ie, clairvoyance, telepathy, or a 6th sense) social isolation, suspiciousness, and distortions of cognitive reference.

In many instances, the schizoid and avoidant personalities are difficult to distinguish because both tend to be socially hesitant and minimally responsive. Yet, the key to differentiation lies in the notion that although socially withdrawing, the avoidant feels a need to exhibit affect and to be socially accepted. The schizoid is intrinsically flat in affect and is socially indifferent. So, we see that the avoidant desires social exchange but is fearful of rejection and humiliation. The schizoid simply does not desire meaningful interaction.

ETIOLOGY AND DEVELOPMENT

Schizoid personalities are emotionally bland, interpersonally indifferent, and are intrapersonally absorbed. In short, they are asocial individuals. What background factors can account for the emotional and social deficits represented in the schizoid personalities such as Roy L. and Margaret L.?

Biogenic Factors

Because children inherit many overt physical features from their parents, it would seem safe to assume that features of internal morphology, physiology, and biochemistry may also be, to one degree or another, inherited. Extrapolating further, it would seem plausible that parents who are biologically limited in their capacity to experience intense emotions or to be vigorous and active possess certain associated structural and physiological deficits that may be genetically transmitted to their children. What we are proposing, then, is that some aspects of the schizoid personality disorder may arise because of biological deficiencies that are capable of being genetically transmitted. This hypothesis is based on extrapolations of the research on the biological bases of schizophrenia and, therefore, must be considered extremely speculative.

What is the nature of potential biogenic factors in the schizoid personality? One biogenic factor that may be genetically transmitted would be the proliferation of dopaminergic postsynaptic receptors located in the limbic and frontal cerebral cortices. In that, the catecholamine dopamine acts as an inhibitory neurotransmitter, it seems reasonable that an excessive number of these receptors at the postsynaptic membranes of the limbic and cortical dopaminergic pathways would contribute to excessive inhibitory functions within these dopaminergic areas. The anticipated result would be unusual cognitive activities and inhibited emotional behavior.

Another biogenic factor, which may also be inherited, would be the ectomorphic body structure. Numerous theorists have proposed that individuals with thin and fragile body structures are shy and introversive. It is unclear, of course, whether the body structure caused the schizoid behavior or is merely highly correlated with it. Furthermore, we are unsure as to whether such observed phenomena are indeed genetically linked.

Finally, Millon (1969) has hypothesized that the schizoid personality represents an individual who is suffering from an excessive degree of trophotropic domination in the autonomic nervous system. Such a condition would result from excessive parasympathetic nervous system activity. Trophotropic domination would easily result in apathy, underresponsiveness, and emotional flatness, as is characteristic of the schizoid personality.

Although several biogenic hypotheses seem to have merit, at best, biogenic factors lay the foundation for the schizoid personality. Environmental factors will shape its ultimate expression.

Environmental Factors

As we have repeatedly noted, biogenic factors, when present, probably serve to create the biological foundations for environmental experiences to build on. This interaction of biogenic and environmental factors act to shape the ultimate formulation of the schizoid personality disorder.

Formal or Rigid Family Atmosphere. Children learn to imitate the pattern of interpersonal relationships to which they are repeatedly exposed. Learning to be extremely formal in relationships as well as emotionally undemonstrative can be an incidental product of participating in, or merely observing, the everyday relationships within a family setting.

Families that are characterized by interpersonal reserve, superficiality, formality, or just an interpersonally bleak or cold atmosphere may be pathogenic. In such families, the members often relate to each other in disaffiliated and remote ways. The family becomes not a family in the social sense but merely a basis for cohabitation—a reason for living together and sharing expenses. Such familial conditions are often the breeding grounds for asocial children who develop ingrained habits of social ineptness, insensitivity, aloofness, and minimal feelings of interpersonal affiliation. The following case describes such a situation:

CASE 10.3

Another Variation of the Schizoid Personality Disorder

Lester M., Age 19, College Student

Lester "wandered in" the door of his college's counseling service, and stood about for over an hour before arranging an appointment. In his first counseling session, he spoke of his inability "to feel" and his awareness that he could not carry on a conversation with his peers of more than a few words at a time. In later sessions, he recounted the impersonal atmosphere of his childhood; rarely was he allowed to speak unless spoken to, and he could not recall any occasion when he experienced or witnessed affection or anger among members of his family.

(From T. Millon, Modern Psychopathology: *A Biosocial Approach to Maladaptive Learning and Functioning.* Philadelphia: Saunders, 1969, Used with permission of the author.)

We see in the case of Lester M. that his familial environment was a rather cold and aloof environment. Although family members did not express hostility, they did not express affection either. Interpersonal exchange was kept to a minimum and was extremely formal when it did occur. It is interesting to note that this very characteristic is what drove Lester M. to seek counseling. That is, once Lester was removed from a noncommunicative family and placed in social situations that required interpersonal communication, he was unable to communicate. Lester had never learned to be sociable.

Fragmented Family Communication. Some individuals fail to learn how to attend to, and interpret, the signals that others communicate. Or they may fail to learn how to respond in meaningful or rational ways. Both of these traits are characteristic of the schizoid personality disorder.

Learning the skills of interpersonal communication is a requisite to shared social behavior. Without the ability to communicate, the individual cannot function effectively with others. Such individuals will appear detached, unresponsive, cold, and insensitive. All of these traits are, again, characteristic of the schizoid pattern.

Fragmented patterns of family communication are not only dysfunctional, but they teach the children similar communicative behaviors. Fragmented communication refers to patterns of communication in which complete thoughts are aborted; transmission of thoughts may be concealed in rhetoric or may be circumstantial. Children raised in environments characterized by fragmented communication are likely to become vague, abortive, and circumstantial in their own communications. After all, this is how they were taught.

By attending to, thinking about, and communicating in disjointed, vague, and abortive patterns, individuals are prone to begin to function both cognitively and affectively in similar patterns. As a result, the pattern of fragmented communication is allowed to extend beyond the family into all spheres of the individual's life. These patterns of meaningless and disjointed communications tend to confuse others, who may react somewhat adversely. Thus, the individual is prone to seek further isolation and social distance feeling that others simply do not understand him/her. Case 10.4 is somewhat characteristic of this phenomenon.

CASE 10.4

Another Variation of the Schizoid Personality Disorder

Chester A., Age 39, Married, No Children

Chester, an engineering professor of my acquaintance, would stop by my office repeatedly to chat about "our mutual interests in psychology and philosophy," oblivious of the fact that I thought his ideas obscure and archaic, at best, and that I found him personally tiresome and boring. Despite his obvious competence in engineering and mathematical matters, he seemed completely incapable of formulating his thoughts in a logical manner, let alone of conveying them to others. His superficial grasp and naivete regarding worldly and social affairs were quite striking, and he appeared totally devoid of any recognition that people might "feel" one way or another about him as a person. He was an extremely inept teacher, a fact he could not understand but nevertheless accepted

(From T. Millon, Modern Psychopathology: *A Biosocial Approach to Maladaptive Learning and Functioning.* Philadelphia: Saunders, 1969, Used with permission of the author.)

In summary, then, we see that the schizoid personality may be formed by an interaction of biogenic and environmental factors. Formal familial atmospheres as well as fragmented communication patterns superimposed over deficient excitatory or excessive inhibitory biochemical substates may ultimately act to help shape the schizoid personality disorder. Furthermore, we must note that the inability to interact interpersonally or to perform in socially competent manners is likely to contribute to a punishing or otherwise hostile environment. That is, the apathetic attitudes, aloof and formal interpersonal dispositions, and often dysfunctional communicative behavior of the schizoid personalities are likely to foster misunderstanding, lack of tolerance, frustration, or even hostility on the part of others. Such behavior is punishing to most. Yet, schizoid personalities are usually incapable, on their own, of correcting the problem. As a result, they seek further isolation and social withdrawal. Thus, we see that the role of operant conditioning clearly enters into the formation or exacerbation of the schizoid personality disorder.

Neuropsychological Development

One of the conditions that appears to set the stage for later learning of schizoid behavior is insufficient stimulus nutriment received by the child in the first year of life. Insufficient stimulation during this critical developmental period is likely to result in various maturational and learning deficits. In addition, the emotional centers in the limbic brain are unlikely to develop fully.

Constitutionally unresponsive or trophotropically dominated infants are likely to evoke few reactions from their environment. In such cases, the maturational underdevelopment is likely to be compounded.

Such children are unlikely to receive much attention or affection. As a result, they are likely to be deprived of the social and emotional cues necessary to learn human-attachment behaviors. In many cases, these children will turn to autostimulation through fantasy, daydreaming, and so on. Their objects of affection are likely to be dolls, blankets, blocks, and so forth, rather than other human beings. Thus, neuropsychologically, we see the stage set for the development of the schizoid personality.

SELF-PERPETUATION OF THE SCHIZOID PERSONALITY DISORDER

Having described the clinical picture and development of the schizoid personality, let us now turn to a discussion of the self-perpetuation of this personality disorder.

Infrequent Social Activities

Schizoid individuals perpetuate their own disorder by restricting their social contacts and keeping emotional involvements to a minimum. They tend to engage in only those activities necessary for performing their jobs or fulfilling the most minimal of family obligations. By reducing and restricting their interpersonal environment, they are able effectively to prevent new and different experiences that might threaten or inconvenience them. This, of course, is their preference. Schizoid personalities prefer social isolation, but such isolation also serves to foster the continuation of the isolated and withdrawn existence because it serves to exclude any new events that might serve to alter their asocial existence.

We see in the case of Roy L. that his wife tried to get him involved in numerous and diverse social activities, for example, bridge clubs, sports, and so on. These attempts served to make Roy L. even more "grumpy and antagonistic." As a result, he was allowed to continue in his isolation.

Reinforcement of Social Isolation

The apathetic, noncommunicative, and affective unresponsiveness that characterize the schizoid personalities do little to make them attractive to others. Most people are minimally inclined to respond to such asocial behavior. As a result, schizoid individuals are overlooked and ignored in many social situations. When others do communicate with them, the communication tends to be on the most superfical of levels.

The fact that others view them as boring and colorless appears to suit the schizoid personalities' desire to remain apart and alone. However, these desires, as they are reinforced by others, serve only to perpetuate the disorder.

Social and Cognitive Insensitivity

Schizoid personalities are not only socially insensitive and imperceptive, but they also tend cognitively to homogenize stimuli of a varied nature and to flatten affective responsiveness. Such cognitive and affective strategies serve to simplify complex cognitive and social conditions. These strategies tend to make the world easier to understand and less threatening. Obviously, however, in doing so, these individuals become grossly naive and insensitive to important distinctions in the people, places, and things that make up their world.

Chester A. was an example of a socially naive individual who simply failed to grasp many of the subtle differences in his world that others not only see but find stimulating and rewarding.

In summary, we see that schizoid personalities tend to perpetuate their own disorder through seeking to avoid social activities, by having their social isolation reinforced, and by their social and cognitive insensitivity. Their infrequent social activities limit their ability to grow by new experience. Their social isolation is frequently reinforced by others who tend to ostracize asocial individuals. And their social and cognitive insensitivity tends to oversimplify and make boring a world that is rich in diversity and subtle variety. Thus, the pattern is perpetuated.

ASSOCIATED DISORDERS

We now examine the Axis II and Axis I disorders that are related to the schizoid pattern.

Mixed Personality Disorders

The theoretical and empirical work of Millon (1969 and 1982, respectively) indicates that the schizoid personality disorder is likely to fuse with two other personality disorders: the dependent disorder and the schizotypal disorder. Therefore, in addition to the schizoid disorder, in its pure sense, one is likely to encounter the schizoid-dependent and the schizoid-schizotypal mixed disorders. Let us briefly examine these mixed personality disorders that seem to be anchored in the schizoid pattern. Schizoid-Dependent Mixed Personality Disorder:

The schizoid-dependent mixed personality disorder is the most commonly encountered blend of schizoid disorders. It is likely to be encountered among long-term institutionalized patient populations as well as patients found in halfway houses.

Case 10.5 summarizes a common manner in which the schizoid and dependent disorders combine and present themselves clinically. The case is that of a veteran of World War II. He has been an ambulatory outpatient for 30 years. However, on three occasions, he has experienced extended psychotic episodes during which time he was hospitalized and diagnosed as a chronic undifferentiated schizophrenic. His first hospitalization was for a period of three years, the other two were for 3-month periods each. He has been ambulatory for the last 8 years, having recently remarried. He is currently experiencing marital difficulties.

CASE 10.5

The Schizoid-Dependent Mixed Personality Disorders

54-Year-Old Man; World War II Veteran

This patient's life-style is typified by a quiet, colorless, and dependent way of relating to others. His introversive pattern covaries with a general lack of vitality, deficits in social initiative and stimulus-seeking behaviors, impoverished affect, and a cognitive vagueness regarding interpersonal matters. Fatigability, low energy level, and weakness in motoric expressiveness and spontaneity are notable. He prefers a peripheral but dependent role in social and family relationships. There is a desire for social isolation that conflicts with strong dependency needs. Both stem from low self-esteem and inadequacies in autonomy and social competence.

The patient is inclined to be self-belittling and possesses a self-image of a weak and ineffectual person. Life is experienced as uneventful, with periods of passive solitude interspersed with feelings of emptiness and depersonalization. He evidences an indifference to social surroundings, is minimally introspective and generally insensitive to the subtleties of emotional life. Thought processes, though not deficient, are unfocused, particularly with regard to interpersonal matters. Social communication is often strained, self-conscious, and tangential.

There is a deficiency in the expression of affection, which may stem from an anhedonic inability to display enthusiasm or experience pleasure. He does exhibit a chronic but mild depressiveness. There is a marked tendency to keep to a simple, repetitive, and dependent life pattern. He avoids self-assertion, abdicates autonomous responsibilities, and is content to remain aloof from normal social aspirations. Disengaged from and disinterested in most of the rewards of active human relationships, he appears to others as apathetic and asocial. By restricting social and emotional involvements to a minimum, he perpetuates a life pattern of isolation and dependency.

(From T. Millon, *Disorders of Personality: DSM-III, Axis II.* New York: Wiley, 1981, Used with permission of the author.)

The noteworthy aspects of this veteran's case are the manner in which the schizoid and dependent characteristics blend. His colorless affect, low energy, self-belittling, social incompetence, and dependent attitude and behavior make the prognosis for this individual rather bleak.

Schizoid-Schizotypal Mixed Personality Disorder

Perhaps the second most commonly encountered blend of schizoid disorders is the schizoid-schizotypal mixed personality disorder. This variant is more severe than the previously discussed schizoid and schizoid-dependent disorders. It is commonly encountered among institutionalized populations and among the residents of halfway houses.

Case 10.6 is that of a patient who has been hospitalized several times since her adolescence, with a diagnosis of schizophrenia. Currently, she is residing in a halfway house in a large city, going through what her supervisors call a quiet, if eccentric adjustment.

CASE 10.6

The Schizoid-Schizotypal Mixed Personality Disorder

44-Year-Old Woman, Unmarried

This patient's way of life is characterized by a quiet and inexpressive dependency. A marked deficit in social interest is notable, as are frequent behavioral eccentricities, occasional autistic thinking, and depersonalization anxieties. This intensely introversive pattern covaries with a lack of energy, deficits in social initiative and stimulus-seeking behaviors, impoverished affect, and confused thinking regarding interpersonal matters. She is likely to have acquired a peripheral but dependent role in social and family relationships. Her desire for social isolation conflicts with her strong dependency on others for support. Both stem from low self-esteem and inadequacies in autonomy and social competence.

The patient remains a detached observer of the passing scene, is characteristically self-belittling, and possesses a self-image of being a weak and ineffectual person. Rather than venturing outward, she has retreated defensively, increasingly remote from others and from sources of potential growth and gratification. Life is uneventful, with extended periods of solitude interspersed with feelings of being disembodied, empty, and depersonalized. She evidences a pervasive inadequacy in most areas, and there is a tendency to follow a meaningless, ineffectual, and idle pattern, drifting aimlessly and remaining on the periphery of social life.

Thought processes are unfocused, particularly with regard to emotional and interpersonal matters. Her estrangement from others has led to a loss of touch with reality. Social communication is often strained, self-conscious, and tangential, further alienating her from others. There is hesitation in expressing affection, which may stem from an anhedonic inability to display enthusiasm or experience pleasure.

She exhibits a distinct depressive tone, is occasionally morose, and is likely to display an erratic moodiness with multiple complaints. Beneath her more typical apathetic exterior, there are intense feelings of discontent and anger. This is evident in periodic displays of passive-aggressive, petulant, and fault-finding behaviors. More commonly, she is self-deprecating and self-punitive, and is disposed to constant but quiet worrying. There is a marked tendency to keep a simple, repetitive, and depen-dent life pattern with avoidance of self-assertion and indifference to normal social aspirations. Disengaged from and disinterested in most of the rewards of active human relationships, she appears to others as an unobtrusively strange, discon-nected, and lifeless person. By restricting social and emotional involvements to a minimum, she perpetuates her life pattern of isolation and dependency.

(From T. Millon, *Disorders of Personality: DSM-III, Axis II*. New York: Wiley, 1981, Used with permission of the author.)

Associated Axis I Disorders

Having reviewed the most common mixed personality disorders that appear to be anchored in the schizoid personality, let us turn to a discussion of the Axis I major clinical syndromes that are associated with the schizoid disorder.

Affective Disorders. Surprisingly, schizoid personalities do experience a few of the major affective disorders from *manic disorders* to *depressive disorders*. Manic excitation may occur as a result of the avoid-ant's attempts to break out of his/her characteristic states of stagna-tion and interpersonal barrenness. Wild and irrational exuberance tends to run a brief but erratic course before collapsing into a more typical reserved and inexpressive state. Depressive symptoms may emerge as a result of these individuals' realization of the socially iso-lated and empty existence they actually lead.

Dissociative Disorders. *Depersonalization disorders* are not uncommon among schizoid individuals. As an elaboration of their characteristic

state, these individuals often experience altered perceptions of themselves. States of self-estrangement, including "mechanical" feelings or
disembodied feelings, are likely to occur. These conditions are best
understood as extensions of the common schizoid pattern. As decompensation occurs, social withdrawal is extended into intrapersonal
withdrawal. As described by Millon (1981) "Empty or devoid of a past,
deficient in 'psychic' cohesion, and insensitive to external prompting,
they are subject to the kind of splitting or disintegration that inclines
them to dissociative states" (p. 287).

Schizophrenic Disorders. Schizoid individuals are prone to a wide range
of schizophrenic disorders. Most notable among them are *disorganized schizophrenia* and *catatonic schizophrenia.* The most characteristic features of these schizophrenic disorders, as they apply to
schizoids, are profound lethargy, indifference, even stuporous behavior. Speech patterns are usually slow and labored, often difficult to
comprehend. Passively withdrawn and unresponsive, these individuals seldom participate in their surroundings. Once again, these
disorders may be best understood as syndromal elaborations, or extensions, of the basic schizoid pattern that has emerged as a result of
pathogenic biological and environmental factors.

It should be noted that *schizophreniform disorder* and *brief reactive psychosis* are also potential syndromal elaborations of the schizoid personality disorder. These reactions are less prolonged and are
characteristically transient disorders compared to the other disorders
described.

Summary

In this chapter we have reviewed the last of the basic eight mildly severe personality disorders—the passive-detached, schizoid personality. Let us review
some of the main points:
1. The clinical picture of the schizoid personality is one characterized by cognitive and emotional deficits. More specifically:
   a. Behaviorally, schizoids tend to range from being lethargic to sluggish.
   They appear fatigued and lacking vitality.
   b. Interpersonally, they appear to range from being aloof to interpersonally
   remote. They have few, if any, close friends.
   c. Cognitively, schizoids range from impoverished to barren.
   d. Their ability for affective expression ranges from flat to bleak. They often
   seem cold, unresponsive, and unfeeling.
   e. Their self-perception appears to range from complacent to lifeless. They
   have a minimal awareness of self.
   f. The primary defense mechanism employed by schizoids is
   intellectualization.

  g. Differential personality diagnosis would include the avoidant personality
      disorder and the schizotypal personality disorder.
2. Etiological and developmental factors in the schizoid disorder include hypo-
      active physiological substrates (limbic or ascending reticular activating sys-
      tem deficits as well as parasympathetic nervous system dominance) com-
      bined with environmental factors such as parental indifference and
      fragmented familial communication patterns.
3. The schizoid disorder appears to be self-perpetuating through factors such
      as infrequent social interaction, reinforcement of social isolation, and so-
      cial and cognitive insensitivity.
4. Mixed personality disorders that seem to be anchored to the schizoid per-
      sonality include the schizoid-dependent mixed personality disorder and the
      schizoid-schizotypal mixed personality disorder.
5. Associated DSM-III, Axis I disorders include affective disorders, dissociative
      disorders, schizophrenic disorders as well as schizophreniform and brief
      reactive psychotic disorders.

Six

THE MORE SEVERE PERSONALITY DISORDERS

In Part Six, we have chosen to separate out what we feel are the more severe personality disorders: the schizotypal disorder, the borderline disorder, and the paranoid disorder. DSM-III makes no such distinction along the lines of severity, yet we have chosen to treat the material in such a fashion because Millon's theoretical work (1969, 1981) and clinical work (1982) has led to the differentiation of the major personality disorders, not only on the basis of reinforcement processes (described in Chapter 2), but in terms of their level of severity as well.

Continuing the theme of syndromal continuity presented earlier, the three more severe personality disorders to be discussed may be thought of as elaborations of the eight more basic, less severe personality disorders examined earlier. That is to say, they may be thought of as syndromal continuations of the less severe disorders. The same clinical symptomatology and the same constellations of etiological and development factors that are present in the less severe disorders are present in extended elaborations (i.e., with greater frequency, intensity, and chronicity) in the more severe disorders. "No matter how extreme of maladaptive these behaviors may become, they are best understood as extensions and distortions that derive from, and are fully consonant with, the basic personality style" (Millon, 1982, p. 34).

In summary, then, we see that these three more serious disorders are to be conceived of as syndromal elaborations of the eight more basic personality disorders; the schizotypal represents a deterioration of the less severe schizoid or avoidant disorders; the borderline represents a deterioration of the less severe dependent, histrionic, or passive-aggressive disorders; and the paranoid represents a deterioration of the less severe narcissistic, antisocial, or compulsive

Eight Basic Personality Disorders	*More Severe Personality Disorders*
Schizoid personality disorder	
Avoidant personality disorder	Schizotypal personality disorder
Dependent personality disorder	
Histrionic personality disorder	Borderline personality disorder
Passive-aggressive personality disorder	
Narcissistic personality disorder	
Antisocial personality disorder	Paranoid personality disorder
Compulsive personality disorder	

Figure 1

disorders (see Figure 1). Thus, the individuals discussed in the following chapters differ from those discussed in the previous chapters by the frequency, intensity, and chronicity with which their symptoms arise.

11

The Schizotypal Personality Disorder

The first of the more severe personality disorders to be examined in Part Six will be the schizotypal personality disorder. It should be noted, however, that the format we will employ to present the three remaining personality disorders will vary somewhat from the format used to present the preceding eight disorders. Because each of the remaining disorders is believed, by the authors, to represent a syndromal deterioration of one or more of the eight basic matrix-derived personality disorders (see Chapter 2), we will first present the generic clinical picture for each personality disorder and then describe, with relevant case material, the clinical variations in which the personality disorder under discussion is likely to manifest itself, considering its premorbid foundations.

CLINICAL PICTURE

The schizotypal personality disorder is best understood as a more severe syndromal extension, or deterioration, of either the schizoid or avoidant personality disorders. As such, it represents many of the same characteristics found in the schizoid and avoidant disorders, but in greater intensity, or severity. Several features, however, are found generically common among individuals ultimately diagnosed as

Table 11.1   A Multidimensional Appraisal of the Generic Schizotypal Personality Disorder

1. Behavioral appearance: eccentric to bizarre.
2. Interpersonal conduct: detached to inaccessible.
3. Cognitive style: ruminative to deranged.
4. Affective expression:
   a. apprehensive to frantic
   b. apathetic to deadened
5. Self-perception: forlorn to vacant.
6. Primary defense mechanism: undoing.
7. Differential personality diagnosis: borderline personality disorder.

schizotypal. Let us review these basic similarities (summarized in Table 11.1) before going on and examining the major clinical variations of the schizotypal disorder.

Behavioral Appearance

To those who find themselves in contact with schizotypal individuals' they often range from appearing eccentric and aberrant to outright bizarre in their actions. Their behavior is clearly erratic. School and employment histories of these individuals show marked deficits and irregularities. Not only are they frequent dropouts, but they drift from one source of employment to another. If married, they are often separated or divorced.

At times, their behavior appears eccentric, that is, they prefer social isolation and may engage in activities that others find curious. In more severe cases, their behavior may seem clearly bizarre. The presence of odd speech patterns is an example. Schizotypal individuals may verbally digress or become metaphorical in their expressions. According to the DSM-III, "Often, speech shows marked peculiarities; concepts may be expressed unclearly or oddly or words used deviantly, but never to the point of loosening of associations or incoherence (American Psychiatric Association, 1980, p. 312).

Interpersonal Conduct

Interpersonally, schizotypals experience a life of isolation, with minimal personal attachments and obligations. As their lives progress it is not uncommon to find these individuals drifting into increasingly superficial and peripheral social and vocational roles. These individuals have virtually no close friends or confidants. They have great difficulty with face-to-face interaction. They commonly experience intense social anxiety at relatively minimal social challenge. For these reasons, we believe the interpersonal conduct of schizotypals may be categorized as ranging from being interpersonally detached and secretive to inaccessible.

Cognitive Style

The cognitive style of schizotypal individuals may be ruminative and autistic in less severe variations to blatantly deranged in more severe forms of the disorder. The cognitive slippage and interference that characterize the thought processes of this disorder in its milder forms are simply amplified here. Schizotypals are frequently unable to orient their thoughts logically. They tend to become lost in a plethora of irrelevancies. Their thinking appears scattered and autistic as the disorder manifests itself in its more severe variations.

According to the DSM-III, these individuals may report "magical thinking" (i.e., clairvoyance, telepathy, a sixth sense, or just extreme superstitious behavior). Similarly schizotypals may experience recurrent illusions where they report the presence of a person or force not actually there. Psychotic thought, when it does occur, is transient and not indicative of a diagnosis of schizophrenia.

Affective Expression

The deficient or disharmonious affect of many of these patients deprives them of the capacity to relate to people, places, or things as anything but flat and lifeless phenomena. Their affective expression ranges from being apathetic to insentient and deadened. On the other hand, some schizotypal individuals seem in a constant state of agitation. Their affective expression ranges from being apprehensive to distraught and frantic.

One is likely to ask at this point how it can be that schizotypals can present two very different affective pictures? The answer lies in the fact that schizotypals who evolve from a distribution of milder schizoid traits which present themselves as apathetic, perhaps even affectively deadened, whereas schizotypals who evolve from a distribution of milder avoidant traits will present themselves as apprehensive, perhaps even frantic in their affective expression. We will present more on these clinical variations later.

Self-Perception

Schizotypal individuals often view themselves as forlorn and lacking meaning in life or, in more severe cases, on introspection, they may see themselves as vacant. They may experience recurrent feelings of emptiness or of estrangement. Experiences of depersonalization and dissociation may also be present in these patients. In sum, schizotypals appear virtually "self-less" as they look inward towards self-appraisal.

Primary Defense Mechanism

The schizotypal personality disorder is characterized by extreme social and affective isolation as well as autistic and bizarre cognitive functioning. The defense mechanism commonly used by individuals who possess this disorder is *undoing.*

Undoing is a self-purification mechanism in which individuals attempt to repent for some undesirable behavior or "evil" motive. In effect, undoing represents a form of atonement. In severly pathological forms, undoing may take the form of complex and bizarre rituals, or "magical" acts. These rituals, such as compulsive hand washing, are designed to cleanse or purify the individual. These compulsions not only cause these individuals discomfort, but they may also consciously recognize them as absurd. Nevertheless, individuals employing such a mechanism appear to have lost the ability to control these acts as well as the ability to see their real meaning.

Differential Personality Diagnosis

The schizotypal personality disorder is likely to be confused with another severe personality disorder, the borderline disorder. Both the schizotypal and the borderline patterns represent severe personality disorders. Furthermore, according to the present biosocial learning theory, they both emerge when the less severe personality variants decompensate. Yet, there are marked differences in these two disorders.

The schizotypal disorder features schizophrenic-like symptoms. These symptoms reflect disturbances in cognitive processes. Thus, the schizotypal is characterized by perceptual pathology as well as social withdrawal and isolation.

The most obvious feature of the borderline disorder, on the other hand, is instability of mood. The symptoms of the borderline reflect disturbances in affect rather than cognition. Finally, the borderline individual is interpersonally dependent, unlike the socially isolated schizotypal.

A final note should be made regarding the schizotypal disorder in contrast to the Axis I *schizophrenic disorders.* Axis I disorders are characteristically more severe and of relatively shorter duration. The Axis II schizotypal disorder represents the operation of internal, ingrained, and more enduring defects in the patient's personality. Although schizophrenic episodes often reflect a psychosocial stressor, the schizotypal disorder represents an underlying and persistent characterological pattern.

CLINICAL VARIATIONS

The description of the schizotypal personality disorder presented in the previous section portrays the generic aspects of this disorder. It is more common, however, to see the schizotypal pattern manifest itself in one of two major variations. The two major clinical variations of the schizotypal disorder are (1) the schizotypal-schizoid pattern and (2) the schizotypal-avoidant pattern.

Schizotypal-Schizoid Variation

Schizotypal-schizoid individuals are characteristically drab, sluggish, and inexpressive. They display a marked deficit in their affective expression and appear bland, untroubled, indifferent, and unmotivated by the outside world. Their cognitive processes seem obscure and vague. Such individuals seem unable to experience the subtle emotional aspects of social exchange. Interpersonal communications are often vague and confused. The speech patterns of these individuals tend to be monotonous, listless, or at times, inaudible. Most people consider these individuals as strange, curious, aloof, and lethargic. In effect, they become background people satisfied to live their lives in an isolated, secluded manner. Case 11.1 portrays such an individual.

CASE 11.1

The Schizotypal-Schizoid Variation

Jane W., Age 27, Unmarried, Hospitalized

Jane was the youngest of three sisters. Since early life, she was known to be quiet and shy, the "weakest" member of the family. Jane's father was a chronic alcoholic who, during frequent drinking sprees, humiliated and regularly beat various members of his family. Her mother seemed detached from Jane, but she often would be critical of her for being "stupid and slow."

Jane completed the tenth grade with better than average grades; however, she had to leave school shortly thereafter because of her mother's death. Jane was given a job as a seamstress as a means of contributing to the family income since her father had abandoned his family two years prior to his wife's death, never to be heard from again.

Unfortunately, Jane was unable to hold her position since the factory in which she worked had closed down; she failed to keep the next three jobs her sisters got for her over a two year period; as Jane put it, "I was not interested and slow."

Following dismissal from her last position, Jane simply withdrew from work, becoming entirely dependent on her older sister. Jane claimed that work was too difficult for her and, more significantly, that she thought that everyone felt, "I was stupid and would mess up the job." In a similar vein, several young men sought to court her, but she persistently refused their overtures since she knew "they wouldn't like me after they took me out."

For the next seven years, Jane took care of the house for her unmarried sister; however, Jane felt that she had never done a "good job" since, "I spent most of my time sleeping or watching TV." She reported further, "I don't like to read or to watch TV, but it's better than thinking about people or myself."

Upon her older sister's marriage, it was decided that Jane, who was both afraid and incapable of being on her own, should be institutionalized. The decision, made by both her sisters, was not responded to by Jane as a painful rejection; she accepted it, at least overtly, without protest.

Upon entrance to the hospital, Jane seemed hazy and disconnected, although she evidenced no hallucinations or delusions. She spoke minimally, answered questions with a yes or no, seemed rational, took care of herself reasonably well and fitted quietly into the admissions ward. She voiced relief to an attendant at being away from the expectations and demands of the outer world; however, she established no personal relationships with other patients or with the hospital personnel.

Were it not for the fact that no one wanted to assist her in making the transition back to society, Jane would have been recommended for discharge. Lacking such environmental support and recognizing her inability to relate easily with others or to assume independence, there was no option but to keep her hospitalized.

(From T. Millon, Modern Psychopathology: *A Biosocial Approach to Maladaptive Learning and Functioning.* Philadelphia: Saunders, 1969, Used with permission of the author.)

The case of Jane W. demonstrates the classic self-absorbed, lethargic, hypoactive, and minimally communicative schizotypal-schizoid individual. Jane W. presents a personality clearly deficit in both cognitive and affective functioning.

Schizotypal-Avoidant Variation

Schizotypal-avoidant individuals are restrained and isolated. Similarly, they are apprehensive, guarded, and interpersonally withdrawing. As a protective device, they seek to eliminate their own desires and feelings for interpersonal affiliation, for they expect only rejection and pain from interacting with others. Thus, apathy, indifference, and impoverished thought, which we saw in the cognitive and affective insensitivity, is presented here as a result of an attempt to dampen an intrinsic oversensitivity. The case of Harold T. is a study of a schizotypal-avoidant individual.

CASE 11.2

The Schizotypal-Avoidant Variation

Harold T., Age 27, Unmarried, Hospitalized

Harold was the fourth of seven children. His father, a hard-drinking coal miner, had been on relief throughout most of Harold's early life; his mother died giving birth to her seventh child when Harold was 8. The family was raised by two older sisters, ages 15 and 11 at the time of their mother's death; partial household assistance was provided by a widowed maternal aunt with eight children of her own.

"Duckie,"as Harold was known, had always been a withdrawn, frightened and "stupid" youngster. The nickname "Duckie" represented a peculiar waddle in his walk; it was used by others as a term of derogation and ridicule. Harold rarely played with his sibs or neighborhood children; he was teased unmercifully because of his "walk" and his fear of pranksters. Harold was a favorite neighborhood scapegoat; he was intimidated even by the most innocuous glance in his direction.

His father's brutality toward the other children of the family terrified Harold. Although Harold received less than his share of this brutality, since his father thought him to be a "good and not troublesome boy," this escape from paternal hostility was more than made up for by resentment and teasing on the part of his older siblings. By the time Harold was 10 or 11, his younger brothers joined in taunting and humiliating him.

Harold's family was surprised when he performed well in the first few years of schooling. He began to falter, however, upon entrance to junior high school. At about the age of 14, his schoolwork became extremely poor, he refused to go to classes and he complained of a variety of vague, physical pains. By age 15 he had totally withdrawn from school, remaining home in the basement room that he shared with two younger brothers. Everyone in his family began to speak of him as "being tetched." He thought about "funny religious things that didn't make sense"; he also began to draw "strange things" and talk to himself. When he was 16, he once ran out of the house screaming "I'm gone, I'm gone, I'm gone . . .", saying that his "body went to heaven" and that he had to run outside to recover it; rather interestingly, this event occurred shortly after his father had been committed by the courts to a state mental hospital. By age 17, Harold was ruminating all day, often talking aloud in a meaningless jargon; he refused to come to the family table for meals.

The scheduled marriage of his second oldest sister, who had been running the household for five years, brought matters to a head. Harold, then 18, was taken to the same mental hospital to which his father had been committed two years previously.

When last seen, Harold had been institutionalized for nine years; no appreciable change was evident in his behavior or prognosis since admission. Most notable clinically is his drab appearance, apathy and lack of verbal communication; on rare occasions he laughs to himself in an incongruous and peculiar manner. He stopped soiling, which he had begun to do when first admitted, and will now eat by himself. When left alone with pencil and paper, he draws strange religious-like pictures but is unable to verbalize their meaning in a coherent fashion. Drug therapy has had no effect upon his condition; neither had he responded to group therapeutic efforts.

(From T. Millon, Modern Psychopathology: *A Biosocial Approach to Maladaptive Learning and Functioning.* Philadelphia: Saunders, 1969, Used with permission of the author.)

Harold T.'s developmental history was characterized by painful interpersonal experiences from his parents to his siblings and his peers. The characteristic pattern of interpersonal withdrawal appears throughout his life. So, despite the obvious schizotypal veneer, we are able to detect the fine threads of the avoidant personality that serve as a more subtle, yet central, theme in the case of Harold T.

ETIOLOGY AND DEVELOPMENT

The etiology and development of personality disorders seems most reasonably viewed as an interaction of biogenic and environmental factors. The schizotypal disorder is no exception.

The schizotypal personality may be viewed as a syndromal continuation of the less severe schizoid and avoidant personality disorders. As a result, we would expect to find generically the same clinical symptomotology and the same etiological and developmental factors— only in greater intensity or chronicity, that is, with greater severity. From an etiological and developmental perspective, we would expect to see the same basic constellation of determinants in the schizotypal disorder as in the schizoid and avoidant disorders but in greater severity. Therefore, where we find biogenic factors in operation, we would expect to see more severe physiological dysfunction in the schizotypal disorder compared to the schizoid or avoidant disorders. Similarly, where we find environmental factors operative, we would expect to see more severe and persistent environmental turmoil present in the schizotypal disorder compared to the less severe variants (Millon & Millon, 1974).

Because the schizotypal personality disorder manifests itself in two major variants: (1) the schizotypal-schizoid variant and (2) the schizotypal-avoidant variant, we will discuss two major processes of pathogenic development.

First, the passive variant of the schizotypal disorder, here referred to as the schizotypal-schizoid variant, appears to be affected through an interaction of biogenic and environmental factors.

There is a reasonable likelihood that genetic factors conducive to affective and cognitive deficits exist. Many individuals have shown a passive infantile reaction pattern that, in turn, may have initiated a sequence of impoverished infantile stimulation and parental indifference. More biogenically, the possibility exists that these individuals may suffer from hypostimulation deficits or dysfunctions in the ascending reticular activating system (ARAS) or the limbic circuitry. Such dysfunctions in the ARAS or limbic brain would lead to diminished activation in these critical neuroanatomical centers. The results of such problems are likely to be reduced potentials for cognitive and affective input from environmental activity. The result might then be the need for these individuals to rely on autostimulation, fantasy, or even hallucinations.

In their social learning background, there is a reasonable probability of marked stimulus impoverishment during the sensorimotor attachment stage, reflecting either parental neglect or parental indifference. In the case of Jane W., her father was an abusive alcoholic and her mother was clearly "detached" from her. This left Jane frequently neglected and deprived of stimulation. Experiences such as these may lay the groundwork for an underdevelopment of affectivity and a deficit learning of interpersonal attachment behaviors. A family atmosphere of cold formality may serve as such a model for interpersonal detachment as well. We may also see fragmented or amorphous styles of parental communication that may prompt the development of disjointed or fragmented patterns of thought.

Repeated exposures to such conditions may create a web of significant psychopathology. Once established, early styles of behavior and coping may perpetuate and intensify past problems. In the case of Jane W., her past passivity precluded any possibility of social or intellectual development. As a result, she was content simply to live off her family and basically vegetate. When the recommendation for hospitalization was presented to her, she accepted without protest. Thus, her passive attitude and behavior patterns prevented any meaningful form of development or rehabilitation.

Second, the active variant of the schizotypal personality disorder, referred to here as the schizotypal-avoidant variant, seems similarly affected through an interaction of biogenic and environmental factors but to somewhat dissimilar outcome.

The background of schizotypal-avoidant individuals is often marked by evidence of apprehensive or cognitively muddled relatives. Such evidence points to, at least, a possible contribution of genetic factors to the existing pathology. Apprehensive, tense, and fearful infantile patterns are often in evidence among schizotypal-avoidant individuals. Such behavior often precipitates parental tension and derogation, which may serve to aggravate the existing temperament. Biogenically, we would not be surprised to find dysfunction in the ARAS or limbic neuroanatomical centers. However, in the case of the active, schizotypal-avoidant disorder, we would be most likely to see hypersensitivities to external stimulation as opposed to the hyposensitivities to external stimulation that might be encountered in the passive, schizotypal-schizoid disorder. The social-learning histories of the schizotypal-avoidant personalities often show a background of parental deprecation and sibling or peer-group humiliation that typically result in lowered self-esteem and interpersonal distrust. These experiences often begin as early as the sensorimotor-attachment stage of development, thus leading the child to protectively insulate his/her feelings. The persistence of belittling and derogating attitudes through childhood and adolescence leads eventually to self-criticism and self-deprecation. For example, in the case of Harold T., he was subjected to relentless criticism and harassment at home and cruel humiliation at school. By the time he was 13 or 14 years of age, Harold T. had accepted the inevitability of his fate. He referred to himself as stupid and ugly and ultimately he withdrew from all of social contacts in an attempt to protect himself from further pain and humiliation. As Harold T. withdrew further from social contact, he began stimulating himself through the use of fantasy and delusion. The subsequent development of hallucinations would not be a surprise in cases such as Harold T.'s.

Thus, we see the strategies employed to protect against further social ridicule usually only serve to perpetuate and intensify the original problem. Harold T. denied himself opportunities for remedial and growth opportunities when young because he perceived threats where none really were. He also tended to dwell on past ridicule. To protect himself against this cognitive tendency to dwell on painful experiences in the past, Harold T. began to distort and block his own cognitive clarity. This, in itself, fostered self-estrangement. As these self-estranged feelings grew, periodic psychotic episodes began to blend into one another until he deteriorated into a more chronic decompensated state requiring hospitalization.

SELF-PERPETUATION OF THE SCHIZOTYPAL PERSONALITY DISORDER

The prognosis for the schizotypal personality disorder is perhaps the least promising of all the personality disorders discussed in this text. Let us examine why.

The self-perpetuating spiral of deterioration that occurs in the schizotypal disorder is fostered by three major factors: (1) social isolation, (2) dependency training, and (3) self-insulation.

Social Isolation

Individuals who possess the schizotypal disorder are often segregated from social contact. They are kept at home or hospitalized with minimal encouragement to progress on a social basis. Social isolation such as this serves not only to perpetuate the difficulties these individuals have with cognitive organization and social skills, but also serves to worsen the status of both. In many instances, the social isolation seems to stimulate a regression on the part of these individuals. They will tend to lose what cognitive and social abilities they may have had before the isolation. Jane W. was clearly capable of returning to society if she had been provided adequate social support. Without such support, the only option was to keep her institutionalized.

Dependency Training

Often found in conjunction with social isolation is the tendency on the part of those around schizotypal individuals to be overly protective. They will tend to patronize or coddle them. Such overprotection tends to reinforce dependent behavior on the part of the schizotypal. According to Millon (1981), "Prolonged guidance and shielding of this kind may lead to a progressive impoverishment of competencies and self-motivation, and result in a total helplessness. Under such ostensibly 'good' regimens, schizotypals will be reinforced to learn dependency and apathy" (p. 427).

Self-Insulation

Finally, not only through mismanagement and neglect will the schizo-typal disorder be perpetuated, but also through the tendency of these individuals to insulate themselves from outside stimulation. As we described earlier, to protect themselves from painful humiliation, re-jection, or excessive demands, schizotypals have learned to withdraw from reality and disengage themselves from social life. Even though exposed to active social opportunities, most of these individuals will participate only reluctantly. They prefer to keep to themselves—to withdraw. Without active social relationships, these individuals will simply recede further into social isolation, apathy, and dependency. Thus, the disorder is perpetuated.

The case of Harold T. demonstrates a condition in which his abil-ity to insulate himself has served as an effective barrier to rehabilita-tion. His apathy, lack of verbal communication, and habit of drawing strange and religiouslike pictures has effectively insulated him from others and has removed any hope of improvement for almost 10 years.

So, in summary, we see that through social isolation, dependency training, and self-insulation, the schizotypal disorder is perpetuated. Although the motives for socially isolating and overprotecting these individuals are usually good, that is, with the best interests of the patient in mind, the tactics are actually counterproductive for they deprive the patients of the opportunity to develop social skills while reinforcing dependency. The schizotypal's own tendency to insulate himself/herself from social contact serves to exacerbate the disorder even further. Such self-insulation serves to foster and further perpetu-ate the spiral of cognitive and social deterioration that typifies the schizotypal disorder.

ASSOCIATED DISORDERS

Earlier we described the theoretically "pure" schizotypal personality disorder. We then presented the schizotypal personality disorder as it most commonly appears *in vivo*, which is in combination with either the schizoid or the avoidant personality disorders. Having already pre-sented the most frequently encountered mixed schizotypal personality disorders, we will limit the present discussion to the DSM-III, Axis I clinical syndromes that are most commonly associated with the schizotypal personality.

Associated Axis I Disorders

Schizotypal personalities are likely to experience *anxiety disorders,
somatoform disorders,* and *dissociative disorders.* Yet, the major Axis
I associations will be with the psychotic schizophrenic disturbances
that schizotypals find themselves particularly prone to experience, especially under extreme environmental pressure or strain.

Disorganized Schizophrenic Disorders. DSM-III describes the key clinical
features of *disorganized schizophrenia* as frequent incoherence and
flat, inappropriate, or silly affect, all with the absence of systematized
delusions. Schizotypals are particularly subject to experience this psychopathological condition. Under perceived stress that is intense and
enduring, schizotypals may decompensate into such a disorganized
state. At these times, they may seem totally disoriented and confused,
they are unclear as to time and place and even identity. They may
exhibit grimacing, posturing, incoherent neologisms (word salads),
and other peculiar mannerisms. Fragmentary delusions may be
present, but no systematized delusions are apparent during these
states.

Catatonic Schizophrenia. Another schizophrenic disorder that schizotypals may slip into is *catatonic schizophrenia.* Under extreme environmental duress, schizotypals may have a tendency to lose what
minimal cognitive and affective control they may have been maintaining. Once controls are abandoned, random thoughts and emotions are
likely to break loose. There is no apparent reason or logic behind their
behavior at this point. Unable to grasp reality or coordinate thoughts
and feelings, these schizotypals may regress into a helpless catatonic
state.

Residual Schizophrenia. In *residual schizophrenia,* "thoughts and emotions churn close to the surface but are managed and held in check by
the schizotypal patient. However, should these feelings overpower the
patient's tenuous controls, particular disorders are likely to occur,
such as hebephrenic states or brief schizophreniform episodes" (Millon, 1981, p. 416). By discharging these tensions, the schizotypal is
able to release temporarily much of the cognitive and affective turmoil
he/she has been undergoing. However, the prognosis usually anticipates further schizophrenic episodes.

Summary

In this chapter, we have presented the first of the more severe personality disorders—the schizotypal personality disorder. Let us review our main points:

1. The generic clinical picture of the schizotypal personality disorder may be described as follows:
   a. Behaviorally: eccentric to bizarre, for example, socially gauche, odd, or aloof.
   b. Interpersonally: detached to inaccessible, for example, a preference for isolation.
   c. Cognitively: ruminative to deranged, for example, self-absorbed, lost in fantasy.
   d. Affectively: apathetic to deadened (schizoid variation), apprehensive to frantic (avoidant variation).
   e. Self-perception: forlorn to vacant.
   f. Primary defense mechanism: undoing.
   g. Differential personality diagnosis: borderline personality disorder.
2. The schizotypal disorder has two major clinical manifestations within which the disorder presents itself:
   a. The schizotypal-schizoid variation.
   b. The schizotypal-avoidant variation.
3. Developmentally, the schizoid variation is shaped through an interaction of biogenic and environmental factors. Biogenically, dysfunctions in the ARAS or limbic brain seem plausible. Environmentally, a cold and formal familial environment accentuated with fragmented parental communication seems to set the stage for this variation.
4. The development of the avoidant variation may represent a similar biogenic and environmental mix. Yet, environmentally, we would expect to see parental deprecation, sibling rivalry, and perhaps antagonism from peers as primary factors.
5. Factors such as social isolation, overprotection, and self-insulation seem to be perpetuating aspects of this disorder.
6. Common DSM-III, Axis I related disorders include anxiety disorders, somatoform disorders, dissociative disorders, and various schizophrenic disorders.

12

The Borderline Personality Disorder

The borderline personality disorder is best conceived of as a patholog-ical syndromal continuation of the less severe dependent, histrionic, or passive-aggressive personality disorders. As such, we would expect to find many of the same characteristics appearing in the borderline disorder as we find in its three less severe precursors but in greater severity.

CLINICAL PICTURE

According to the DSM-III, the key feature in the borderline personality disorder is its "instability in a variety of areas, including interpersonal behavior, mood, and self-image" (American Psychiatric Association, 1980, p. 321). Although no single factor defines this disorder, its true essence can be captured in the capriciousness of its overt behavior and the lability of its moods. The borderline personality may be thought of as an extreme extension of less severe personality patterns, but it, too, will present a range of diverse symptoms and symptom intensities. Table 12.1 summarizes many of the generic aspects of this personality disorder.

Table 12.1   A Multidimensional Appraisal of the General Borderline Personality Disorder

1. Behavioral appearance: spontaneous to chaotic.
2. Interpersonal conduct: oppositional to mercurial.
3. Cognitive style: inconstant to disorganized.
4. Affective expression: temperamental to volatile.
5. Self-perception: troubled to conflicted.
6. Primary defense mechanism: regression.
7. Differential personality diagnosis: schizotypal personality disorder.

Behavioral Appearance

An important feature in the makeup of the borderline personality disorder is how borderline individuals appear to others. Their appearance ranges from being spontaneous to precipitous in less severe variations to virtually chaotic in more severe variations.

Borderlines often appear impulsive. They display abrupt unexpected and apparently spontaneous outbursts. This characteristic lends an unpredictability to their behavior. These individuals may also exhibit irregular sleep-wake cycles that suggests some form of instability in regulated patterns of arousal. They frequently appear anxious to those who have contact with them.

At times, the borderline may engage in self-damaging behaviors such as recurrent accidents, fights, self-mutilation, or suicidal gestures. Similarly, the borderline may engage in an excessive pattern of self-defeating behaviors such as overeating, gambling, spending sprees, shoplifting, or sexual behavior (American Psychiatric Association, 1980).

Interpersonal Conduct

Interpersonally, borderline individuals behave erratically, this behavior may range from oppositional to paradoxical to mercurial. In general, although borderlines require attention and affection, they still behave impulsively and tend to manipulate others. This interpersonal pattern often elicits rejection rather than the support these individuals need.

Separation anxiety is a prime motivator in the interpersonal behavior of borderline patients. These individuals are exceedingly dependent on others. As a result, they are especially vulnerable to a chronic fear of being separated from, or abandoned by, their interpersonal sources of support.

In sum, borderlines behave in an interpersonally paradoxical manner, although they need affection from others, they behave in unpredictable, contrary, manipulative, and, at times, volatile ways. The more mercurial the behavior of these individuals, the more confusing they appear to others. As a result, they tend to be rebuffed and rejected and to experience intense anxiety on being abandoned.

Cognitive Style

Borderline patients typically experience some degree of conflict over their obvious dependency needs coupled with their occasional flair for self-assertion. As a result, cognitively, these individuals range from being inconsistent to capricious and disorganized.

Their cognitive processes display a rapidly changing pattern of oppositional and antithetical thoughts. Such fluctuation often confuses others and results in a further muddling of cognitive processes as the borderline patient attempts to organize the perceptions and feedback in his/her world.

In their quest for security and support from others, borderlines are likely to have been subjected to isolation, separation, and disapproval. As a result, many have acquired feelings of distrust and hostility towards others. Chronic feelings of emptiness and boredom are also not uncommon.

Affective Expression

Another key feature in the borderline disorder is the marked lability of mood. These patients will range from being temperamental to labile to being highly volatile in their affective displays.

Borderline patients characteristically shift from experiencing normal mood on one hand to inappropriately intense anger and rage and then to excitement or euphoria. These shifts may last several hours or several days, but they invariably end up back at some normal expression of affect as long as the disorder does not deteriorate further.

These individuals, in addition to their vacillating and labile mood, also seem to experience a chronic anxiety. They seem to be anxiously ambivalent about their contradictory needs for dependency, on the one hand, and their inability to trust others and the resultant desire to be self-assertive and self-controlling, on the other hand.

In sum, the affective picture of borderline individuals is a complex one. These patients appear caught in a web of chronic anxiety over fear of being left alone and abandoned and at the same time experience anger towards those on whom they depend for "forcing" them to be dependent. This deeply rooted ambivalence manifests itself in the form of volatile, impulsive outbursts that seem unpredictable and distressing to others.

Self-Perception

Identity disturbances are common in borderline patients. They are uncertain about who they are and where they are headed in life. As a result their self-perceptions tend to range from being troubled to uncertain to contradictory and conflicted.

With so shaky a basis for self-esteem to be built and lacking the ability for self-determination, these patients remain chronically on edge. They are prone to anxiety attacks based on their fear of abandonment and interpersonal isolation. They commonly encounter problems with gender identity, career planning, long-term values, and loyalties (American Psychiatric Association, 1980). As a result of this seemingly chronic state of intrapersonal confusion, they usually lack the strength and stability to withstand environmental adversity. Virtually any intense psychosocial stimulus, therefore, has the potential to initiate a psychotic tirade in these patients.

Primary Defense Mechanism

We have seen the borderline personality disorder as an affectively labile and unstable pattern. The borderline personality is particularly vulnerable to environmental pressure and stress. As one might predict, therefore, the defense mechanism commonly employed by borderline individuals is a mechanism that specifically avoids pressure and strain—regression.

Regression represents a retreat, under stress, to developmentally earlier stages. Unable to cope with the anxiety and stress of adulthood, the individual chooses to revert to an earlier, less mature level of functioning when life was not so complex nor stressful. The signs of regression may begin as simple decreases in impulse control, daydreaming about childlike experiences or desires, or the need to be nurtured. Advanced regressive signs may include thumb sucking, baby talk, incontinence, and womblike posturing.

Differential Personality Diagnosis

According to Millon (1981), "Borderlines typically manifest so many and so wide-ranging a group of associated disorders that differential diagnosis becomes an academic matter of minor clinical significance" (p. 362). Yet, as we have stated in Chapter 11, the borderline personality may be confused with the schizotypal disorder.

It may be of value to mention briefly that the borderline personality disorder is similar to the Axis I class of disorders known as affective disorders. Affective disorders and the borderline personality both reflect disturbances in mood. However, affective disorders have a relatively more abrupt onset than the borderline personality disorder. The borderline personality results from a complex integration of biogenic and environmental factors that have been allowed to intertwine developmentally over the course of years. The transitory nature of the affective disorders must be contrasted to the enduring nature of the borderline personality.

Despite the distinctions noted, "the line between Axis I affective disorders and the Axis II borderline personality is often a blurred one. Diagnostic complications are compounded further in these cases by the fact that episodes of a symptom disorder may gradually blend into a more permanent borderline pattern" (Millon, 1981, p. 363).

CLINICAL VARIATIONS

Having described the generic aspects of the borderline personality disorder, let us now turn our attention to a discussion of the major clinical variations within which the borderline disorder is most likely to manifest itself.

The borderline personality is likely to assume three clinical variations: (1) the borderline-dependent variation, (2) the borderline-histrionic variation, and (3) the borderline-passive-aggressive variation.

Borderline-Dependent Variation

Borderline-dependent individuals tend to be characteristically helpless, impotent, and depressed. They appear to be convinced of their unworthiness and the inevitability of abandonment and desertion. As a result of these beliefs they commonly crumble and sink into a state of perceived hopelessness. These individuals, once hospitalized, often regress to a childlike dependency in what appears to be a total attach-

ment to the nurturing and supportive aspects of the institutional setting. The case of Helen A. represents one example of the borderline-
dependent disorder.

CASE 12.1

The Borderline-Dependent Variation

Helen A., Age 32, Married, No children

This . . . woman decompensated over several years . . . following persistent quarrels
with her exasperated husband, a man she married in her teens who began to spend
weeks away from home in recent years, presumably with another woman. For brief
periods, Helen sought to regain her husband's affections, but these efforts were for
naught, and she became bitterly resentful, guilt-ridden and self-deprecating. Her
erratic mood swings not only increased feelings of psychic disharmony, but further
upset efforts to gain her husband's attention and support. As she persisted in vacillating between gloomy despondency, accusatory attacks and clinging behaviors, more
of her sources of support were withdrawn, thereby intensifying both separation anxieties and the maladaptive character of her behaviors. The next step, that of a regression to invalidism, was especially easy for her since it was consistent with her lifelong
pattern of passive-dependence. Along with it, however, came discomforting feelings
of estrangement and the collapse of all self-controls, as evidence in her ultimate
infantile-like behaviors and the total disorganization of her cognitive processes.

(From T. Millon, *Modern Psychotherapy: A Biosocial Approach to Maladaptive Learning and
Functioning.* Philadelphia: Saunders, 1969, Used with permission of the author.)

On reading the case of Helen A., it is easy to recognize the characteristically labile and impulsive behaviors of the borderline. Yet, almost
as a more subtle central theme, the basic dependent pattern can be
detected in her case presentation.

Borderline-Histrionic Variation

Borderline-histrionics are social invalids. They engage in bizarre behavior and cognitive processes. Despite these handicaps, they frequently make an attempt to be charming, gay, and attractive. Their
lifelong pattern of soliciting attention, approval, and support re-
emerges periodically in displays of irrational conviviality, often accom-
panied by garish clothes and extreme degrees of makeup (in the case of
women patients). During these brief hyperactive periods, there is a
euphoric mood, frenetic conversation, and a craving for interpersonal
interaction. These hyperactive episodes are characteristically short-

lived, and the patient tends to fall once more into a less agitated and more downcast state of being. Even during prolonged somber periods, these patients will exhibit their classic exhibitionistic attention-seeking behavior. The case of Olive W. exemplifies the borderline-histrionic disorder.

CASE 12.2

The Borderline-Histrionic Variation

Olive W., Age 49, Separated, Three children

Olive has been institutionalized three times, the first of which, at the age of 24, was for eight months; the second, at 31, lasted about three years; this third period has continued since she was 37.

Olive was the fifth child, the only girl, of a family of six children. Her early history is unclear, although she "always was known to be a tease" with the boys. Both parents worked at semiskilled jobs throughout Olive's childhood; her older brothers took care of the house. By the time she entered puberty, Olive had had sexual relations with several of her brothers and many of their friends. As she reported it in one of her more lucid periods, she "got lots of gifts" that would not otherwise have been received for "simply having a lot of fun." Apparently, her parents had no knowledge of her exploits, attributing the gifts she received to her vivaciousness and attractiveness.

A crucial turning point occurred when Olive was 15; she became pregnant. Although the pregnancy was aborted, parental attitudes changed, and severe restrictions were placed upon her. Nevertheless, Olive persisted in her seductive activities, and by the time she was 17 she again had become pregnant. At her insistence, she was married to the father of her unborn child. This proved to be a brief and stormy relationship, ending two months after the child's birth. Abandoned by her husband and rejected by her parents, Olive turned immediately to active prostitution as a means of support. In the ensuing six years, she acquired another child and another husband. Olive claims to have "genuinely loved" this man; they had "great times" together, but also many "murderous fights." It was his decision to leave her that resulted in her first, clear, psychotic break.

Following her eight month stay in the hospital, Olive picked up where she left off—prostitute, dance-hall girl and so on. Periods of drunkenness and despondency came more and more frequently, interspersed with shorter periods of gay frivolity and euphoria. For a brief time, one that produced another child, Olive served as a "plaything" for a wealthy ne'er-do-well, traveling about the country having "the time of her life." She fell into a frantic and depressive state, however, when he simply "dumped her" upon hearing that she was pregnant.

Hospitalized again, this time for three years, Olive's personality was beginning to take on more permanent psychotic features. Nevertheless, she was remitted to the home of her father and older brother; here she served as a housemaid and cook. Her children had been placed in foster homes; her mother had died several years earlier.

The death of her father, followed quickly by the marriage of her brother, left Olive alone again. Once more, she returned to her old ways, becoming a bar-girl and prostitute. Repeated beatings by her "admirers," her mental deterioration and her growing physical unattractiveness, all contributed to a pervasive despondency which resulted in her last hospitalization.

For the past several years she has been doing the work of a seamstress in the institution's sewing room; here, in addition to her mending chores, she makes rather garish clothes for herself and others. Every now and then, she spruces herself up, goes to the beauty parlor, puts on an excess of make-up and becomes transformed into a "lovely lady." More characteristically, however, her mood is somber; though responsive and friendly to those who show interest in her, her ideas almost invariably are bizarre and irrational.

(From T. Millon, *Modern Psychotherapy: A Biosocial Approach to Maladaptive Learning and Functioning.* Philadelphia: Saunders, 1969, Used with permission of the author.)

Olive W. presents the characteristic borderline features of such cases. Yet, once again, looking beyond the most obvious emotional and behavioral lability, we are able to see a central theme very different from that seen in Case 12.1. In Case 12.2, we are able to observe the threads of the histrionic personality intertwined in the more obvious borderline characteristics.

Borderline-Passive-Aggressive Variation

Borderline-passive-aggressive individuals seem especially prone to episodes of agitated depression. These disorders can be seen as extensions of their less severe passive-aggressive foundations, that is, chronic complaining, irritability, and discontent usually interwoven with hypochondriacal preoccupations and periodic expressions of guilt and self-condemnation. These patients exhibit a characteristic style of acting out their conflicts and ambivalent feelings, but to a far greater degree and intensity than is found in the less severe passive-aggressive disorders. The common result is extreme vacillations between bitterness and resentment, on the one hand, and self-deprecation, on the other hand. Self-pity and somatic anxieties are extremely common. The case of Ethel S. represents one example of the borderline-passive-aggressive disorder.

CASE 12.3

The Borderline-Passive-Aggressive Variation

Ethel S., Age 53, Married, Three children

Ethel, a markedly ambivalent personality with a prior history of several psychotic breaks, became increasingly irritable, despairing and self-deprecating over a period of one or two months: no clear cause was evident. She paced back and forth, wringing her hands and periodically shouting that God had forsaken her and that she was a "miserable creature, placed on earth to make my family suffer." At times, Ethel would sit on the edge of a chair, nervously chewing her nails, complaining about the disinterest shown her by her children. Then, she would jump up, move about restlessly, voicing irrational fears about her own and her husband's health, claiming that he was a "sick man," sure to die because of her "craziness."

Ethel's agitated and fretful behavior took on a more contentious and hypochondriacal quality in the hospital to which she was brought. During a course of electroconvulsive treatments and a regimen of antidepressant drugs, Ethel's composure gradually returned, and she came home seven weeks following hospitalization.

(From T. Millon, *Modern Psychotherapy: A Biosocial Approach to Maladaptive Learning and Functioning.* Philadelphia: Saunders, 1969, Used with permission of the author.)

Once again, in the case of Ethel S., we find the characteristic borderline expressions of lability of mood, cognition, and behavior. However, what differentiates this syndrome from other borderline variants is the marked passive-aggressive agitation, discontent, irritability, and conflict that seems to serve as a subtle central theme.

ETIOLOGY AND DEVELOPMENT

Having reviewed the clinical picture of the borderline personality disorder, we have found the essential features of the disorder to be the general instability of cognitive, affective, and interpersonal and intrapersonal behavior. Yet, no single symptom or feature appears to be consistently present. Let us now examine the processes by which the borderline personality disorder is likely to develop. According to Millon (1981):

It is the author's contention that we will find the same complex of determinants in the borderline syndrome as we do in its less severe variants: the dependent, histrionic, . . . and passive-aggressive personalities. The primary differences between them are the intensity, frequency, timing, and persistence of a host of potentially pathogenic factors. Those who function at the borderline level may begin with less adequate constitutional equipment or be subjected to a series of more adverse early experiences. As a consequence of their more troublesome histories, they either fail to develop an adequate coping style in the first place or decompensate slowly under the weight of repeated and unrelieved difficulties. It is the author's view that the most borderline cases progress sequentially through a more adaptive or higher level of functioning before deteriorating to the advanced dysfunctional state. Some patients, however, notably childhood variants, never appear to "get off the ground" and give evidence of a borderline pattern from their earliest years (pp. 363–364).

We will now describe the developmental history of the borderline personality disorder by subdividing the presentation into three major subtypes of the borderline disorder: (1) the borderline-dependent, (2) the borderline-histrionic, and (3) the borderline-passive-aggressive personality disorders.

First, the biogenic backgrounds of the borderline-dependent personalities typically include disproportionately high numbers of bland and unenergetic relatives. As children, these individuals often manifest a sad, almost pitiful, gentility. This infantile pattern often evokes parental warmth and overprotection. Such influences in the neuropsychological development process are likely to result in very attached and dependent children who fail to develop a sense of autonomy.

The central social-learning influence appears to be parental overprotection that leads to an unusually strong attachment to, and dependency on, a single caregiver. The perpetuation of overprotection throughout childhood fosters a lack of development of autonomous behaviors and a self-image of incompetence and inadequacy. By allowing themselves to become dependent on others, these individuals restrict their opportunities to learn skills for themselves and to establish any sense of social independence and self-efficacy.

In contrast to the less severe dependent personalities who stabilize at milder levels of psychopathology, the borderline-dependents often find themselves rebuffed by those on whom they have become dependent. Intense separation anxiety and trauma from rejection seem to fuel the deterioration process that leads to the borderline-dependent condition.

Second, in contrast to the borderline-dependents who possess a family history of low energy levels, the borderline-histrionic often possesses a family history characterized by high autonomic reactivity. As children, these individuals often exhibit hyperresponsiveness in early childhood. The result is often that these children are exposed to high levels of stimulation. Such stimulation, from a neuropsychological perspective, is likely to result in pronounced stimulus-seeking behavior on the part of the child. In effect, we might expect to see such children develop a "need" for stimulation.

From a learning perspective, parental control by contingent and variable ratio reinforcement may also have occurred. As a result, these children are likely to feel personally competent and accepted *only* if their behavior is explicitly approved of by others. Many of these children may have been exposed to histrionic parental models as well. Thus, we see the borderline-histrionic is likely to see his/her attempts at attention-seeking, approval-seeking behavior stifled. As they become unable to sustain a consistent external source of nurturing and their ability to elicit attention and support wanes, these individuals are likely to experience the cyclic mood swings that are characteristic of borderline-histrionic functioning. As the decompensation process becomes more pronounced, their mood swings become more dramatic and extended. Ultimately one begins to expect a pervasive decompensation that typifies the borderline-histrionic.

Third, borderline-passive-aggressive individuals appear to suffer from parental inconsistency during their upbringing. As children these individuals were likely to have been exposed to vacillations between extreme affection (often guilt laden), on the one hand, and verbal or physical abuse on the other hand. Many of these children were products of schismatic families. In addition to the emotional consequences of these pathogenic conditions, the parental roles these individuals observed as children were likely to have served as models for learning the erratic, vacillating, passive-aggressive behavior they display as adults.

The major difference between the milder passive-aggressive disorder and the more severe borderline-passive-aggressive disorder may be that, in the more severe cases, personality deterioration occurred as a result of prolonged and pathogenically extended conflicts and disappointments, combined with consistently ineffective coping. Rarely can borderline-passive-aggressive patients sustain a prolonged harmonious interpersonal relationship. As a result of their erratic, negative, and moody behavior, they alienate the very sources of attention, affection, and support they so desparately need. Obviously, the problem disorder is then intensified.

As borderline-passive-aggressives deteriorate further, they can be expected to exhibit irrational and sometimes violent outbursts. It is not uncommon, however, to see these outbursts interspersed with bizarre episodes in which these patients appear remorseful and guilt ridden. During such periods as these, the patients will likely condemn their own outrageous behavior and ask for forgiveness.

If the deterioration continues, cyclic swings of extreme behavior become more frequent and chronic; psychotic vacillations may then replace reality.

SELF-PERPETUATION OF THE BORDERLINE PERSONALITY DISORDERS

It is difficult to understand what reinforcements are gained through the prolongation of the borderline personality disorder. Helplessness, depression, resentfulness, stubbornness, hostile outbursts, and guilt seem clearly self-destructive. On the one hand, genuine emotions such as these do, indeed, elicit attention and approval. Furthermore, they do release tensions and they do avoid permanent rejection when they are followed by genuine derogation and guilt, as in the case of this disorder and its less severe variants. Yet, prolonged and intense use of these tools ultimately serve to erode the borderline's search for happiness. So, although these strategies are useful for short-term gains, they are health eroding and self-defeating in the long run.

A common tactic used by borderlines to seek relief, when it becomes obvious other coping mechanisms are failing, is reversal. Reversal refers to the tendency to reverse previous roles totally. "Thus, when these patients exaggerate or intensify their habitual style of soliciting their needs, and fail to gain what they sought, they may renunciate their characteristic coping style, even for a brief period. For example, the borderline-dependents, rather than acting weak and submissive, will reverse their more typical behaviors and assert themselves, becoming gay and frivolous or demanding and aggressive" (Millon, 1981, p. 368). By using reversal, these patients attempt a new and unusual coping tactic designed to provide them what their older, more commonly used tactics failed to achieve.

The use of reversal only seems to perpetuate the problem. The use of new and unusual coping tactics distances these patients from their more accustomed tactics and predictable outcome. To maintain the use of such tactics requires considerable energy on the part of these patients as well. Soon, their energy begins to run out without having achieved the ends desired. "As these 'last ditch' means of coping prove self-defeating, the patients' tensions and depressions mount beyond tolerable limits and they may begin to lose control. Psychotic behaviors may burst forth and discharge a torrential stream of irrational emotions" (Millon, 1981, p. 369). The reactions on the parts of others, combined with the sense of self-impotence, perpetuates and intensifies the borderline condition.

ASSOCIATED DISORDERS

Because we have already discussed the borderline personality disorder as it most commonly combines with other personality disorders, we will limit our discussion here to the DSM-III, Axis I clinical syndromes with which the borderline personality disorder is most commonly associated.

Associated Axis I Disorders

The borderline personality disorder has been referred to as the unstable pattern. It has been described in such a manner because of its affective lability. Such lability makes the borderline highly prone to a host of Axis I syndromes. Let us briefly describe some of the more commonly encountered Axis I syndromes associated with the borderline personality disorder.

Anxiety Disorders. The affective instability of borderline personalities makes them vulnerable to brief eruptions of uncontrollable emotion. These emotional eruptions are often an affective overlay on prolonged *generalized anxiety.* For varied reasons related to their inability to cope effectively with environmental pressure, borderlines often experience this diffuse, generalized apprehension. As this condition persists, the tenuous emotional controls of the borderlines are eroded. As a result, we would expect to see borderlines subject not only to generalized anxiety, but to a *panic disorder* as well. In extreme cases, the borderline's emotional controls may completely disintegrate and he/she is overwhelmed by a wild rush of irrational and chaotic behavior as would be characteristic of *brief psychotic episodes.*

Dissociative Disorders. Borderline personalities appear to have a propensity to display brief but highly charged outbursts during *psychogenic fugue* states. These fugue states usually represent the ventiliation of repressed resentments or frustrations occurring most commonly when these patients have felt overwhelmed, confused, trapped, or generally out of control.

Affective Disorders. Borderline personalities are known for their propensity to express impulsively anger and frustration through brief but hostile outbursts. The remainder of the time, the individuals expend considerable effort attempting to control these negative feelings for fear others will reject them.

A major hostility control mechanism employed by these individuals is to turn the feelings inward into *hypochondriacal disorders* and *depressive episodes.* These symptoms are often effective in eliciting the aid and support of others. Soon, however, those who have turned to assist these borderlines become exasperated at their own ineffectiveness and the passive resistance they often meet from the patients themselves.

If these borderline patients are unsuccessful at eliciting support from those around them, they often experience more severe depression. It is common to see guilt, self-derogation, and self-disparagement being expressed by these borderline patients. Feelings of emptiness, boredom, and worthlessness are also voiced. Not infrequently, this sadness and sorrowful condition is successful in enlisting the aid, nurture, and support of others. According to Millon (1981), "As in other symptom disorders, this is a subtle and indirect means of venting hidden resentment and anger. Helplessness and self-destructive acts make others feel guilty and burden them with extra responsibilities and woes" (p. 355).

In general, we find the affective characteristics of borderline patients erratic and varied according to the patient's unique learning histories and vulnerabilities. To summarize these erratic and varied displays, it may be suggested that they consist primarily of depression intertwined with hostility.

Schizoaffective Disorder. Should the borderline patient ultimately be unable to elicit the support and nurture from others that he/she usually seeks, major decompensation processes are likely to follow. These patients are prone to decompensate into schizoaffective states. They appear to behave in a bizarre manner, often showing regressive tendencies. Yet, underlying these symptoms, there will likely be a desire for approval and nurturance—the same needs that motivated the patient's behavior before such gross decompensation.

Summary

In this chapter, we have presented the borderline personality disorder. Let us review our main points:

1. The generic clinical picture of the borderline personality disorder may be summarized as follows:
   a. Behaviorally: spontaneous to chaotic, unpredictable.
   b. Interpersonally: oppositional to mercurial, changeable, volatile.
   c. Cognitively: inconstant to disorganized, inconsistent, dysfunctional.
   d. Affectively: temperamental to volatile, highly labile.
   e. Self-perception: ranges from troubled to conflicted, confused.
   f. Primary defense mechanism: regression.
   g. Differential personality diagnosis: schizotypal personality disorder.
2. The borderline personality disorder has three major clinical manifestations:
   a. The borderline-dependent variation.

b. The borderline-histrionic variation.

c. The borderline-passive-aggressive variation.

All of these variations may be best conceived of as syndromal extensions of the three less severe personalities, respectively.

3. Developmentally, the dependent variation of the borderline disorder appears to be shaped by parental overprotection, which later sets the stage for rejection by those on whom these patients have come to rely.

4. The histrionic variation of the borderline disorder appears to be shaped by inconsistent variable ratio reinforcement patterns that leave these individuals continually "performing" in order to secure support, attention, and nurturance.

5. The passive-aggressive variation appears to be shaped through environmental, especially parental, inconsistency.

6. The borderline disorder is self-perpetuated through the positively reinforcing release of inner tensions as well as the utilization of self-defeating coping strategies, for example, reversal.

7. Common DSM-III, Axis I related disorders include anxiety disorders, dissociative disorders, affective disorders as well as schizoaffective states.

13

The Paranoid Personality Disorder

The final personality disorder to be addressed in our text is the paranoid personality. This personality disorder is best conceived of as a pathological syndromal continuation of the less severe narcissistic, antisocial, or compulsive personality disorders. As a result, we would expect to find many of the same characteristics appearing in the paranoid personality disorder as we find in its three respective precursors but in greater severity.

CLINICAL PICTURE

According to the DSM-III, the key feature of the paranoid personality disorder is "a pervasive and unwarranted suspiciousness and mistrust of people, hypersensitivity, and restricted affectivity not due to another mental disorder, such as Schizophrenia, or a Paranoid Disorder" (American Psychiatric Association, 1980, p. 307). So, we see the most prominent feature of this personality disorder is a mistrust of others combined with a desire to remain free of close personal relationships in which there is a chance of losing power or self-determination and self-control.

Characteristically, paranoid individuals are suspicious, resentful, and hostile. They tend to respond with anger to anything that even

**Table 13.1   A Multidimensional Appraisal of the Generic Paranoid
Personality Disorder**

1. Behavioral appearance: wary to vigilant.
2. Interpersonal conduct: quarrelsome to acrimonious.
3. Cognitive style: incredulous to conspirative.
4. Affective expression: sullen to fractious.
5. Self-perception: formidable to embittered.
6. Primary defense mechanism: projection.
7. Differential personality diagnosis: antisocial personality disorder.

approaches ridicule, deception, deprecation, or betrayal. This readiness to perceive deceit and aggression precipitates innumerable intrapersonal and interpersonal difficulties. Although the paranoid personality disorder is best conceived as an extreme extension of less severe
disorders, it, too, will present a range of diverse symptoms and symptom intensities. The generic aspects of the paranoid personality disorder are summarized in Table 13.1. Let us review these generic components before going on to examine the three major clinical variations of
the paranoid personality disorder.

Behavioral Appearance

Paranoid individuals appear to be constantly on guard, mobilized and
ready for any emergency or perceived threat. Therefore, depending on
the severity of the disorder, paranoids appear to range from being wary
and defensive to vigilant.

Whether these individuals are faced with real dangers or not, they
maintain a steady state of preparedness. They seem ever-vigilant
against the possibility of attack and derogation.

Paranoid individuals detest being dependent, not only because it
signifies weakness and inferiority, but also because these individuals
are unable to trust anyone. As a result, they are tenaciously resistant
to sources of external influence and control.

Interpersonal Conduct

Paranoid individuals are interpersonally provocative, quarrelsome,
abrasive, and fractious. They precipitate exasperation and anger in
others by continually testing loyalties and searching for hidden mean-
ings and hidden motives. For this reason, we see the paranoid as

ranging interpersonally from quarrelsome and provocative to acrimonious.

Beneath a surface of interpersonal mistrust and defensiveness lies a current of deep resentment towards others who have made it. To many paranoids, most people who are successful have attained that status unjustly. Thus, these paranoids are likely to feel mistreated, overlooked, and generally bitter at having been slighted.

Paranoids tend to be interpersonally hypersensitive. They may have a tendency to be easily offended, to catastrophize, that is, to make mountains out of molehills, and they may have a tendency to be vindictive for perceived transgressions against them.

In sum, the interpersonally suspicious nature of the paranoid is compounded by their quarrelsome disposition and their absolute disdain for interpersonal dependency.

Cognitive Style

Cognitively, paranoid individuals range from being incredulous to suspicious to conspirative. These persons are skeptical, cynical, and mistrustful. Their tendency is to misconstrue innocuous events as signifying some form of criticism or derogation. This incredulous nature may become conspirative in severe forms of this disorder. In other words, they may exhibit tendencies to be secretive, questioning, and irrationally concerned with the motives of others, and they may possess delusions of persecution.

This basic lack of trust colors the paranoid's entire world. It effects perceptions, cognitions, and memories. So powerful are these mistrusting preconceptions that they lead paranoid individuals to disregard any evidence to the contrary. Delusions are a natural outgrowth of the paranoid personality disorder. Insisting on retaining independence, paranoids isolate themselves from others and become unwilling to share the perspectives and attitudes of others. Left alone, the paranoid may naturally evolve a delusional cognitive structure.

Affective Expression

Affectively, paranoids express themselves in a manner that may range from sullen to irascible to fractious. These individuals are characteristically cold, sullen, humorless, and quick to react angrily.

The anxiety experienced by paranoids is generally related to the fear of being used or of losing perceived control over their lives. Ever-fearful of being dominated, paranoid individuals constantly scan the horizon for signs of treachery. This process leaves them hypersensitive, on edge, and in a chronic state of tension, despite attempts to appear unemotional and fully in control.

Self-Perception

Unable to accept their own faults and weaknesses, paranoids maintain their self-esteem by attributing their shortcomings to others. They repudiate their own shortcomings and failures while ascribing them to someone else through a process of projection. They possess a talent for spotting even the most subtle deficiencies in others. Many paranoids seem chronically envious, hostile, and irascible. For these reasons we see the paranoid's self-perception as ranging from formidable to unviolable and embittered.

Primary Defense Mechanism

The paranoid personality disorder, when fully developed, is clearly one of the most unpleasant and recalcitrant personality disorders with which to deal. We have seen that it can be characterized by suspiciousness, hostility, defensive vigilance, and impulsive aggressive acts. The paranoid individual will frequently employ *projection* as a defense mechanism.

Projection involves two processes: first, the individual will repress or disown undesirable traits and motives that he/she may possess; second, the individual will then attribute those same traits or motives to others. Projection allows individuals to ventilate as well as disclaim objectionable, undesirable behavior. Furthermore, by attributing hostile motives to others paranoids may claim the right to persecute others. So, projection may not only serve as a tool to disown and ventilate undesirable behaviors, but it may also serve as a tool to justify aggression or retaliation towards others. Such a mechanism would obviously serve the already suspicious and defensive paranoid individual extremely well.

Differential Personality Diagnosis

As the two disorders sometimes combine, the paranoid personality disorder may be confused with another personality pattern—the antisocial personality disorder.

As we described in Chapter, the paranoid personality disorder may be considered a more extreme syndromal elaboration of the antisocial personality. The paranoid exhibits far fewer emotional controls than the antisocial individual. As a result, paranoid individuals are more prone to irrational behavior, especially wild, chaotic outbursts. Finally, although both paranoids and antisocials are vigilant and mistrusting, paranoids are far more so, expecting to be deceived at every turn.

Brief mention should be made of the difference between the paranoid personality disorder and the Axis I categories *paranoid disorders* and *schizophrenic disorder, paranoid type.* The Axis I paranoid categories are distinguished from the Axis II paranoid personality disorder by the presence of persistent psychotic symptoms such as delusions and hallucinations. In the case of the paranoid personality disorder, delusions and hallucinations are *not* intrinsic to this personality variant. Furthermore, the paranoid personality represents an ingrained and enduring characterological pattern that, in most cases, has a significant developmental history. The Axis I paranoid categories represent, for the most part, rather abruptly occurring symptomatology that is less persistent than the symptomatology found in those with the personality disorder. Of course, as described earlier, the paranoid personality may decompensate. As this process occurs, the lines of distinction between Axis I and Axis II begin to fade.

CLINICAL VARIATIONS

Having described the prototypal aspects of the paranoid personality disorder, let us now turn our attention to a discussion of the major clinical variations of the paranoid personality.

The paranoid personality disorder is likely to manifest itself in the form of three clinical variations: (1) the paranoid-narcissistic variation, (2) the paranoid-antisocial variation, and (3) the paranoid-compulsive variation.

Paranoid-Narcissistic Variation

Paranoid-narcissistic individuals are similar to their less severe counterparts, the narcissistic personalities. They seek to retain their admirable self-image. They behave in a pretentious manner, and they are naively self-confident. Yet, the paranoid-narcissistic individual, despite the pompous veneer, has had his/her delusions of grandeur challenged and frequently shattered. This often proves devastating to these individuals. Not only must they now counter their apparent failures, but they must also somehow cope with the humiliation of apparent failures. The generic paranoid pattern may be seen as one set of behaviors used to salvage their threatened self-esteem. The case of Charles W. describes one variation of the paranoid-narcissist.

CASE 13.1

The Paranoid-Narcissistic Variation

Charles W., Age 36, Married, No Children

Charles, an only child of poorly educated parents, had been recognized as a "child genius" in early school years. He received a Ph.D. degree at 24, and subsequently held several responsible positions as a research physicist in an industrial firm.

His haughty arrogance and narcissism often resulted in conflicts with his superiors; it was felt that he spent too much time working on his own "harebrained" schemes and not enough on company projects. Charles increasingly was assigned to jobs of lesser importance than that to which he was accustomed. He began to feel, not unjustly, that both his superiors and his subordinates were "making fun of him" and not taking him seriously. To remedy this attack upon his status, Charles began to work on a scheme that would "revolutionize the industry," a new thermodynamic principle which, when applied to his company's major product, would prove extremely efficient and economical. After several months of what was conceded by others as "brilliant thinking," he presented his plans to the company president. Brilliant though it was, the plan overlooked certain obvious simple facts of logic and economy.

Upon learning of its rejection, Charles withdrew to his home where he became obsessed with "new ideas," proposing them in intricate schematics and formulas to a number of government officials and industrialists. These resulted in new rebuffs which led to further efforts at self-inflation. It was not long thereafter that he lost all semblance of reality and control; for a brief period, he convinced himself of the grandiose delusion that he was Albert Einstein.

(From T. Millon, *Modern Psychopathology: A Biosocial Approach to Maladaptive Learning and Functioning*. Philadelphia: Saunders, 1969, Used with permission of the author.)

The case of Charles W. shows us an example of a basically arrogant narcissistic pattern that deteriorated into a paranoid personality disorder under repeated rejections and failures.

Paranoid-Antisocial Variation

Paranoid-antisocial personalities exhibit a more hostile appearance than their narcissistic counterparts. Usually because of repeated humiliations and failures, these individuals drift into patterns of suspiciousness and persecution. The case of Joseph M. is one such example.

CASE 13.2

The Paranoid-Antisocial Variation

Joseph M., Age 52, Separated, Four Children

Joseph lived in foster homes since the age of 3 months; at 8 years of age he settled with one family, remaining there until he was 15, when he left to go on his own. Eventually enlisting in the Navy, he was given a medical discharge on psychiatric grounds, after three years of service.

As a child, Joseph was known to be a "bully"; he was heavy, muscular, burly in build, had an inexhaustible supply of energy and prided himself on his physical strength and endurance. Though quite intelligent, Joseph was constantly in trouble at school, teasing other children, resisting the directives of teachers and walking out of class whenever he pleased.

Joseph was the foster son of a manager of a coal mine, and spoke with great pride of his capacity, at the age of 12, to outproduce most of the experienced miners. When he was 14, his foster mother died, leaving Joseph alone to take care of himself; his foster father, who lived periodically with a mistress, rarely came home. Joseph worked at the mine and quarreled bitterly with his father for a "fair" wage; when he was 15, he got into one of his "regular fights" with his father and beat him so severely that the man was hospitalized for a month. After this event, Joseph left his home town, wandered aimlessly for two years and enlisted in the Navy. In the service, Joseph drank to excess, "flew off the handle at the drop of a hat" and spent an inordinate amount of time in the brig. The persistence of this behavior and the apparent bizarre features which characterized some of these episodes resulted in his discharge.

For several years thereafter, Joseph appeared to make a reasonable life adjustment. He married, had four sons and started a small trash collecting business. Drinking was entirely eliminated, though Joseph remained a "hot-headed" fellow who happily "took on all comers" to prove his strength.

Greater success—and difficulty—followed when Joseph "took up" with a teenage girl; this younger woman was quite attractive and built up Joseph's self-image. More importantly, she bore him, illegitimately, what his own wife failed to—a little girl. With mistress and child in hand, he left his legal family, moving some 600 miles to a new city where he "started life again." Within three years, Joseph founded a successful contracting company and became moderately wealthy; at 36, he ran for a local political office, which he won.

Trouble began brewing immediately thereafter. Joseph was unable to compromise in the give-and-take of politics; he insisted at public meetings, to the point of near violence, that his obviously impractical and grandiose plans be adopted. After many outbursts, one of which culminated in the assault of a fellow official, Joseph was asked to resign from office, which he refused to do. To assure his resignation, as he put it, "They dredged up all the dirt they could get to get rid of me"; this included his Navy psychiatric discharge, his abandonment of his legal family, his illicit "marriage," illegitimate child and so on. The final collapse of his world came when his present "wife," in whose name alone his business was registered, rejected him, sold the company and kept all of the proceeds.

Joseph became physically violent following these events, and was taken to a state institution. Here, his well-justified feelings of persecution were elaborated until they lost all semblance of reality. Joseph remained hospitalized for two years during which time he managed gradually to reorient himself, although still retaining his basic, aggressive paranoid pattern. Upon remission, he returned to his legal family, working periodically as a driver of heavy contracting equipment. He began drinking again and got involved in repeated fist fights in local bars. When Joseph came home after a night's drinking, he frequently attempted to assault his wife. To his dismay, his teen-age sons would come to their mother's defense; Joseph invariably was the loser in these battles.

After living with his family for four years, Joseph disappeared, unheard from for about 18 months. Apparently, he had lived alone in a metropolitan city some 90 miles from his home; the family learned of his whereabouts when he was picked up for vagrancy. After he was bailed out, it was clear that Joseph was a beaten and destitute man. He returned to the state hospital where he has since remained. Although subdued and generally cooperative, Joseph is still suspicious, tends to be easily affronted and occasionally flares up in a hostile outburst. He ruminates to himself all day, occasionally speaking in an angry voice to hallucinated images.

(From T. Millon, *Modern Psychopathology: A Biosocial Approach to Maladaptive Learning and Functioning.* Philadelphia: Saunders, 1969, Used with permission of the author.)

Paranoid-Compulsive Variation

Paranoid-compulsive individuals represent ambivalent individuals who have chosen to abandon their dependency roles and assert themselves. In this process, these individuals begin to discharge the feelings of tension and hostility that were ubiquitous for so long. Yet they retain their basic rigidity and perfectionism. In this process they typically go to pathological extremes. The case of Martin is a brief example of this process.

CASE 13.3

The Paranoid-Compulsive Variation

Martin, Age 50, Married, No Children

This passive-ambivalent paranoid, although known as a harsh, perfectionistic and overly legalistic probation officer, managed to maintain a moderately acceptable veneer of control and propriety in his relationships with his neighbors. In recent years, however, he became convinced that youngsters who "smoked pot" were part of a

"Communist plot to undo this great country." Whenever a "hippie" was brought to court on any charge, he would "make it his business to talk to the judge" about the plot, and attempt to ensure that he would impose a "proper jail sentence." After repeated failures to persuade the judge to see things his way, he began a personal campaign in the community to impeach the judge and to place "all hippies in a federal jail."

(From T. Millon, *Modern Psychopathology: A Biosocial Approach to Maladaptive Learning and Functioning.* Philadelphia: Saunders, 1969, Used with permission of the author.)

ETIOLOGY AND DEVELOPMENT

Having reviewed the clinical picture of the paranoid personality disorder, we see the essential features to be a pervasive suspiciousness and mistrust of others, a general hypersensitivity, and restricted, dysfunctional affect.

According to the present theory, we would expect to find the same constellation of determinants in the paranoid disorder as we do in its less severe variants: the narcissistic, antisocial, and compulsive personality disorders.

We will now describe the developmental history of the paranoid personality disorder by subdividing the presentation into the three major subtypes of the disorder: the paranoid-narcissistic, the paranoid-antisocial, and the paranoid-compulsive.

First, parental overevaluation and indulgence is the common pattern of parental behavior in the case of the paranoid-narcissist variant of the paranoid disorder. As a result, these children fail to learn interpersonal responsibility. They rarely seem to consider the rights, feelings, or welfare of others. Generally speaking, they are deficient in social cooperation and interpersonal skill.

The lack of parental control not only inhibits social development and interpersonal cooperation, but seems to give rise to cognitive tendencies towards fantasy. Many of these individuals, through excessive self-reinforcement, tend to weave glorious fantasies concerning their own achievements and power. Most of them, however, lack true skill or innate ability to support their illusions and aspirations.

Once outside the domestic environment, these individuals are perceived as egotistical and selfish. Compared to their less severe variant (the narcissistic personality), paranoid-narcissists are far more grandiose and blatantly selfish. As a result, they are more often humiliated and rejected by their peers. Often the outcome is the tendency of these individuals to withdraw interpersonally and to seek refuge intrapersonally, that is, within a world of fantasy. Thus, we see interpersonal rebuff followed by increased isolation and fantasy.

As the isolation and fantasy increase, a more clear-cut propensity for paranoia emerges. These individuals begin to suspect that others are out to harm them or to exploit them. As fantasy replaces reality and as their delusions lead them further into fantasy, the decompensation process accelerates until hospitalization often becomes the only option available to these patients.

Second, the paranoid-antisocial variant of the paranoid disorder may be based on biogenic factors. This is suggested by the frequent presence among family members of high levels of activation and high-energy temperaments. Along these lines, many of these patients exhibited a vigorous and aggressive obtrusiveness as children, as in the case of Joseph M.

Most paranoid-antisocials have been exposed to harsh parental treatment. As a result, they acquire a deep mistrust of others, a desire for self-determination and a confident sense of competence and autonomy. With this as a base, they frequently reject parental controls and social controls at the same time. Instead, they develop an impulsive, aggressive, and hedonistic style of life.

The anticipation of attack from others combined with arrogance tends to provoke tensions with others on an interpersonal basis. Differing from the less severe antisocial personality, the paranoid-antisocial variant of this paranoid disorder decompensates into a state of irrational persecutory and vindictive delusions. Unable to cope directly with the perceived threats that surround them, tensions increase and tend either to erupt into overt hostility or into further delusional fantasy.

Unrelieved stress may prompt a marked withdrawal from social and reality contact. Bizarre delusions and hallucinations may then emerge in severely decompensated cases. Again, hospitalization is often the only option for treatment at this point.

Third, with the exception of divergency in coping aims, the developmental histories of the compulsive and the paranoid-compulsive are essentially alike. Refer to Chapter 8 for a review. The paranoid-compulsive differs from its less severe variant, the basic compulsive disorder, in that the former is far more rigid and tends to decompensate into delusions marked by irrationally rigid, inflexible behavior.

SELF-PERPETUATION OF THE PARANOID PERSONALITY DISORDER

By ascribing slanderous and malevolent attitudes and motives to others, paranoid individuals are likely to stay in a defensive or vindictive posture the majority of the time. Such behavior, although it may reduce the chances of being harmed by the intentional malevolent actions of others, it also alienates other individuals who intend no harm. After awhile, those persons alienated are likely to experience feelings of exasperation and even anger directed towards the paranoid person. In some cases, these feelings may actually lead to malevolent motives. So, we see a self-fulfilling prophecy emerging from the paranoid pattern of behavior. In other words, as they expect others to be, that is, hostile and malevolent, so they often become.

The paranoid's characteristic attitudes of independence and self-confidence are largely spurious. These individuals maintain their illusions of superiority by rigid self-conviction and exaggeration. Time and time again, their competencies are shown to be minimal or defective, and they are made to look foolish. This leads them to become even more defensive and hostile. They look to redeem themselves and to punish those responsible for their embarrassment. Thus, to regain a belief in their superiority or invincibility, they are driven to extremely pathological measures. The most common measure is to blame some alien being or force for their dilemmas. They deny the possibility that their failures are self-determined or, at least, that they contributed to by their own behaviors. As their dilemmas increase in severity, paranoids ascribe their failures to more complex and powerful forces. For example, it is not uncommon to see delusions of persecution involving intricate multinational conspiracies, the use of "secret" technologies, and even beings from other worlds. One delusion feeds into another, unchecked by the controls of reality. As these paranoid individuals continue to fail, their delusions increase. Unable to see any self-contributing components to their failures, these individuals continue to blame more frequent and complex delusional entities. Thus, the disorder goes on.

ASSOCIATED DISORDERS

In the beginning of this chapter, we described the paranoid personality in its theoretically "pure" form. Following that description, we presented the paranoid personality disorder as it most commonly appears among actual patient populations, that is, in combination with either the narcissistic, antisocial, or compulsive personalities. Because we have already described the most frequently encountered mixed paranoid personality disorders, we will restrict our discussion of associated disorders to the DSM-III, Axis I clinical syndromes that are most commonly found to emerge from, or at least be correlated with, the paranoid personality disorder.

Associated Axis I Disorders

The paranoid personality is considered by the authors as being a more severe personality disorder when compared to the first eight personality disorders described in this text. We are, therefore, likely to observe the emergence of a host of more severe Axis I clinical syndromes should the paranoid personality begin to deteriorate under extreme duress.

Anxiety Disorders. Although not as severe as the disorders to be described later in this section, the paranoid personality is likely to experience *generalized anxiety.* At first, this anxiety may manifest itself in the form of diffuse apprehensions of the unknown. These patients may complain of their inability to concentrate or to enjoy previously enjoyable activities. Later, these symptoms may progress to a preoccupation with the experienced anxiety and its physical symptoms. Finally, this preoccupation becomes an obsession that threatens ultimately to overwhelm these individuals. The expected result would be acute anxiety attacks or *panic disorder* as the last remnants of self-control are exhausted.

Affective Disorders. Paranoids, especially those containing a substantial narcissistic component, may develop a self-exalted and pompous variant of *manic disorder.* Mania is a condition in which "the predominant mood is either elevated, expansive, or irritable . . ." (American Psychiatric Association, 1980, p. 206). Furthermore, there will be symptoms, including hyperactivity, rapid speech, inflated self-concept, racing of thoughts, and an inability easily to fall asleep. These symptoms, then, are likely to emerge intertwined with pompous, egocentric behaviors during situations in which these individuals are faced with realities that confront or contradict their illusions of superiority. We see, then, that when confronted with extreme pressure or failure, the paranoid may engage in behavior designed to reestablish, or reconfirm, his/her illusion of superiority; and the manner in which this is attempted may approach manic intensity.

Paranoid Disorders. Perhaps the most readily anticipated outcome from deterioration of the paranoid personality disorder is one or more aspects of the Axis I *paranoid disorders.* Acute paranoid episodes may result from the shock of an unanticipated failure or perceived betrayal. Paranoid delusions may also result from such occurrences. During episodes such as these, previously repressed resentments may overwhelm the individual's cognitive and emotional self-controls and emerge as delusional beliefs and dramatic, impulsive ventilations of overt behavior. For the most part, however, the deterioration from paranoid personality to Axis I paranoid disorder is a subtle one. It is the predominant nature of these individuals to remain secretive, withdrawing, irritable and persistently suspicious.

Schizophrenic Disorders. Earlier, we described the tendency of the paranoid-narcissist to display buoyant and even manic hyperactivity. In contrast, we would expect to find the paranoid with antisocial components deteriorate into varied *schizophrenic disorders*, given unmanageable environmental events. More specifically, we would expect to find paranoid-antisocials deteriorate into *excited catatonic schizophrenic episodes*. The aggressive, antisocial characteristics when combined with the paranoid symptoms tend to unleash themselves as aggressive and abusive and as threatening verbal and overt behavioral expressions. It is this quality of irrational belligerence and fury that distinguishes these paranoids from others.

On the other hand, the paranoid when combined with the compulsive personality deteriorates in a different manner. We would expect to see the paranoid-compulsive deteriorate into a *catatonic stupor*. The "normal" rigidity and restraint of the compulsive combines with the suspicious qualities of the paranoid to create an individual who, under extreme duress, cognitively, emotionally, and physically withdraws. Although typically unexpressive, the grimaces and postures that are displayed by these patients may well be a symbolic way of communicating the aggressive urges that exist within.

Summary

This chapter has addressed the paranoid personality disorder. Several key points have been made regarding this disorder, let us review them at this time:
1. The generic clinical picture of the paranoid personality disorder may be summarized as follows:
    a. Behaviorally: wary to vigilant; alert to derogation and deception.
    b. Interpersonally: quarrelsome to acrimonious, for example, abrasive.
    c. Cognitively: incredulous to conspirative, for example, doubting, cynical.
    d. Affectively: sullen to fractious, for example, cold, humorless, quick to anger.
    e. Self-perception: formidable to embittered.
    f. Primary defense mechanism: projection.
    g. Differential personality diagnosis: antisocial personality disorder.
2. The paranoid personality disorder has three major clinical manifestations:
    a. The paranoid-narcissistic variation.
    b. The paranoid-antisocial variation.
    c. The paranoid-compulsive variation.

3. Developmentally, the narcissistic variation of the paranoid disorder may be highly contributed to by parental overevaluation and indulgence.
4. The antisocial variation of this disorder may be thought of as being contributed to by an interaction of biogenic and environmental factors. The primary environmental contributor appears to be harsh parental treatment.
5. The developmental history of the compulsive variation of the paranoid personality disorder appears to be influenced by parental rigidity and overcontrol.
6. The paranoid personality disorder appears to be self-perpetuated by their own rigidity and their interpersonal suspicion that tends to breed the same in others.
7. Common DSM-III, Axis I disorders associated with the paranoid personality disorder include anxiety disorders, affective disorders, paranoid disorders, and schizophrenic disorders.

Seven

CONCLUDING REMARKS

14

Reflections on Personality and Its Disorders

As noted among the initial pages of this volume, humankind has since the beginning of recorded history been engaged in a quest for understanding. We have explored the continents, the seas and oceans, and even worlds beyond our own. Yet, one of the greatest mysteries still remaining must certainly be why people behave in the relatively consistent patterns that they do. The construct of personality offers us a tool for integrating not only evidence from the social sciences, but also the biologic sciences and specific clinical sciences to cast a revealing light on the enigma at hand. As Hall and Lindzey (1957) noted, the study of personality does, indeed, reveal an "Order and congruence" that integrates the vast realm of human behavior.

Conceptually, it is helpful to see human personality as the basic foundation on which transituational behavior may be recast in a more illuminating and integrating perspective. Such a perspective ultimately reveals a series of patterns and traits that now add order to, and make sense of, what had previously appeared to be only unrelated, situationally contingent behavior. A truly multidimensional formulation of personality may then give us a powerful tool for understanding, predicting, and even altering human behavior in all its diversity. In this volume, we have described what we believe is an integrative, multidimensional model for understanding human personality. The utility of such an integrative biosocial model becomes obvious. For clinically oriented students, the DSM-III's compendium of clinical syndromes (Axis I) becomes far better understood in relation to the underlying personality structures that we believe ultimately serve to support and shape the manifestation of these Axis I syndromes. In the final analysis, however, whether the student of human behavior finds himself/herself in clinical settings, in the classroom, or in the high-pressure arenas of business and industry, the quest for an understanding of human behavior continues. The following summary tables are designed to be useful pedagogical tools as well as quick reference guides in that quest.

Table 14.1 Independent Personality Disorders

	Antisocial	Narcissist
I Clinical Picture		
Behavioral Appearance	Ranges from fearless to reckless, e.g., daring, thickskinned, undaunted by danger or punishment, seeks challenge, power oriented.	Ranges from arrogant to pompous, e.g., flouts conventional rules of shared social living, disregards personal integrity and rights of others.
Interpersonal Conduct	Ranges from antagonistic to belligerent, e.g., likes intimidating others, is contemptuous of compassion, mistrusting, derogating.	Ranges from exploitive to shameless, e.g., expects special favors without responsibility, takes others for granted and uses them to indulge himself/herself.
Cognitive Style	Ranges from personalistic to bigoted, e.g., construes words and actions of others in terms of own needs.	Ranges from expansive to undisciplined, e.g., undisciplined imagination, takes liberty with facts often lying to redeem self-illusions of grandeur.
Affective Expression	Ranges from hostile to malevolent, e.g., temper flares readily into argument; frequently verbally abusive, physically cruel.	Ranges from insouciant to exuberant, e.g., airs of nonchalance or bouyant optimism, except when uncertain—then feels shame, emptiness, or rage.
Self-perception	Ranges from competitive to domineering, e.g., independent; values tough, domineering, power-oriented aspects of self.	Ranges from admirable to wonderful, e.g., acts in self-assured manner, confidently displaying achievements, despite being seen as egotistic or arrogant.

Defense Mechanism	Acting out: inner tensions rarely constrained; socially undesirable impulses expressed directly, usually without guilt feelings.	Rationalization: is self-deceptive, devising plausible reasons to justify inconsiderate behavior; puts self in best light despite shortcomings.
Differential Diagnosis	Narcissistic personality disorder.	Histrionic personality disorder.
II Etiology and Development Biogenic Factors	Low thresholds for limbic system stimulation and inefficient inhibitory centers, mesomorphic-endomorphic build, ill-tempered infantile pattern.	No factors hypothesized.
Environmental Factors	Parental hostility, deficient parental models, operant conditioning of vindictive behavior, disorganized family and social systems.	Parental overvaluation and indulgence, only-child status in many cases.
III Self-perpetuation Mechanism	Consistent perceptual distortions; demeaning attitude towards affection and interpersonal cooperation; antagonistic behavior towards others, which breeds antagonism in return; negative reinforcement of antisocial behavior. The apparent motivation sustaining this aggressive pattern is a fear of being used, taken advantage of, or humiliated; a need to achieve, or remain in, powerful, superordinate positions vis-à-vis others.	Self-reinforcing illusions of competence, lack of self-control, deficient sense of social responsibility, positive reinforcement of narcissistic behavior itself. The apparent motivation sustaining this narcissistic pattern is the need to be seen and accepted as a truly unique, gifted, or superior individual, i.e., one who is entitled.

Table 14.2 Dependent Personality Disorders

	Histrionic	Dependent
I Clinical Picture		
Behavioral Appearance	Ranges from affected to theatrical, e.g., overreactive, responding impulsively; penchant for excitement and short-sighted hedonism.	Ranges from incompetent to helpless, e.g., unable to assume independent role, docile, passive, avoids self-assertion.
Interpersonal Conduct	Ranges from flirtatious to seductive, e.g., solicits praise, manipulates others to gain attention, demanding, exhibitionistic.	Ranges from submissive to clinging, e.g., subordinates own needs to stronger, nurturing figure; compliant and self-sacrificing.
Cognitive Style	Ranges from flighty to scattered, e.g., avoids introspection, attending to superficial events; integrates experience poorly; poor judgment.	Ranges from naive to gullible, e.g., easily persuaded, waters down objective problems, Pollyanna attitude towards interpersonal problems.
Affective Expression	Ranges from fickle to impetuous, e.g., dramatic emotions, exhibits tendencies to be easily enthused, angered, or bored.	Ranges from pacific to timid, e.g., warm and noncompetitive, avoids social tension and interpersonal conflicts.
Self-perception	Ranges from sociable to hedonistic, e.g., charming, enjoys attracting others and maintaining pleasure-oriented social life.	Ranges from inept to inadequate, e.g., views self as weak, fragile; belittles own competencies and aptitudes; self-doubting.
Defense Mechanism	Dissociation: alters self-perception, resulting in changing facade; dis-	Introjection: firmly devoted to another and denies independent

Differential Diagnosis	tracts self to avoid reflecting on unpleasant thoughts and feelings. Narcissistic personality disorder.	views to prevent conflicts or threats to this relationship. Histrionic personality disorder, avoidant personality disorder.
II Etiology and Development Biogenic Factors	Hyperresponsive infantile pattern, low excitability thresholds for limbic and posterior hypothalamic nuclei, low threshold for ascending reticular system activation.	Fearful, sad, or even withdrawn at infancy; hypometabolic condition mediated through chronic thyroid insufficiency, yet within "normal" limits; endomorphic or ectomorphic builds; low-energy threshold.
Environmental Factors	Parental reinforcement of attention-seeking behavior; histrionic parental role models; operant conditioning of interpersonally manipulative behavior; enriched, diverse sensory attachment stage; parental control by contingency and irregular reward: sibling rivalry; shifting values and standards.	Parental overprotection, competitive deficits among peers and siblings, social-role programming.
III Self-perpetuation Mechanisms	Preoccupation with external stimuli, short-lived social relationships, massive repression, operant conditioning of histrionic behavior pattern itself. The apparent motivation sustaining this histrionic pattern is a need for interpersonal affiliation, approval, support and affection.	Positive and negative reinforcement of dependent behavior, avoidance of competitive activities and deprecation, plaintive behavior provokes exasperation and rebuffs. The apparent motivation sustaining this dependent pattern is a need for interpersonal affection and support.

Table 14.3 Ambivalent Personality Disorders

	Passive-Aggressive	Compulsive
I Clinical Picture		
Behavioral Appearance	Ranges from stubborn to contrary, e.g., resists fulfilling others' expectations, procrastinating, likes demoralizing others.	Ranges from disciplined to perfectionistic, e.g., maintains repetitive, structured life pattern; insists subordinates adhere to rules.
Interpersonal Conduct	Ranges from ambivalent to uncooperative, e.g., changes from dependent to independent roles, is unpredictable.	Ranges from respectful to ingratiating, e.g., unusual adherence to convention; prefers formal, polite relationships; is highly loyal; rigid.
Cognitive Style	Ranges from inconsistent to disorienting, e.g., thinks and expresses attitudes contrary to feelings, experiences incompatible urges and needs.	Ranges from constricted to blocked, e.g., is unimaginative and upset by new ideas and customs, methodical, narrow-minded, dogmatic.
Affective Expression	Ranges from irritable to agitated, e.g., frequently touchy, fretful, impatient followed by expressions of guilt.	Ranges from solemn to grave, e.g., unrelaxed, tense, joyless; keeps emotions under tight control; grim; cheerless.
Self-perception	Ranges from discontented to mistreated, e.g., sees self as misunderstood and demeaned by others, feels pessimistic, disillusioned.	Ranges from conscientious to righteous, e.g., sees self as reliable and efficient, fearful of error, values self-discipline.
Defense Mechanism	Displacement: shifts anger from instigator to persons of lesser sig-	Reaction formation: presents positive thoughts and behaviors

Differential Diagnosis	nificance; expresses resentment passively, e.g., being forgetful. Antisocial personality disorder, avoidant personality disorder.	that are opposite to deeper contrary, forbidden feelings. Dependent personality disorder, paranoid personality disorder.
II Etiology and Development Biogenic Factors	Low stimulation thresholds in limbic circuitry structures, uneven maturational process, irregular infantile pattern.	No factors hypothesized.
Environmental Factors	Parental inconsistency, family schisms, sibling rivalry, learned vacillation, guilt and anxiety training, contradictory family communication, reinforcement of contradictory behavior.	Parental overcontrol, learned compulsive behavior, training in being responsible to others.
III Self-perpetuation Mechanisms	Absence of emotional controls, anticipation and creation of disappointment, positive reinforcement of passive-aggressive behavior itself, erratic and negativistic behaviors provoke inconsistent and rejecting reactions creating unresolvable conflicts. The sustaining motivation of this pattern is most likely the desire to behave in a manner contrary to the existing reinforcement history, therefore, the creation of ambivalence and negativism.	Cognitive and behavioral rigidity, dogmatic adherence to rules and regulations, tendencies to be self-critical, operant conditioning of compulsive behavior itself. The apparent motivation sustaining this pattern is a need to be "proper," to avoid mistakes, and to behave in socially sanctioned ways.

Table 14.4 Detached Personality Disorders

	Avoidant	Schizoid
I Clinical Picture		
Behavioral Appearance	Ranges from guarded to alarmed, e.g., scans environment for potential threats, overreacts to innocuous events, viewing them as threats.	Ranges from lethargic to sluggish. e.g., appears fatigued; lacks energy, vitality: deficits in motoric expressiveness and spontaneity.
Interpersonal Conduct	Ranges from aversive to withdrawn, e.g., history of pananxiety and distrust, seeks acceptance while maintaining distance.	Ranges from aloof to remote, e.g., rarely responds to actions or feelings of others, fades into background, few close relationships.
Cognitive Style	Ranges from distracted to perplexed, e.g., preoccupied with inner thoughts, upsurge of irrelevant ideation interrupts communication.	Ranges from impoverished to barren, e.g., deficient across broad spheres of knowledge, communication may lose its sequence of logical progression.
Affective Expression	Ranges from anguished to overwrought, e.g., constant underlying tension, sadness, anger; desires affection yet fears rebuff.	Ranges from flat to bleak, e.g., emotionally impassive; seems unfeeling, cold, unable to experience pleasure or sadness: weak affectionate needs.
Self-perception	Ranges from alienated to rejected, e.g., sees self as isolated and empty, devalues own achievements.	Ranges from complacent to lifeless, e.g., minimal introspection, awareness of self; seems blind to emotional and personal aspects of everyday life.

Defense Mechanism

Fantasy: depends heavily on imagination for gratification of needs and conflict resolution.

Intellectualization: describes interpersonal and affective experiences matter-of-factly, pays most attention to formal, objective aspects.

Differential Diagnosis

Schizoid personality disorder, schizotypal personality disorder, borderline personality disorder.

Avoidant personality disorder, schizotypal personality disorder.

II Etiology and Development

Biogenic Factors

Hyperirritable infantile pattern, maturational irregularities, low arousal thresholds for the autonomic nervous system.

Hypoactive physiological substates (limbic and ascending reticular activating system deficits as well as parasympathetic nervous system dominance), passive infantile pattern, ectomorphic build, probable dopaminergic excesses in mesolimbic system.

Environmental Factors

Parental rejection or deprecation, peer-group alienation.

Parental indifference, impoverished sensory attachment stage, fragmented family communication patterns.

III Self-perpetuation Mechanisms

Hypersensitivity to social rejection, restricted social experience, excessive introspection, cognitive interference, alienated feelings of self, operant conditioning of avoidant behavior itself. The motivation sustaining this avoidant pattern is a fear of social rejection, humiliation.

Impassivity, infrequent social interaction, social and cognitive insensitivity, reinforcement of social isolation. Major factors sustaining this pattern include a lack of reinforcing social history and dampened biologic reactivity.

Table 14.5 More Severe Personality Disorders

	Schizotypal	Borderline	Paranoid
I Clinical Picture			
Behavioral Appearance	Ranges from eccentric to bizarre, e.g., socially gauche, peculiar habits and mannerisms; odd; curious; aloof.	Ranges from spontaneous to chaotic, e.g., desultory energy level with sudden, unexpected outbursts.	Ranges from wary to vigilant, e.g., alert to derogation and deception, very resistant to external control.
Interpersonal Conduct	Ranges from detached to inaccessible, e.g., prefers isolation, highly tentative attachments, personal obligations.	Ranges from oppositional to mercurial, e.g., needs affection but is often volatile eliciting rejection, changeable.	Ranges from quarrelsome to acrimonious, e.g., abrasive, causes anger by testing others' loyalty and hidden motives.
Cognitive Style	Ranges from ruminative to deranged, e.g., self-absorbed and lost in daydreams, blurring of fantasy and reality.	Ranges from inconsistent to disorganized, e.g., rapidly changing, antithetical thoughts about past that confuse others.	Ranges from incredulous to conspirative, e.g., cynical, magnifies minor social problems into proof of malice, conspiracy.
Affective Expression	Ranges from apprehensive to frantic or apathetic to deadened, e.g., wary of others, anxious; spiritless; affectless.	Ranges from temperamental to volatile, e.g., mood level not in accord with reality, can shift from depression to excitement.	Ranges from sullen to fractious, e.g., cold, humorless; appears unemotional but is edgy, envious, quick to anger.

Self-perception	Ranges from forlorn to vacant, e.g., thoughts of meaninglessness, permeable ego boundaries, experiences of depersonalization, dissociation.	Ranges from troubled to conflicted, e.g., wavering sense of identity leads to confusion, redeems actions with self-punitive behaviors.	Ranges from formidable to embittered e.g., pridefully independent but very fearful of losing identity.
Defense Mechanism	Undoing: bizarre, ritualistic behaviors in attempt to nullify assumed misdeeds or "evil" thoughts.	Regression: retreats under stress to earlier developmental levels of anxiety tolerance, impulse control and social adaptation.	Projection: attributes undesirable traits and motives to others, blind to own unattractive qualities.
Differential Diagnosis	Borderline personality disorder.	Schizotypal personality disorder.	Antisocial personality disorder.
II Etiology and Development Biogenic Factors	Low arousal thresholds for the autonomic nervous system (schizotypal-avoidant), hypoactive physiological substrates (schizotypal-schizoid).	Low autonomic nervous system reactivity (borderline-dependent), high autonomic nervous system reactivity (borderline-histrionic), low stimulation thresholds in limbic system and uneven maturational process (borderline-passive-aggressive).	Low thresholds for limbic system stimulation and inefficient limbic inhibitory centers.

(continued)

Table 14.5 *(Continued)*

	Schizotypal	*Borderline*	*Paranoid*
Environmental Factors	Cold and formal familial environment accentuated with fragmented parental communication.	Parental overprotection leading to rejection by those on whom they come to rely (borderline-dependent); inconsistent, variable ratio reinforcement patterns causing need to "perform" for attention (borderline-histrionic); environment inconsistency (borderline-passive-aggressive).	Parental overvaluation and indulgence (paranoid-narcissistic), harsh parental treatment (paranoid-antisocial), parental rigidity and overcontrol (paranoid-compulsive).
III Self-perpetuation Mechanisms	Social isolation, overprotection, self-insulation.	Positively reinforcing release of inner tensions, utilization of self-defeating coping strategies.	Rigidity and interpersonal suspician that breeds the same in others.

REFERENCES

Allport, G. (1937). *Personality: A psychological interpretation.* New York: Holt.

American Psychiatric Association. (1980). *Diagnostic and statistical manual of mental disorders* (3rd ed.). Washington, DC.

Bandura, A. (1974). Behavior theory and the models of man. American Psychologist, 29, 859–869.

Bayley, N. (1970). Development of mental abilities. In P. Mussen (Ed.), *Carmichael's Manual of Child Psychology* New York: Wiley.

Beck, A. T. (1967). *Depression.* New York: Harper & Row.

Brown, T. and Wallace, P. (1980). *Physiological Psychology,* New York: Academic Press.

Child, C. M. (1941). *Patterns and problems of development.* Chicago: University of Chicago Press.

Cooper, T., (1981). Coronary-prone behavior and coronary heart disease: A critical review. *Circulation, 63,* 1199–1245.

Diagram Group. (1977). *Woman's body.* New York: Paddington.

Ellis, A. (1962). *Reason and emotion in psychotherapy.* New York: Lyle Stuart.

Endler, N., & Magnusson, D. (1976). Toward an interactional psychology of personality. *Psychological Bulletin, 83,* 956–974.

Epstein, S. (1979). The stability of behavior: I. *Journal of Personality and Social Psychology, 37,* 1097–1126.

Erikson, E. (1950). Childhood and Society. New York: Norton.

Escalona, S. (1968). *Roots of individuality.* Chicago: Aldine.

Everly, G., & Rosenfeld, R. (1981). *The nature and treatment of the stress response: A practical guide for clinicians.* New York: Plenum.

Farber, S. (1982). Genetic diversity and differing reactions to stress. In L. Goldberger and S. Breznitz (Eds.), *Handbook of stress* (pp. 123–133). New York: Free Press.

Fenichel, O. (1945). *The psychoanalytic theory of neurosis.* New York: Norton.

Freud, S. (1957). *Standard edition of the works of Sigmund Freud.* London: Hogarth.

Fromm, E. (1955). *The sane society.* New York: Rinehart.

Gellhorn, E. (1957). *Autonomic imbalance and the hypothalamus: Implications for physiology, medicine, psychology, and neuropsychiatry.* Minneapolis: University of Minnesota Press.

Goffman, E. (1973). The inmate world. In T. Millon (Ed.), *Theories of psychopathology and personality* Philadelphia: Saunders.

Goldstein K. (1939). *The organism.* New York: American Book.

Goldstein, K. (1959). The organismic approach. In S. Arieti (Ed.), *American handbook of psychiatry* (pp. 1333–1347). New York: Basic Books.

Gottesman, I., & Shields, J. (1972). *Schizophrenia and genetics.* New York: Academic Press.

Hall, C., & Lindzey, G. (1957). *Theories of personality.* New York: Wiley.

Harlow, H. F. (1963). The maternal affectional system. In B. M. Foss (Ed.), *Determinants of infant behavior* New York: Wiley.

Heymans, G., & Wiersma, E. (1906). Beitrage zur speziellen Psychologie auf Grund einer Massenuntersuchung. *Zeitsehrift fuer Psychologie, 42.*

Horney, K. (1939). *New ways in psychoanalysis.* New York: Norton.

Kallmann, F. J. (1953). *Heredity in health and mental disorder.* New York: Norton.

Kollarits, J. (1912). *Charakter und Nervositat.* Budapest: Knoedler.

Kovach, J. (1970). Critical period or optimal arousal? *Developmental Psychology, 3,* 88–97.

Kretschmer, E. (1925). *Physique and character.* New York: Harcourt Brace.

Lazarus, R. (1976). *Patterns of adjustment.* New York: McGraw-Hill.

Lazarus, R. (1966). *Psychological stress and the coping process.* New York: McGraw-Hill.

Leary, T. (1957). *Interpersonal diagnosis of personality.* New York: Ronald.

Lewin, K. (1935). *A dynamic theory of personality.* New York: McGraw.

Lewin, K. (1936). *Principles of topographical psychology.* New York: McGraw.

Lorr, M., Klett, C., & McNair, D. (1963). *Syndromes of psychosis.* New York: Macmillan.

Marx, J. (1973, April). Drugs during pregnancy: Do they affect the unborn child? *Science, 174–175.*

McClelland, D. (1951). *Personality.* New York: Dryden.

McDougall, W. (1908). *Introduction to Social Psychology.* New York: Scribners.

McGraw, M. B. (1943). *The neuromuscular maturation of the human infant.* New York: Columbia University Press.

Millon, T. (1981). *Disorders of Personality: DSM-III, Axis II.* New York: Wiley.

Millon, T. (1982). *Millon Clinical Multiaxial Inventory Manual.* Minneapolis: National Computer Systems.

Millon, T. (1969). *Modern psychopathology: A biosocial approach to maladaptive learning and functioning.* Philadelphia: Saunders. (Reprinted, 1983, Prospect Heights, ILL.: Wareland Press.)

Millon, T., & Klerman, G. (Eds.). (in press). *Contemporary directions in psychopathology.* New York: Guilford Press.

Millon, T., & Millon, R. (1974). *Abnormal behavior and personality.* Philadelphia: Saunders.

Murphy, G. (1947). *Personality: A biosocial approach to origins and structures.* New York: Harper.

Murphy, L., & Moriarty, A. (1976). *Vulnerability, coping and growth.* New Haven, Conn.: Yale University Press.

Murray, H. (1938). *Explorations in personality.* New York: Oxford University Press.

Piaget, J. (1956). The general problems of the psychobiological development of the child. In J. M. Tanner & B. Inhelder (Eds.), *Discussions on child development*, Vol. 4, New York: International Universities Press.

Rapaport, D. (1958). The theory of ego autonomy: A generalization. *Bulletin of the Menninger Clinic, 22*, 13–35.

Sarbin, T., & Mancuso, J. (1970). Failure of moral enterprise. *Journal of Consulting and Clinical Psychology, 35*, 159–173.

Scheff, T. (1973). The role of the mentally ill and the dynamics of mental disorder. In T. Millon (Ed.), *Theories of psychopathology and personality*. Philadelphia: Saunders.

Sheldon, W. (1940). *The varieties of human physique: An introduction to constitutional psychology*. New York: Harper.

Sheldon, W., & Stevens, S. (1942). *The varieties of temperament: A psychology of constitutional differences*. New York: Harper.

Simmel, E. C. (1970). The biology of socialization. In R. A. Hoppe (Eds.), *Early experiences and the processes of socialization*. New York: Academic Press.

Skinner, B. F. (1953). *Science and human behavior*. New York: Macmillan.

Slater, E., & Cowie, V. (1971). *The genetics of mental disorder*. London: Oxford University Press.

Sorochan, W. (1981). *Promoting your health*. New York: Wiley.

Stuart, R. B. (1970). *Trick or treatment: How and when psychotherapy fails*. Champaign, IL: Research Press.

Szasz, T. (1960). The myth of mental illness. *American Psychologist, 15*, 113–118.

Thomas, A., & Chess, S. (1977). *Temperament and development*. New York: Brunner/Mazel.

Thomas, A., Chess, S., & Birch, H. (1963). *Behavioral individuality in early childhood*. New York: New York University Press.

Thompson, W., & Grusec, J. (1970). Studies on early experience. In P. Mussen (Ed.), *Carmichael's Manual of Child Psychology*. New York: Wiley.

Thorndike, E. L. (1935). *The psychology of wants, interests, and attitudes*. New York: Appleton, Century.

Venables, P. H. (1968). Experimental psychological studies of chronic schizophrenia. In M. Shepard & D. Davies (Eds.), *Studies in Psychiatry*. London: Oxford University Press.

Weil, J. L. (1974). *A neurophysiological model of emotional and intentional behavior*. Springfield, IL: Charles C Thomas.

Werner, H. (1940). *Comparative psychology of mental development*. New York: Follett.

Williams, R. (1983). The biological approach to the study of personality. In T. Millon (Ed.), *Theories of Personality and Psychopathology* (pp. 14–24). New York: Holt, Rinehart & Winston.

ABOUT THE AUTHORS

Theodore Millon, Ph.D. is Professor of Psychology and Director of Graduate Clinical Training at the University of Miami, Coral Gables, Florida. Dr. Millon served continuously on the American Psychiatric Association's Task Force on Nomenclature and Statistics since it undertook responsibility for developing the DSM-III in 1974. Dr. Millon is also noted for his other major works including *Modern Psychopathology, Theories of Psychopathology and Personality* and, *Disorders of Personality, DSM-III: Axis II;* as well as three computer-diagnostic self-report inventories, the Millon Clinical Multiaxial Inventory, the Millon Behavioral Health Inventory, and the Millon Adolescent Personality Inventory.

George S. Everly, Jr., Ph.D. is Associate Professor of Psychology and Director of the Psychophysiological and Health Psychology Research Laboratory at Loyola College in Baltimore, Maryland. Dr. Everly is a Diplomate of the American Academy of Behavioral Medicine and is author or coauthor of six other textbooks including *The Nature and Treatment of the Stress Response* and *Occupational Health Promotion,* as well as more than 50 scientific and professional papers.

INDEX